By Wallace Stegner

Novels:

ALL THE LITTLE LIVE THINGS
A SHOOTING STAR
THE PREACHER AND THE SLAVE
SECOND GROWTH
THE BIG ROCK CANDY MOUNTAIN
FIRE AND ICE
ON A DARKLING PLAIN
THE POTTER'S HOUSE
REMEMBERING LAUGHTER

Short Stories:

THE CITY OF THE LIVING
THE WOMEN ON THE WALL

Non-Fiction:

THE SOUND OF MOUNTAIN WATER
BEYOND THE HUNDREDTH MERIDIAN
ONE NATION (WITH THE EDITORS OF *Look*)
THE GATHERING OF ZION
MORMON COUNTRY
WOLF WILLOW

The Sound of
Mountain Water

WALLACE STEGNER

The Sound of Mountain Water

1969

DOUBLEDAY & COMPANY, INC.
GARDEN CITY, NEW YORK

Library of Congress Catalog Card Number 69–12196

Contents

Introduction

Some Geography, Some History

In most parts of the West (Utah is one exception) a child is likely to learn little in school about the geography and history of the region that is shaping him. He gets them through the pores if he gets them at all. Many never get them, some get them in excess: it is not uncommon for grown men to develop a monomaniac interest in local history that as children they never heard of. The discovery that it has been around them all the time, and they deprived of it, forever shatters their ability to take it for granted as inheritors of a stabler tradition might do.

I suppose the essays in this volume demonstrate some aspects of that process of learning to *know* what one spontaneously responds to because it is what one grew up in. They were written over a period of more then twenty years, and they reveal, I am sure, no systematic approach and develop no coherent thesis. I have tried the systematic approach and the developed thesis in *Beyond the Hundredth Meridian* and *Wolf Willow,* the first wholly impersonal, the second colored by personal experience and feeling. These essays, mainly personal, were written during the years I was gathering material for those two books, and they probably show me getting my education in public. For example, I am dismayed to find myself, in "The Rediscovery of America," speaking admiringly of Hoover Dam and Lake Mead. I know better now, or at least know enough not to speak well of reclamation dams without looking closely at their teeth. But I have not changed the essay, or any of the essays, except to cut away a little dullness and update a few facts. They represent the way I felt when I wrote them. So be it. Later ones will perhaps correct their errors.

Physically and socially, the West does not remain the same from decade to decade any more than other places do. Some of the places spoken of here—Glen Canyon, for instance—no longer exist. Others, such as Las Vegas, exist in continual flux. All exist within the warping influence of great in-migration, uninterrupted boom, and unremitting technological tinkering. But these essays on country are to be understood in relation to Professor Webb's view of the West as an oasis civilization—a generalization that applies as truly to Los Angeles as to Las Vegas or Albuquerque. *Limitation, deprivation,* are words we must keep in mind when speaking of the reputedly limitless West. Even a state with only a half million people in it may be overpopulated. Even an oasis civilization, if it tinkers enough with the environment, may be in danger of depleting or destroying it.

So if these essays begin in innocence, with a simple-minded love of western landscape and experience, they move toward the attempt, more systematically made in other books of mine, to understand what it is one loves, what is special or fragile about it, and how far love alone will take us.

In gathering things together for a book, I have omitted a good many essays on the subject of conservation, which, being polemics, have dated badly as the controversies that evoked them died down. I have also omitted a good many purely literary essays that have nothing to do with the West. So this is not a volume of conservation essays or literary essays, though it contains some of both. It is a book of confrontations (not in the contemporary sense!) with the West, a series of responses and trial syntheses. The West being what it is, a Westerner trying to examine his life has trouble finding himself in any formed or coherent society (again Utah is an exception). His confrontations are therefore likely to be with landscape, which seems to define the West and its meaning better than any of its forming cultures, or with himself in the context of that landscape.

So here. The first group of these essays are personal responses to landscape—or perhaps one should say geography—and they conclude with a personal expression of faith in the importance of geography, and especially wilderness, to human personality and culture. In making wilderness the geography of hope, I have undoubtedly revealed myself: there is nothing so desperately demoralizing to a New World optimist as the sight of the New World floundering toward total reunion with Europe's cynicism, belligerence, and despair.

I am aware that the literary essays of Part II, historical in their bias and realistic in their intention, conform to none of the contemporary fashions. That fact does not bother me so long as they conform to authentic western experience and deal truthfully with the quandary of the western writer, past and present. No matter how I try, I cannot believe in the "liberated" consciousness that is the subject of so much contemporary writing. Though I may enjoy these productions, and may even myself play games with Kronos as a literary exercise, I want a foot on earth, I am forced to believe in Time. I believe we are Time's prisoners, I believe Time is our safety and strength. I think we build our little huts against it as the latter-day Illyrians built their huts within and against the great palace of Diocletian at Split. One of the deprivations of people in western America is that Time in their country is still not molded by human living into the forms of sanctuary, continuity, and confidence that it is the ambition of all human cultures to create.

Hence this general, inadequate summary of some of the things that too many Westerners do not know about their West. Known, they can be built on.

Let us discriminate among the parts of what we are talking about. The Pacific Northwest and California are separate sub-regions, earlier settled and more amenable to settlement than the interior West. The Southwest is historically and ethnically another country. The states that are left—Montana, Wyoming, Colorado, Utah, Idaho, and Nevada—comprise the Rocky Mountain West, but they are by no means all mountains. The whole eastern side of Montana, Wyoming, and Colorado is high plains, the gently sloping "long hill" which the swinging rivers have built. Montana, named for its mountains, is three fifths high plains, Wyoming about a quarter, Colorado about a third. Southern Idaho, western Utah, and all of Nevada are desert.

Different as they are, and different as any part is from the Pacific slope or the Southwest, they are all the West. They lie beyond the unmarked boundary that crudely corresponds with the 100th meridian, and that is a dividing line more surely than Mason and Dixon's. It marks the isohyetal line of twenty inches, beyond which unassisted agriculture is dubious or foolhardy and beyond which one experiences the western *feel*—a dryness in the nostrils a cracking of the lips, a transparent crystalline quality of the light, a new palette of gray, sage-green, sulphur-yellow, buff, toned white, rust red, a new flora and fauna, a new ecology. If political boundaries were logically drawn, our western states, and the recognized West, would begin about a third of the way across Kansas, Nebraska, and the Dakotas.

But the quintessential West begins at the mountains. Walling the sunset side of the plains, tilting the earth violently upward, they reach down out of the northwest corner of Montana, from where Chief Mountain is overthrust onto the short-grass prairie at the gateway of Glacier National Park. Widening as they go, they run south-southwest, a chain of interlocking ranges with several isolated outliers—the Sweetgrass Hills, the Highwoods, the Bearpaws, the Little Rockies, the Little Belts, the Big Snowies, and farther south the Big Horns and the Black Hills—until they reach a corner at the Laramie Range, north and west of Cheyenne. There the whole system, now at its widest spread, turns due south. The ranges that leap up behind Boulder, Denver, and Colorado Springs are the highest in the whole American Rockies, with fifty-four peaks over fourteen thousand feet. Front Range, Park Range, Sawatch, Sangre de Cristo, San Miguel, La Plata, they fill western Colorado nearly to the Utah border, where the plateaus intrude, and southward they continue down into New Mexico to link the Rocky Mountain region with the Southwest.

The eastern tier of western states is plains on the east, mountains on the west; the western tier is mountains and plateaus on the east and deserts on the west. Nevada's mountains lift out of the Great Basin to real altitudes, but they are nearly uniformly barren; they make a transition between the Rockies and the Sierra as Oregon's scablands make a transition between the Rockies and the Cascades.

Throughout the West, altitude has both favorable and unfavorable effects. The mountains catch moisture, but they also throw a rain shadow. As the Montana, Wyoming, and Colorado plains lie in the rain shadow of the Rockies, the deserts of Oregon, Idaho, Nevada, and Utah lie in the shadow of the Sierra-Cascades. These deserts, said the late Walter Webb, are the truest West, its dead and arid heart. The rest is a semi-arid fringe subject to cyclic dust bowls and a chronic and only partly curable water shortage.

Webb's thesis, which was first stated in John Wesley Powell's extraordinary *Report on the Lands of the Arid Region* in 1878, needs periodic and stentorian restating in a region where optimism consistently outruns resources. But I would put it in a slightly different way. Instead of a country with a dead heart and semi-arid fringes, I conceive the West to be two long belts of alternating mountains and lowlands, fountains with arid lands in their rain shadow. Even if every reclamation proposal should be implemented —and it shouldn't be—the fountains could water only a fraction of the lands lying below them. Nevertheless their importance cannot be overstated. A simple comparison of annual rainfall figures, such as that between the thirty-five-inch precipitation of the Yellowstone Plateau and the six-inch precipitation of the Bighole Basin, tells only part of the story. The difference is more than the apparent six-to-one, for in the higher altitudes the snow pack melts more slowly, the forest cover retards the runoff, and the evaporation rate is much lower than down below. Both surface streams and the underground water table for hundreds of miles may depend upon the fact that water is not only made in the mountains but stored there. When those fountains fail, the lowlands suffer ruin, as in the 1880's and early 1890's, in the 1930's, and again in the 1950's.

That is the West's ultimate unity: aridity. In other ways it has a bewildering variety. Its life zones go all the way from arctic to sub-tropical, from reindeer moss to cactus, from mountain goat to horned toad. Its range of temperatures is as wide as its range of precipitation. It runs through twelve degrees of latitude and nearly three miles of altitude. It is short-grass plains, alkali flats, creosote-bush deserts, irrigated alluvial valleys, sub-arctic fir forests, bare sun-smitten stone. From the 100th meridian to the Pacific is two fifths of the United States, by common consent of the local booster clubs the biggest, widest, highest, hopefulest, friendliest region on the footstool. The statistics quoted about it are as uniformly the statistics of the Promised Land as they were a hundred years ago when Governor William Gilpin of Colorado Territory was tooting the horn of Manifest Destiny. The song is persistent, they never play anything but "Old Zip Coon"; one hears perennially the words of a self-conscious provincialism hopefully clamoring for its turn to be swamped by the populations and the industries that have made so much of America so nearly unbearable to live in. As for me, I share the enthusiasm for the country without sharing the eagerness to spoil it.

Within the six Rocky Mountain states there lived in 1960 less than seven million people. They were densest in Colorado, at 16.9 to the square mile, and thinnest in Nevada at 2.6. Surprisingly, they were more urban than rural. Over half of Colorado's people were packed into the ten counties along the eastern face of the Rockies, the rest were scattered thinly across fifty-three counties. More than two thirds of Utah's population made a narrow dense band of settlement in the six counties at the foot of the Wasatch. The cause for this concentration is the cause that dictates so many aspects of western life: water. As Professor Webb said, the West is an oasis civilization.

Room, then—great open spaces, as advertised. In reality as in fiction, an inescapable fact about the West is that people are scarce. For comparison, the population density of the District of Columbia in 1960 was nearly 13,000 to the square mile, that of Rhode Island was 812, that of New Jersey 806, that of Massachusetts 654. By the criterion of space, California at 100 to the square mile had already in 1960 ceased to be West, if it ever was, and Washington at 42.8 was close to disqualification; but Oregon, thanks to its woods and its desert eastern half, was still part of the family at 18.4, which is less than half the density of Vermont.

The natural resources of these open spaces are such as cause heartburn among corporations and individuals who wish the West were as open as it used to be, and were not watched over by so many federal bureaus. Now that the pineries of Wisconsin and Michigan are long gone, the Northwest holds our most valuable forests. Now that the Mesabi Range approaches exhaustion, Iron County, Utah, becomes a major source of iron ore; the steel industry based upon Utah ore and limestone, and Utah, Colorado, and Wyoming coal is a first step on the road that led to Pittsburgh and Gary. It has been estimated that the Upper Colorado River basin contains a sixth of the world's known coal reserves. The oil shales of Utah and Colorado, already in experimental reduction in Parachute Canyon, lie ready for the time when petroleum reserves decline. The Rocky Mountains contain most of our gold, silver, lead, zinc, copper, molybdenum, antimony, uranium, and these, depending on the market of the moment, may produce frenzies comparable with the gold rushes of last century. A few years ago, on a road across the Navajo Reservation near the Four Corners, I was stalled behind an oil exploration rig that had broken an axle fording Chinle Wash after a cloudburst. Behind me, in the hour I waited, stacked up fifteen or twenty cars and parts of three other exploration outfits. And who pulled the broken-down rig out and let us go on? A truck loaded with twenty tons of uranium ore. This on a road that only a little while earlier had been no more than ruts through the washes, ducks on the ledges, and periodic wallows where stuck travelers had dug and brushed themselves out of the sand.

Enormous potentials for energy—coal, oil, oil shale, uranium, sun. But one source, water, has about exhausted its possibilities. The Rockies form the nation's divide, and on them are generated the three great western river systems, the Missouri, Columbia, and Colorado, as well as the

Southwest's great river, the Rio Grande. Along those rivers and their tributaries most of the feasible power, reclamation, and flood-control damsites have been developed. Additional main-stem dams are not likely to recommend themselves to any close economic analysis, no matter how the dam-building bureaus promote them, and conservationist organizations in coming years can probably relax a little their vigilance to protect the scenery from the engineers.

The scenery is superlative, the greatest we have, and the future is geared to its exploitation, but the greatest scenery does not necessarily draw the greatest crowds. People go where people are; the six sparsely populated mountain states, for all their scenery, drew fewer tourist dollars than California alone in 1955, and there is no reason to suppose that situation has altered since. They are too far from the great centers of population—one is inclined to add "Thank God"—to be overrun—yet. So far people go, not to, but through them, despite Glacier, Yellowstone, Rocky Mountain, Grand Teton, Mesa Verde, Zion, Bryce Canyon, and Canyonlands National parks, two dozen national monuments, and hundreds of square miles of mountain, forest, plateau, and canyon that anywhere else would be called superlative. The ski resorts off the main line, or out of reach from great centers, have been much slower to develop than those which, like Sun Valley and Aspen and the Sierra resorts, are more accessible. So even now, with all the intensive promotion and development since the end of World War II, the tourist business of the truest West remains, like so many of its other resource-based businesses, an enormous potential.

The potentials that bring a gleam to the eye of entrepreneurs may frighten others, for all of the West's resources, even water, even scenery, are more vulnerable than the resources of other regions, and, perhaps as a consequence of that fact, the social and economic structure of the West is tentative, uncertain, and shifting. Short-haul freight rates and distances from sizable markets are a handicap, but a more compelling fact is that the basic resources of water and soil, which can be mismanaged elsewhere without necessarily drastic consequences, cannot be mismanaged in the West without consequences that are immediate and catastrophic, and that reach a long way. Overgrazing or clear-cutting a watershed on the Yampa can send consequences clear to Yuma, abusing the range on the Big Timber can do things to the Missouri that alarm St. Louis. And the entire history of the West, when we hold at arm's length the excitement, the adventure, the romance, and the legendry, is a history of resources often mismanaged and of compelling conditions often misunderstood or disregarded. Here, as elsewhere, settlement went by trial and error, only here the trials were sometimes terrible for those who suffered them, and the errors did permanent damage to the land.

The reason is again that unmarked, wavering, almost mystical line near the 100th meridian that separates wet-enough from too-dry. The history of the West until recently has been a history of the importation of humid-land habits (and carelessnesses) into a dry land that will not tolerate them; and of the indulgence of an unprecedented personal liberty, an atomic individualism, in a country that experience says can only be successfully tamed and lived in by a high degree of cooperation. Inherited wet-land habits have given us a damaged domain. The exacerbated personal freedom of the frontier has left us with myths, a folklore, a set of beliefs and assumptions, that are often comically at odds with the facts of life. Because this folklore has been embedded in a sub-literary tradition, distributed everywhere by dime novels, Wild West shows, movies, and television, this West is a place where life may often be seen copying art. Nobody devours Westerns more hungrily than the bona fide cowhand; nobody is so helplessly modeled by a fictional image of himself. What directly affects the cowhand indirectly affects people who never had a close acquaintance with a horse or cow. A lot of clerks and soda jerks in western cities are partly what fact and history have made them, and partly what the romantic imagination and traditional stereotypes tell them to be.

Bernard DeVoto has described the West as a plundered province. Certainly, until the industrial expansion that began with World War II, its products generally went to provide dividends for corporations chartered in Missouri or Maine or New Jersey, and to enrich investors in Boston and Upper Montclair. And certainly, for at least seventy-five years of its short history, it was not so much settled as raided. Until the 1880's it saw few true settlers except the Mormons, and some of the few it did see should have been talked out of coming, for their heroic efforts to make homesteads in the arid belt succeeded mainly in making dust bowls. What the West generally saw was explorers, through travelers bound for Oregon or California (it is not so different now), and a series of hit-and-run plunderers—picturesque, robust, romantic, and destructive.

Before the beginning of the nineteenth century white men had seen the Rocky Mountains twice. In 1743 Pierre and Chevalier de la Vérendrye, exploring far down into the plains from the Saskatchewan country, described "high" and "well-wooded" mountains that might have been the Big Horns, the Black Hills, or even the Laramie Range. In 1776 Fathers Escalante and Dominguez crossed from Taos to the Utah Valley, turned southwest along the eastern wall of the Great Basin, recrossed the Colorado at the Crossing of the Fathers near the present Glen Canyon Dam, and found their way back across the Painted Desert to New Mexico. They left both Escalante's journal and the map drawn by Bernardo Miera y Pacheco, the civilian leader of the expedition, and both added immeasurably to knowledge. But the history of the Rocky Mountain region for Anglo-Americans begins with the official explorers from the United States, with Lewis and Clark in 1804–6, Zebulon Pike in 1810, and Major Stephen Long in 1820—especially with Lewis and Clark, the first, the most intelligent and resolute, incomparably the most successful. Pike, whose impetuousness got him into difficulties first with the country and then with the Spaniards, has left his name on the great landmark peak above Colorado Springs. Long, as overcautious as Pike was headstrong, retreated without major discoveries, but also left his name on a peak, this one above Estes Park. Lewis and Clark left their names on no such peaks, but they opened the West.

From St. Louis up the Missouri through the plains that would some day be Nebraska, the Dakotas, Montana; past the Great Falls where I once lived for two years without ever being taught one thing about them; through the "Gates of the Rocky Mountains" and up the dwindling forks, they went by water until the streams would no longer float them. Then they stalked Sacajawea's suspicious

Snake relatives until they caught some and made friends, and with a few horses and some information about a difficult way over the mountains, they struggled up over Lolo Pass and stood, the first Americans to do so, on the western slope of the continental divide. Next spring, having passed a dreary winter in the rain at the mouth of the Columbia, they came back over the Bitterroots, split forces so that Clark could explore the Yellowstone while Lewis went up the Marias, and were reunited below the mouth of the Yellowstone, from where—Lewis with an accidental gunshot wound in his thigh—they floated the long river homeward to St. Louis and triumph.

Their word on the unknown reaches of Louisiana and "the Oregon" was added to by Pike and Long as well as by Frémont, who surveyed the Oregon Trail in 1842 and other parts of the West in 1844–46. It was given detail by the Pacific Railroad surveys of the 1850's, and topographical knowledge was brought close to its final form by Major John W. Powell's brilliant exploration down the Green and Colorado rivers in 1869. The last act of all in the record of official exploration belonged to Powell's brother-in-law, Almon Thompson, who in 1871 added to the map of southern Utah the last-discovered river, the Escalante, whose mouth Powell had missed. But long before the 1870's, when explorers had become surveyors and the King, Hayden, Powell, and Wheeler surveys were triangulating the West, another breed had lived its short hot life and disappeared: the first of the raiders, the picturesque and destructive ones, the first shapes of myth—the mountain men.

Returning out of the wilderness on Clark's heels in 1806, Lewis had met, below the mouth of the Yellowstone, two trappers named Dickson and Hancock, the first to follow upriver the path the explorers had opened. One of the expedition's men, John Colter, turned out to be still unsated with wilderness after two years of hardship, starvation, wounds, scurvy, and venereal Chinook squaws. He asked leave to turn back with the trappers, and having been a faithful man, was granted it. He helped build in 1807, at the mouth of the Big Horn, the fort that was the first building in Montana and probably the first in the Rocky Mountain states. That same year he returned from a trip up the Yellowstone with tales of boiling springs, fountains of steam, quaking and smoking earth, mountains of glass. Sixty-five years later a body of enthusiasts assisted by members of the Hayden Survey and armed with photographs by William Henry Jackson and watercolors by Thomas Moran would succeed in having Congress set aside Colter's Hell as Yellowstone National Park, the first of a great system. Both the discovery and the reservation are significant points of reference; they bracket a substantial part of the West's history, from exploration through exploitation to federal reservation and management. A hundred and fifty years after Colter made the first white tracks in the Yellowstone country, an annual invasion of nearly two million tourists would be threatening to trample it to death, and would have done so long since except for the protection provided by the National Park Service.

After 1808 the Northwest Company had posts in western Montana, in 1810 Andrew Henry built his post on Henry's Fork of the Snake, in 1829 the American Fur Company erected Fort Union at the mouth of the Yellowstone, and this was for a time the ultimate outpost of the raiders in a hostile country. But the trade was already shifting westward, away from the river that was so unreliable and dangerous a highway, with so many belligerent tribes in a constant boil along its banks. Soon the raiders would operate without bases, and in their wanderings they would locate a road. Wilson Henry Hunt led his fifty Astorians down the Snake and the Columbia in 1811, following roughly the route of Lewis and Clark. Next year, Robert Stuart led a small party back, swerving southward in search of an easier way. Crossing the mountains to the south and east of the Tetons, he may have made the first crossing of South Pass. The effective discovery of that route, the one with consequences, was made by a party of General Ashley's trappers under Thomas Fitzpatrick and Jedediah Smith in 1824. Intent upon new beaver country, they prepared the way for a new phase of the frontier.

Over the same featureless plateau, Jason Lee and the Spaldings and Marcus and Narcissa Whitman would go missionarying to the Oregon. Whitman would drag a wagon all the way to Fort Hall in 1836; in 1840 mountain men and missionaries would print the mark of wheels all the way to Whitman's mission at Waiilatpu. While fixed posts such as Fort Laramie and Fort Hall began to take over from the annual rendezvous of the fur brigades, and while Nathaniel Wyeth disputed the Snake River country with Peter Skene Ogden and John Work of the Hudson's Bay Company, the fur trade guttered out. Marcus Whitman enforced the new order on the imagination of the country, first making his epic journey from the west coast to preach the gospel of Oregon into eastern ears, and then on his return taking a wagon train all the way through, to show that it could be done. That was almost two decades after the discovery of the easy wagon pass, but the discovery made it all inevitable. There lay the open track to—or through—the West: the route of the Donner-Reed party doomed to their grisly ordeal in the snow-blocked Sierra in 1846, the way of the Mormon pioneer company, moving out of the infested Missouri River bottoms in 1847; the road of the Gold Rush; the road of the handcart companies walking to their snowdrift graves along the Sweetwater in 1856.

Stand on South Pass now and you will find it as still and peaceful as if no clamor of empire had ever surged through it. Antelope will drift close to see what you are up to. No smokes stain the dark blue sky. The riotous rendezvous of the fur hunters, held in this vicinity for a dozen years after 1825, have left neither echo nor mark, not even a tepee ring. The wheels that between 1836 and 1869 rocked and creaked and squealed up the Sweetwater and down past the westward trickle of Pacific Creek have left ruts that still braid among the sage and bunchgrass, but modern travel does not go this way. Both U.S. 30 and the Union Pacific cross the divide at Creston; all that crosses South Pass now is Wyoming 28, a secondary road.

And here is a lesson not only in history but in the fallibility of prophecy. In 1860 William Gilpin foresaw South Pass as a gateway more thronging then Gibraltar, and the population of the Rocky Mountain region as hundreds of millions.

Ask the antelope, coming back after near-extinction, where those hundreds of millions are. Ask the people from the Soil Conservation Service, the Bureau of Land Management, the Forest Service, who have the job of restoring and protecting the overgrazed ranges, how they would like that many guests. Look eastward, back to where the

Sweetwater flows into the North Platte, and see in the Seminole, Kortes, and Pathfinder dams one of the salient reasons why this part of what Gilpin called the Great Cordilleran Region is habitable even by a thin population. The dams represent the act of acquired wisdom, the acknowledgement of inexorable aridity. Gilpin made one error: he forgot that people live on water as much as on land.

Nobody stopped here to accommodate Gilpin's prophecies. Except for the Mormons who after 1847 were building an agricultural society in the valleys of Utah and southern Idaho and the western edge of Nevada, nobody stopped here in the mountain country—especially after John Marshall stooped to examine the glitter in the bottom of Sutter's millrace at Coloma, California, in January 1848. For a round decade everybody went straight on through, cursing every dusty mile between him and the Pacific coast. From John Colter on, men with wild blood in them had found the Rockies a place of savage freedom, but the mountains apparently offered nothing to the homemaker, and their minerals had not yet been discovered. Oregon wagons and Forty-niners were part of the history but not the life of the Rocky Mountains. The Mormons were another kind. On their very first day in Salt Lake Valley they made their peace with one of the West's inflexible conditions—they diverted the water of City Creek and softened the ground for a potato field, and thus began Anglo-American irrigation on this continent, admitting what Indian and Spaniard had already had to learn.

The ferocious partisans of the fur companies had cleaned out the beaver, or lost their market, or both, by 1840, and turned to guiding wagon trains, scouting for the cavalry, or hunting buffalo for the hides. Nearly twenty years before they had the buffalo wiped out and the cavalry had suppressed the last desperate Indian uprisings, a new wave of raiders swept in on the Rockies from both east and west. The year 1858 saw gold strikes on Clear Creek, near modern Denver, and on Cripple Creek back of Pike's Peak, and on Gold Creek in Montana. The next year the fabulous Comstock sucked half the miners in California over the mountains into Nevada, and intercepted most of the travelers from the East. Idaho joined the excitement with the strike on Orofino Creek in 1861, and in 1862 with strikes in the Boise Basin and at Bannack in the Beaverhead country. In 1863 the discovery of the richest of all placers brought into existence a Montana Virginia City to match the Nevada town of the same name on the Comstock. By that time General Connor's soldiers, posted in Salt Lake City to keep an eye on the Mormons, had been turned loose to find gold in Bingham Canyon and in the Wasatch; and a Gentile society of raiders, which gradually transformed itself into a more permanent cluster of camps to exploit lode mines, developed in competition with the Mormon society of irrigation farmers.

Insofar as the non-Mormon West was settled at all by 1869, when the Union Pacific and Central Pacific bumped cowcatchers at Promontory and opened a new age of accessibility for the mountains, it was settled by miners, and miners are notoriously prone to vanish from their mushroom towns as quickly as they gather. Quartz mines can last a long time—one summer forty years ago I mucked in one that is still producing. New discoveries and new mining and smelting methods have kept alive such towns as Bingham, Butte, Anaconda, Park City, Ely. For that matter Salt Lake City, the heart of Mormon agrarianism, is the largest non-ferrous smelting center in the world. But if the West depended entirely on minerals to support a civilization, it could look forward to an extinction as complete as that of the Land of Midian, where King Solomon's mines have heard only the dry whisper of blowing sand for millennia. Mineral resources are not renewable; placers especially are resources of a few years at most. The early camps went out like blown matches.

In such of them as now show any standing buildings, doors swing in the wind and snow blows in the broken windows of saloons and stores, the nails are tufted with hair, the gutted gulches spill their gravels into the valleys in cloudbursts, and the mountainsides whose timber went to prop shafts or flumes show now the deep scorings of erosion gulleys. Some lode camps like Virginia City, Nevada, or Leadville, Colorado, survive as fractions or remnants; some, like Virginia City, Montana, Aspen, Colorado, and Alta, Utah, have been rejuvenated as resort or ski towns. But many lode towns, too, are ghosts, leavings of the second careless rush of hit-and-run exploiters, a breed as thoughtless of the future as the mountain men slaughtering their way through a wilderness of animals that seemed inexhaustible and then was suddenly gone. The towns that *did* expect a future, looking upon their mineral wealth as inexhaustible, and so erected opera houses and ice palaces and hotels, and cultivated the high-toned arts (the two Virginia Cities, Leadville, Central City) have a wistful lease on life as quaint tourist traps or as the sites of summer opera festivals. They survive, that is, on transfusions.

Montana, Colorado, most of Idaho, and Nevada all drew their first inhabitants to the mineralized mountains, not to their agricultural land. Utah and its southern Idaho outposts maintained their pastoral and cooperative economy even through the mining excitements, and made money selling services, farm produce, mules, and Valley Tan whiskey to the infidel. Wyoming, with vast grasslands, became above all a cattle country. The raid here, as on the plains of Colorado and Montana, was on the grass. Many of the cattle corporations, like the fur companies and mining companies, were absentee-owned, some in England and Scotland. The men who set out to get rich from western grasslands shared the psychology—and the ignorance of consequences—of the men who had cleaned out the beaver streams, the buffalo, and the precious metals. Who among the mountain men would have paused to consider, or would have cared, that beaver were a water resource, and that beaver engineering was of great importance in the maintenance of stream flow and the prevention of floods? Who among the miners worried about what happened to the watersheds when they logged their timbers or tore up streambeds with their dredges? Who among the cattlemen knew or cared that in a dry land grass, like minerals, might be non-renewable, that some of the best grasses were annuals that reproduced only from seed, that overgrazing both prevented reseeding and encouraged erosion? The cattleman like his predecessors lived a large, free life; he is even more deeply embedded in our folklore than mountain man or miner; in terms of the enduring capacity of the West to sustain a civilization, he did more harm than either.

Late as they came to it, settlers were in the West before much of it was surveyed and before there were laws adequate to its conditions. The public domain lay wide open to anyone with the energy to take it. Also there were, for those who chose to use them, short cuts to empire. By having your cowhands homestead a quarter section apiece and commute it to you for a small consideration, you could assemble the core of a noble range. By homesteading, buying, or merely appropriating the land along the watercourses or around the sources of water, you could dominate many square miles of dry grazing land. By using the public domain as if it were really your own, you could perhaps convince yourself that you had exclusive rights to it, and by intimidation or the method known as dry-gulching you might discourage rivals or sheepmen or nesters, saying in justification that they were trespassers or rustlers. The history of the West is full of murderous quarrels over property that neither of the contestants owned, and over rights that no law had approved. Transformed, these quarrels are often the stuff of horse opera. Read, for instance, the history of the Johnson County War in Wyoming, when cattlemen rode northward from Cheyenne with a list of "rustlers" and "trespassers" they intended to rub out. They rubbed out two, with great difficulty, before the law began belatedly to assert that the rustlers and trespassers had as much right where they were as the cattlemen who were trying to gun them off. That is an ugly story. But put in the terms Owen Wister gave it in *The Virginian*, it takes on all the beguiling qualities of myth. The culture hero, torn between friendship and his duty to "law," does not seem like a lyncher and a vigilante. By such transformations it is even possible to make a sort of hero out of Tom Horn, the cattlemen's hired assassin, or Billy the Kid, a psychopathic killer.

The mythic West is the West that everybody knows. Every American child grows up in it. The dream of total emancipation from inhibition, law, convention, and restraint is a potent dream (I know some hippies who are snuggling up to it in caves and shacks in the California hills at this moment). The West, wide open, has fostered that dream as few environments could. And if emancipated and uninhibited man was also lawless, if he was a scoundrel as so many western characters turn out to be on close inspection, let us make him a rebel against the system, a friend of the poor, according to a formula well known to the folk creators of Robin Hood and Jesse James. If law officials turn out to be bandits with badges on, and if the posse who made themselves judge, jury, legislature, and hangman look sometimes like dupes, sometimes like a bloody-minded rabble, let us put into their mouths such excuses as the Virginian uses, and further palliate their vigilantism by making them courteous to women and tender to little children. Let us give them a stern faith in honesty, property, and the sanctity of contract. Commit them fully to the mores of the middle class community and give them all the lineaments of the Lone Ranger. Let them be lawless in defense of law, unconventional in the service of convention, and the peculiarity of their ethics, like the dubiousness of their exploitation of the natural resources of the West, blurs and disappears in a blaze of picturesqueness.

The mythic western hero, an apostle of the most rugged individualism, is a curious hangover, and may often be caught sanctifying odd practices and policies. He had codified and perpetuated an honor as high-colored as the feudal code of the old South—which, by way of the Virginian and other ex-Confederates among the cattle drovers, was probably its source. He suggests that the resolution of every quarrel is ultimately violence. The walkdown is a fixture of all highbrow horse opera, as the stagecoach chase is of the lowbrow variety. This mythic cowboy is really a citizen of a Poictesme, a Cockaigne, a Never-Never land, but he is propped with the most niggling realism. Try to write a Western with your gun lore crooked, or with holes in your lingo. He is sometimes—and this is the principal danger of what would otherwise be only wistful or amusing— invoked to justify new outbreaks of rugged individualism, irresponsibility, intemperance, and the economics of the raid.

The real people of the West are infrequently cowboys and never myths. They live in places like Denver and Salt Lake, Dillon and Boise, American Fork and American Falls, and they confront the real problems of real life in a real region, and have gone some distance toward understanding the conditions of western life and accepting the agencies that have been slowly created to meet them. But those who live by the myth, or pretend to, have never admitted that they live in a land of little rain and big consequences. Whether they are resisting the gift of Grand Teton National Monument from the Rockefellers to the people of the United States, or maneuvering for the transfer of grazing, timber, oil, or mineral lands from national parks and forests to the state and ultimately to private ownership for the quick profit of a few, they represent the survival of a gospel that left to its own devices would already have reduced the West to a desert as barren as Syria.

Say of the quintessential West that it is extravagantly endowed, but that it has one critical deficiency, water, and that therefore its soil, its watersheds, its timber, and its grass are all vulnerable. There have been man-made deserts before this in the world's history; some, like the valley of Oaxaca, in Mexico, are being made while we watch. The West could be one of those: it is not comforting to know that its grasslands are at least fifty percent deteriorated in the century of our occupancy, and that its rivers run muddy where they used to run clear. The very jokes that strike us as characteristically western are likely to have an edge of grimness: "Throw a gopher in the air, and if he starts to burrow, it ain't a clear day." "The best place to locate a farm in eastern Colorado is in western Kansas."

Say of the West, too, that it has been plundered and has plundered itself, but that little by little whole communities and districts have learned how to manage their environment and have made superb living places out of their oases. Say that the West is everybody's romantic home, for we have all spent a part of our childhood there. And say that in its territory, as in its legendry, much of the West is public domain. Next to aridity, that may be the most important fact about it.

Of the four hundred million acres in the Rocky Mountain states, more than half are federally owned. Of the state of Nevada, you and I own eighty-seven percent. Drive from Glacier Park to the Spanish Peaks, and from the Sierra Nevada to the high plains, and you are never out of sight of lands reserved and managed by public agencies in the public interest. Not because Westerners are more socialist than other Americans: on the contrary. And not because a conspiracy within the federal government is using the West as a pawn in a game to overthrow the American way of life. Some of these lands have been reserved to keep them from ruinous private exploitation, some to protect the regions in which they lie, some as playgrounds and wildlife sanctuaries, some simply because despite all its efforts the government was never able to get anyone to homestead or buy them.

Some of the management is a good deal less effective than it ought to be. The Bureau of Land Management's 116,000,000 acres of range and wasteland are overgrazed, partly because permit holders resist reduction of their stock, partly because the bureau has never had a budget big enough to do more than a token job. If by any miracle of public spirit or through any inconceivable inattention of western Congressmen it *should* get an adequate budget, it would find itself instantly at war with the leaseholders and stockmen's associations.

Who else runs the public West? In the six mountain states the Bureau of Reclamation has 5,500,000 acres reserved for dam and canal sites whose use, considering the finite amount of water available in the streams, would be an expensive misfortune. Reclamation has reached the point of diminishing returns. There are 4,500,000 acres set aside for "use without impairment" as national parks and monuments. There are 3,500,000 acres in game and bird refuges run by the Fish and Wildlife Service. The Bureau of Indian Affairs has 188,000 acres, apart from the Indian reservations themselves, which are not federal but tribal land. The withdrawals for the use of the armed services are large—empty space recommends itself for bombing ranges and A-bomb testing sites as well as for large installations such as the Air Force Academy near Denver. But it is the 75,000,000 acres of national forests in the six mountain states that are probably the most critical acres in the West.

They are important for their resources, their reserves of timber, their annual crop of water, their summer grazing (always too heavy), and their priceless and mushrooming value as places of outdoor recreation. But they are also vital for what they prevent. Forest Service lands lie almost entirely in the high country, on the watersheds where the West's life is made and stored, where floods can begin, where erosion is most disastrous. Both watershed control and recreation are more important functions of western forests these days than anything that can be measured in board feet, and certainly more important than the grazing which is their most harmful use and the cause of most attacks upon the Service.

Attacked or not, the Forest Service is not going to go out of business in the West, and neither are the other federal bureaus, because too many Westerners have come to depend on them. It is not merely a question of federal payrolls in local areas, though those are often a significant element in a community's economic life. Who can measure the importance to Las Vegas of the A-bomb testing range nearby, or to Denver of its more-than-two-hundred federal offices? Neither is it a question of local construction and boondoggles, though no citizen of the West is likely to complain about federal intervention when there is an interstate highway or a flood-control dam in the offing. Few Westerners will deplore the spending of public funds to rescue the trumpeter swan from the edge of extinction, or feed the elk in Jackson Hole, or cure ducks sick with botulism in the Bear River marshes. The collaboration between state fish and game departments, which hatch and plant fish and game birds, and the Forest Service, which maintains much of the habitat, is close and cordial.

But quite apart from these immediate and material bene-fits, no Westerner in his right mind would dream of trying to get along without the constant aid and support of the federal agencies. It is easy to see why. Stand, as I did once, on the high grade of the Union Pacific between Salt Lake and Ogden, and watch a cloudburst roll a fifteen-foot wall of mud and rocks and water down the canyon onto the farmland; and come back later to see houses full to the second story with mud and gravel, and fields covered ten feet deep with rocks and débris. Reflect that floods like that one arise from one cause alone—the stripping of the mountain slopes of timber in the 1880's and after. Then visit the regional forest office in Ogden and learn what they are doing in watershed research in small pilot projects, and in watershed restoration, and you will know why this agency and others have friends when the sniping starts. Watch the parachutes of smoke jumpers balloon out against a sky ominous with smoke, and the lesson acquires excitement, even heroics.

For research that preserves a national forest helps state forests or private forests. Saved watersheds reflect good all around them. A fire halted in your woods and mine is money in the pocket of everyone anywhere near there. To give the public lands to the states, as the raiders peri-odically have suggested and will suggest again—their word is "restore," which is untruthful and unhistorical—could have only one of three effects. The states would go bank-rupt trying to manage and maintain them; they would let them deteriorate according to precedents well known west of the 100th meridian; or they would turn them over to private or corporate hands to be gutted.

Most people in the West desire no such alternatives. They know when they are well off.

There is no Western face, despite the myths and stereotypes. The people of the West come from everywhere, practically, and it takes more generations than they have had, and more isolation than has been vouchsafed to them, to stabilize the breed. Also it takes more generations than they have yet had for the making of a regional culture.

The West is still nascent, still forming, and that is where much of its excitement comes from. It has a shine on it; despite its mistakes, it isn't tired. Even the dubious activities of the boosters reflect an energy that doesn't know what it means to be licked or to give up. The face of the West changes; a decade is much. Generally speaking, the country lives up to its water supply, or somewhat beyond it. So long as there is only so much water for so much land or so many municipalities or industries, Mormon boys and boys from the Montana cow towns and mining towns, boys from Sheridan and Ucross and Twin Falls, will be heading toward the West Coast or the Midwest or the East. By and large, the Rocky Mountain states export manpower.

There will be some continuing open space. Not all the immigration of the next hundred years, as the continent fills and overflows, can do more than overcrowd the oases: the arid backlands will remain essentially unpeopled. Not all the irrigation works of the next century—and let us hope that the West is sane enough to scrutinize them with a skeptical eye before rushing to embrace them—can affect the absolute amount of water that the mountains can produce, nor alter the climate sufficiently to take the dry clarity from the air or change the gray and tawny country to a green one. Despite the dubious contemporary experiment of bulldozing great tracts of sagebrush and juniper land to produce range, there will be enough of the old wild undamaged country left to give us the smell of sagebrush wetted by a shower, the bitter tang of mountain aspen, the smoke of juniper or piñon fires: western smells. Thanks to growing public comprehension of the issues and the continuing work of federal bureaus there will always be some roadless back country. The Wilderness Act put the best of it in deep freeze. And there will always be the accessible national forests, the superlative scenic and archaeological jewels of the national parks, a managed harvest of fish and game, to provide us a touch of the old wonder at mountain water, mountain sky, mountain life.

Angry as one may be at what heedless men have done and still do to a noble habitat, one cannot be pessimistic about the West. This is the native home of hope. When it fully learns that cooperation, not rugged individualism, is the quality that most characterizes and preserves it, then it will have achieved itself and outlived its origins. Then it has a chance to create a society to match its scenery.

Part I

I

~~~~~~

Overture

The Sound of Mountain Water

I discovered mountain rivers late, for I was a prairie child, and knew only flatland and dryland until we toured the Yellowstone country in 1920, loaded with all the camp beds, auto tents, grub-boxes, and auxiliary water and gas cans that 1920 thought necessary. Our road between Great Falls, Montana, and Salt Lake City was the rutted track that is now Highway 89. Beside a marvelous torrent, one of the first I ever saw, we camped several days. That was Henry's Fork of the Snake.

I didn't know that it rose on the west side of Targhee Pass and flowed barely a hundred miles, through two Idaho counties, before joining the Snake near Rexburg; or that in 1810 Andrew Henry built on its bank near modern St. Anthony the first American post west of the continental divide. The divide itself meant nothing to me. My imagination was not stretched by the wonder of the parted waters, the Yellowstone rising only a few miles eastward to flow out toward the Missouri, the Mississippi, the Gulf, while this bright pounding stream was starting through its thousand miles of canyons to the Columbia and the Pacific.

All I knew was that it was pure delight to be where the land lifted in peaks and plunged in canyons, and to sniff air thin, spray-cooled, full of pine and spruce smells, and to be so close-seeming to the improbable indigo sky. I gave my heart to the mountains the minute I stood beside this river with its spray in my face and watched it thunder into foam, smooth to green glass over sunken rocks, shatter to foam again. I was fascinated by how it sped by and yet was always there; its roar shook both the earth and me.

When the sun dropped over the rim the shadows chilled sharply; evening lingered until foam on water was ghostly and luminous in the near-dark. Alders caught in the current sawed like things alive, and the noise was louder. It was rare and comforting to waken late and hear the undiminished shouting of the water in the night. And at sunup it was still there, powerful and incessant, with the slant sun tangled in its rainbow spray, the grass blue with wetness, and the air heady as ether and scented with campfire smoke.

By such a river it is impossible to believe that one will ever be tired or old. Every sense applauds it. Taste it, feel its chill on the teeth: it is purity absolute. Watch its racing current, its steady renewal of force: it is transient and eternal. And listen again to its sounds: get far enough away so that the noise of falling tons of water does not stun the ears, and hear how much is going on underneath—

a whole symphony of smaller sounds, hiss and splash and
gurgle, the small talk of side channels, the whisper of
blown and scattered spray gathering itself and beginning
to flow again, secret and irresistible, among the wet rocks.

The Rediscovery
of America: 1946

Friday: I shall not begin where I probably should begin, with the preparations, with the maps spread all over the living-room rug, or with the late-afternoon start down the Santa Clara Valley and over Pacheco Pass into the San Joaquin, where after dark the power stations in the oil-fields were jeweled clusters and the derricks were like a blasted forest on the hills. Those first hours of any trip are spent largely on the unprofitable pastime of remembering the things that have been left behind or neglected or forgotten. I shall not waste much space on how we drove until ten and then groped our way off the road into an "inner-spring wash" outside Coalinga and unrolled our sleeping bags in the sand; or how I awoke several times during the night to see the moon moving down the sky and feel the little cold wind that crept down the wash and into the neck of my bag. It is comparatively irrelevant how stiff-legged Orion looked, walking over the hills, or how I sleepily tried to find the Little Dipper by climbing up its tail from the Pole Star, but lost it in a sky too milky with moonlight.

These are things one might begin with, but I should rather begin with how it feels to be out on the road again, dry-camping in the desert, hitting the road after five years of rationing and restrictions, doing what a good third of America is doing this summer of 1946, if the polls and the prophecies mean anything. For many people—and I sympathize with them—one of the least-bearable wartime deprivations was the loss of their mobility. We are a wheeled people; it seems to me sometimes that I must have been born with a steering wheel in my hands, and I realize now that to lose the use of a car is practically equivalent to losing the use of my legs.

Returning to the road after a layoff of several years is like reestablishing intimacy with a wife or lover. There are a hundred things once known and long forgotten that crowd forward upon the senses, and there is the sharp thrill of recognition in all of them.

During war years I was luckier than most: I had had a 15,000-mile tour in 1941, and in 1944 I got to drive across the continent again and even to work in many side trips to Indian reservations, Japanese relocation centers, and other compounds where we keep the people we fear or dislike. But that trip was clouded by scarcities, rationing, the pressure of business. It had none of the fine loose-jointed feeling we get on this one, and it did not revive old acquaintance as this one does.

Every five minutes I establish contact in a new area. The smell of wetted dust and wetted sagebrush in a desert thundershower is a fragrance more packed with associations than the most romantic of flowers. The signs that I have seen all my life on roadsides and weathered barn roofs are old friends well met, and I resolve that some day, not for health or enjoyment but for pure love, I shall try Dr. Pierce's Golden Medical Discovery, or Dr. Pierce's Pleasant Pellets. Some day I am going to chew Mailpouch tobacco, and treat myself to the best. Some day I am going to soak in Burma-Shave the whiskers that now are a pleasant untended roughness on my jaws. Some day I may even stop and ponder the signs that in staggering letters, in runny white paint, shout from the granite of dry canyons and the red sandstone of washes, "Jesus Saves," or "Christ Died for *You*." (I wonder who puts those messages up there, and when. Somehow I have a mental image of furtive little men clambering like monkeys after dark, daubing their messages, and then running barefooted and stealthy back to the caves where they must live.)

I have forgotten for too long how the tangled, twisted, warped and bent and bone-dry desert ranges lift out of their alluvial slopes, and how the road droops like a sagging rope from one dry pass to another. It is good to play the old game of guessing how far it is to that point, always foreshortened and looking deceptively close, where the road curves and disappears into the rock. It is good to get out of the monotonous green of tamed land and out among the changeable grays and browns and ochres and rusty reds and glaring whites of the desert. It is a fine and relaxing pleasure to sag into the corner of the seat and feel the hot sun on the bare left arm, the furnace-blast of wind from the flats. The wide sailing of buzzards is poetry.

I have forgotten—though I did not really forget, for

how can one forget the things that at night in his childhood choked him with the sense of the wildness and
strangeness of the world?—the way a car sounds on a
lonely road when it comes fast in the dark, and you hear
the growing hum, sometimes fading behind hills or down
in washes, but coming on again, growing, and the lights
pricking across the plain, until the glare bursts on sage
and mesquite and the hum is a roar and a rush and the
bushes bend and grass flattens, and light is darkness again
and the rush is a roar, and now a hum, a diminishing buzz, a
fading whisper, and then there is only the loneliness where
it passed.

The shocks of remembrance and reminder are constant.
The East does not provide the swift scuttling things that
whip through the glare of the headlights on these night
roads. There you would see a porcupine, perhaps, or a
prowling cat gone wild, or a creeping opossum, but not
this life that fills the lights with its variety and paves the
highway with its rundown bodies. Here they move whitely
and at skittering speed. Little high-tailed geckos, surely
as fast as any footed creature, dart and are gone. A bigger
lizard, looking huge and pleistocene but moving with that
same lizard-speed, makes you jam your foot on the brake
for fear of wrecking yourself. In the white glare he looks
as big as a dog.

Jackrabbits seem not to be as numerous as they used
to be, but on any night drive at least one will jerk into
the magnetic beam and race and dodge ahead of the car,
its ears up and then flat, its movements swift and scared.
But it will not, or cannot, very often leap off into the
dark and be safe. Eventually it will cut across under the

wheels, and there will come the sodden thump and the tug of the steering wheel and the squeamish qualm. Geckos you can run over without feeling, tiny and harmless as they are. You can say, "He's wider than he used to be, but not so thick," and laugh. But being the number one natural enemy of the jackrabbit is a queasier business.

As a matter of fact, the automobile is the natural enemy of dozens of small creatures—rabbits, gophers, snakes, mice, lizards, ground squirrels. The highways throughout the West are practically paved with flattened, crisped, sun-dried rabbits and ribboned snakes and wafered squirrels. By killing off the coyotes and wolves we let the rabbits and rodents mutiply; by building highways we lure them to their death under our furious wheels. "Compensation," says Mr. Emerson. "It all evens up," echoes Mr. Hemingway. I wish I felt it possible to draw a moral about how it does not pay to be a predator in this brave new world, but all I can devise is that it doesn't pay to be anything except man. Maybe it doesn't pay to be man either.

Saturday: At four-thirty, at this date and latitude, the sky is full of light while the earth is still dusky. The horizons are ringed with pure, pale light without shadows; there is no wind or stir. Probably this is the same light Wordsworth saw on Westminster Bridge, but my associations with pre-dawn light have no cities in them. I grew up in the arid lands in close intimacy with grass and horizons and sky, and here they are again, as serene and grave as if they have been waiting for me. There is not a chance to sleep longer. This chilly wash, this air, this light, this brown grass and the gopher-dug dry earth are too like the homestead of my childhood and the mornings when I went up through the pasture after the horses. My rising wakes Dave and Miriam Bonner, sleeping thirty feet away, and then Mary and Page. On this first morning out we cook and break camp so briskly that we are on the road at six.

Technically we have not begun this trip yet, but are merely on our way to it. At Bakersfield we gas up with the feeling that we are about to start. The service station attendant is full of admiration for our water-butt, which used to belong in a Navy lifeboat. He wishes he had one to age whiskey in, though he admits sadly that keeping-whiskey and keeping-money never seem to come his way. All he ever gets is the drinking or spending kind. But he fills our breaker with cold water and we leave his Oklahoma drawl behind and start up Tehachapi Pass, the lowest and southernmost of the Sierra crossings. Now the sense of freedom comes to us undiluted.

I doubt if there is any American with any of his country's history in his blood who is not excited at the crossing of a range. I had the feeling last night, crossing the Diablo Range by way of low, oak-dotted Pacheco Pass. I have it stronger now, on the spring-green slopes of Tehachapi. From Cumberland Gap to South Pass and Weber Canyon and the snowy passes of the Sierra, we have been a pass-surmounting people, fascinated by that newness on the other side, that land "vaguely realizing westward." We have misted our eyes with far-looking and stretched our minds on the high points of the continent. Like the bear who went over the mountain, we have got these crossings in our itchy bones, and perhaps always will have. The other side of the mountain is plenty to see, even if we have seen it before.

Tipping the summit of Tehachapi and rolling down the desert side we ran through acres and square miles of spring flowers, whole hillsides of lavender and white and yellow, and a pair of photographers were out, flattening their tripod almost to the ground to get a shot across the blowing flower-heads. Driving down this side was like discovery, and I kept thinking of other passes I had known and crossed.

There was Elbow Pass in the Canadian Rockies above Banff, and Snoqualmie Pass across the Cascades, looking down into the valley of the Cle Ellum; there was King's Hill Pass in the Little Belt Mountains in Montana, the place where for the first time the prairie child I used to be saw pines, and camped beside a mountain stream; there were Ute Pass and Trout Creek Pass and the Weminuche in Colorado, and the Spearfish Canyon road in the Black Hills; there was Sylvan Pass opening up the whole forested lake-set Yellowstone Basin, and packhorse passes like Hades Canyon up into the permanent wilderness of the Granddaddy Lakes country in eastern Utah. There was the climb between Cheyenne and Laramie where the Lincoln Highway crawled up from the high plains to the Wyoming Plateau; there was San Marcos, switching across the Santa Ynez Mountains and breaking suddenly out high above the long lacy shoreline and peopled rivieras of Santa Barbara; there were little-known dirt-road passes like the Seven-Mile Canyon road over the Fish Lake Hightop to Salina, in south-central Utah—a pass that in the late mountain spring was so paved with flowers that a man could walk twenty miles and never set his foot down without trampling them.

They were fine passes to think of, and fine names to roll on the tongue. And ahead lay Mojave, and beyond Mojave the real desert. The stiff, cold wind blew us down the pass; the broken desert ahead was misted with dust beyond the scattered buildings of the town. But I was perfectly content. I knew that almost anyone in the United States would give his spare tire to be where we were, at the threshold of the dry country, with fifteen hundred miles of it ahead.

Dave is very mellow tonight. He is a back-road fiend, and is relatively unhappy on asphalt. But now we are out in what even he has to call happily the bald-assed desert. From Windmill Station, where we finally turned off Highway 91, we took a dirt road toward Cima, turned off that onto a still smaller road, and off that onto a trail that dwindled out in a wide wash. The wind was still blowing hard, and it was cold. To get the protection of a reef of sandstone, we lugged food boxes and water-butt and sleeping bags two hundred years through the sand. The place was dense with joshua trees and cholla and barrel cactus. Every shrub we touched stabbed. Young Page stabbed himself on a yucca, which is not called Spanish bayonet for nothing, and then was clawed by a cholla. Only his discovery of the bleached and sutured shell of a desert tortoise consoled him for the cold and wind and thorns. The rest of us, trying to get camp set up before dark, and get some food going, fell back on the jug of heavy sweet wine which Dave insisted was the best of all desert giant-killers—swift and potable and uncomplex. Oddly enough, he was right.

Now about sunset there is a kind of miracle. The wind dies. Our blood lifts to the heavily-fortified wine. The steak we picked up in Barstow fills the little cross-wash with delirium, the dehydrated soup bubbles in the kettle. The sleeping bags, laid out in a row under a mesquite bush, look inviting and snug. It comes back to me that of all the places to camp, the desert is probably the friendliest. So far as I know, there are only three indispensable requirements for a campsite: wood, level ground to sleep on, and water. In the desert there is always wood, far more than you ever expect, yucca or sage or greasewood or mesquite, or sometimes the dry stalks of cholla, cleaned of thorns, hollow and bone-dry and perforated with neat surrealist holes, so that every stick looks like the cooling jacket of a machine gun. There is always some sandy wash where sleeping is not only level but soft. There is always water because you bring it with you. And you are pretty certain you won't get rained on.

From a disconsolate improvised shelter, the camp becomes a warm and jovial place. We wolf soup and steak and canned peas and bread and jam, wash the dishes and build up the fire and pull Page's sleeping bag close so that he can drowse in the warmth, and pass the jug again. Miriam declines: she says she has a low emetic threshold.

We sit up till midnight, until the talk has run down and the jug has run out. Up aloft the stars are scoured and glittering, and far down the valley the headlight of a train crawls along the Union Pacific's main line. The tracks probably pass within a dozen miles of our camp, and the main Salt Lake-Los Angeles highway is only another dozen back of us. Yet we are almost as remote as Frémont was in this desert a hundred years ago. The road we came in on won't see a half dozen cars a month, and the highway and the railroad will pour their thousands past without affecting this wash in the slightest.

Somehow the white casing of the turtle, sitting on a rock in the moonlight, is symbolic. Tortoises, like elephants, live a long time and die remotely. In this turtle's deathplace we have come directly and promptly to the ultimate isolation. Snuggled into our bags with the renewed wind in the mesquite over our heads, we do not rise up to watch the headlight creep down the valley, and if it whistles for the crossing at Cima we do not hear it for the wind.

Sunday: Twenty years ago Searchlight had nothing to show but crumbling shanties with lizards on the sills, the sad open mouths of drifts and prospect holes, rusting machinery. Now it lies on a paved highway linking Boulder City and Needles. In the sprawling central square the false-fronts wear new paint, mostly orange. We count seven bar-and-casino joints, and even the cafe where we stop for a beer has a crap table, a twenty-one table, and a battery of slot machines. The population is variously reported at from twenty-nine to forty; the housing shortage is serious.

After one boom and a long decay and a flurry of renewed mining activity during the war, Searchlight is due for another boom as a recreation point for workers on the new Davis Dam. The old ghost town is full of drifters. On top of the most imposing of the casinos sits the buckboard in which a certain frontier lady brought in the bodies of two claim-jumpers back in that other boom.

Everyone in town is dutifully repeating this story as part of the Searchlight build-up.

There is a curiously hectic metabolic rate about Nevada towns. It is as if, in the middle of the unwinking desert, man was forced into alternating periods of hibernation and hysteria. And the preparations for a boom are somehow less picturesque than the left-overs of one. We get off on a dirt road as fast as we can, heading for Boulder City by a roundabout way.

Our map, the Mojave and Colorado deserts map of the Automobile Club of Southern California, is the best of its kind, but it is several years old, and surprising things happen. As we come down El Dorado Wash past abandoned mines and caved-in drifts, new asphalt begins mysteriously in the middle of the gulch. At the mouth of the wash we find the wide clear river, see the ranks of trailers lined up hub to hub, hear the impatience of an Elto Twin as it rushes a boat downriver between the low red cliffs. This is the rainbow trout part of the Boulder Dam Recreational Area. After the desert, it looks as populous as Market Street. Ghost towns with housing shortages, gulches which suddenly develop paved roads and trailer parks, confuse us. Obviously this back road we have been exploring with tourist zeal is familiar to every fisherman within five hundred miles. We give up the notion of a swim and head for Boulder City.

Here is another surprise, but a pleasant one. Ten years ago Boulder City was a temporary work town on the barren desert slope. Now it is as green as Ireland, palpitatingly and tenderly green, and over all the streets and the lush little park fast-growing locust trees, pink and white with blossom, spray the town with fragrance. Even the climate has been built from scratch. While the desert all around simmers and the heat waves beat up from sage, this emerald town blows cool in the face of the tourist, cooled by the evaporation from lawns and trees.

We have an invitation to go up the lake for two days as the guests of the Park Service. When I have called Superintendent Edwards and verified the date, we pull on down the long slope to the green patch of the camp ground, thick with tamarisks and trailers. Without unpacking we try a swim, which is cold, on the beach, which is rocky at this stage of low water. In a few weeks the lake will reach fifty feet higher and several hundred yards further up the shore. It is this annual rise and fall which prevents Lake Mead from developing vegetation along its littoral. The buff and pink and yellow and gray mountains rising up from the improbable cobalt water are as bald as when the water was a muddy red thread far down in the canyons.

Tonight we realize the full implications of being not in the wilderness-desert, but in the tourist-desert. In the wilderness, camping is casual and private. Here, a caretaker comes around to tell us that if we want electric plug-ins we'd better move down a few notches. We want no electric plug-ins, but evidently most of the campers here do, for they are standard equipment, along with camp stoves, water taps, tables, benches, clean washroom-toilets, and bath houses.

Next to us an Illinois car and trailer pull in, and the man goes about plugging in his lights and blocking up his wheels. By the time we have finished our primitive and grubby meal our neighbor and his wife are outside with toothpicks in their mouths. The man brings out something white, and I see that it is a section of folding fence, which he sets up around the end of the trailer, and his wife comes out with two folding chairs, and in the dusk they sit within those palings on a spot of ground that is forever Peoria.

We run a course from amusement to irritation. We miss the freedom of last night's camp, and chafe against this crowded urbanism, and half contemplate breaking the rule against camping outside the designated sites. As sage-brushers, whiskery and with gritty ears, we grow bitter and witty at the regimentation of the tourist. Do Not Pick the Wild Flowers, Do Not Destroy or Injure Shrubs or Trees, Place Garbage in Containers, Park Here. Even the signs in the toilets: "Stand Close."

But by bed-time we have talked away our grouch. We remember the desert east of Mojave, every clump of grease-wood or rabbit brush plastered with clinging papers, every stretch of sand strewn with cans and boxes and bottles and the débris of man. Wherever people come in any numbers, they spoil the land. Unsupervised campers, even such impeccable and responsible campers as we think we are, could spoil the whole desert, and without careful rules the campsites in parks and monuments would quickly become wheeled slums. This camp may be crowded, but it is no slum. It is as clean as a city park. We say goodnight fairly pleasantly to the pair sitting twenty feet away in Peoria.

Monday: In a way, camping by boat is more irresponsible than even sagebrushing in the bald desert. Making lunch in the galley of this ex-Coast-Guard patrol boat, we heave cans and scraps blithely overboard. Lake Mead, which could when full supply every person in the United States with 80,000 gallons of water (the Bureau of Reclamation pamphlets are emphatic on this point), is supposedly too big to be polluted.

We are nearing the upper end of the wide lower basin. Fortification Hill is behind us, and over the barren mountains back of Hemenway Wash the snow-peak of Charleston Mountain dreams in the high blue. Our hosts are Ray Poyser, the boatman, a Coast Guard veteran like his boat, and Wilbur Doudna, ex-Navy, a ranger-naturalist. Through the blue glass of the cabin, which deepens the color of the sky and water to postcard intensity, they point out a cluster of wild burros over on the south shore. The burros are so thick in the Recreational Area, Doudna says, that they sometimes have to be thinned out by slaughtering parties. It is hard to get volunteers. I should think it would be.

The shores begin to close in, and we cut into Boulder Canyon between nearly vertical walls. The rock is iron gray above, but from water's edge to high water mark it is bleached white. We are seeing here what the birds used to see before Boulder Dam filled the canyon with water. On any natural lake this deep there would be legends of holes where no line could find bottom, and those holes would probably turn out to be exactly opposite similar holes in the Dead Sea in Palestine. It is nice to know that if we want to inspect the bottom of this lake we can do it on the pre-dam maps. We even know what the local lost Atlantis looks like: at the bottom of Boulder Canyon, undisturbed by the passage of our hull five hundred feet above it, lies the stone building that was once the Mormon river port of Callville.

At the end of a half hour we break out of the pinching cliffs into what the maps call the Virgin Basin, and what Poyser calls Big Lake, or Middle Lake. History is with us here, as it was over the drowned port of Callville. On August 30, 1869, the remnants of Major John Wesley Powell's party, bearded and dirty and down to their last moldy pounds of provisions, met a party of Mormons seining here at the mouth of the Virgin. That day saw the completion of the first passage of the Colorado River canyons by boat, and ended the last major exploration within the continental United States. Because I have for several years been gathering materials for a biography of Powell, I look around here with interest, but where Powell saw low shores and placid muddy river and muddy banks, there is now an even spread of blue sweeping northward.

Neither Powell's journal nor the journal of Jacob Hamblin, who ran this stretch of river even before Powell, is of any use now except for an occasional identifying landmark like the Temple, opposite Temple Bar Wash, an hour upriver, where we meet a pair of fishing boats. The old road that used to come down to a ferry here lies on the cindery hills and hangs its tongue in the lake like a run dog.

The lake narrows into Virgin Canyon, widens out for a long run up Gregg Basin, then is squeezed into the slot of Iceberg Canyon, where high on the wall a Reclamation Service marker perches like an impossible highway sign. Now we are in Arizona.

There will not be for us the fun of sailing up under

Emery Falls, which we can see in a side canyon across the bar, and filling our drinking cups from the fall. We won't see Rampart Cave, either. Ray feels his way until we have had a look, and that is all we will get. Here at the very threshold of the really stupendous scenery, under the lee of the first mighty walls, we have to turn back. I curse myself that I never got down here when the lake went deep into the cliffs, or when the river ran unimpeded.

Only Page, who has explored the boat from forecastle to propeller, looked out portholes and hung over the bow with his nose in the bow wave, who has had a hundred-mile boat ride and is tired of boat rides, is philosophical. "Now can we go fishing?" he says.

An hour before sunset we anchor in a side canyon and Dave, Ray, and Wilbur go off trolling in the skiff. Page fishes with a minnow off the stern of the big boat. It takes him ten minutes to get his first bass, about a one-pounder. Then he brings up a crappie. Miriam, Mary, and I have a highball with some of Ray's K-rations for canapes. In this still cove we can almost hear the rocks giving up their heat. I have a feeling I can even hear the evaporation (a quarter inch a day from the whole 227 square miles of lake) gradually slow up and stop as the sun goes. There is not a gurgle or a lap from the water, though along shore a carp jumps heavily. Down in the water around Page's lip-hooked minnow we can see the small bass chugging, interested but not excited.

I catch the pole, which Page has put down for a moment, and save it from going overboard. This time the fun is mine, two or two and a half pounds of big-mouthed bass.

When our party returns with five small bass, we chase Page to bed belowdecks, clean fish, and set up cots on the deck. Miriam and Dave carry their sleeping bags ashore, determined not to miss a chance to sleep on the ground. Before we turn in we carry our last jug up on shore and make a fire up by high-water mark, where there is plenty of dry bleached wood snagged among the rocks.

The night, like the day, seems full of an intense purity of light and shadow. The driftwood burns hotly, almost without smoke, and the flames are clean. The moon rises full and round, chasing the dark out of our pocket except under the eastern cliff. Passing the bottle around, we get off on peace pipes, and I tell about Powell's experience with a Shivwits peacepipe, its stem broken and mended with sinew and buckskin rags, the whole making a mouthful oozy with old spittle and goodwill. But I do not seem to drive anyone away from the giant killer. All I get is a story from Doudna about a desert rat in the Panamints who had a little creek with minnows in it. Every night he put his false teeth in the stream to let the minnows clean them. "Did a good job, too," Doudna says.

We get talking of animals, which are Doudna's specialty. He and Dave, who is a micro-biologist, swap learning, but Dave cannot swap bear stories with Wilbur. Wilbur has known a man who killed a grizzly bear with a club. "What was the matter with his teeth?" I say.

"Well," Doudna says, "this fellow was pretty old. Teeth were all gone. He tried gumming the bear for a while, but he didn't seem to be getting anywhere, so he used the club."

I give up and crawl back to the foredeck to my cot. The stay from the bow to the boat's short mast is a black line across the narrow sky, and the sky itself is blue-and-silver with moonlight. Straight overhead the moon is molten, as if someone on the other side had burned a hole through the silver bowl with a blowtorch.

This is the fourth night in a row I have gone to sleep with the moon in my eyes.

Tuesday: Two days on Lake Mead, and an afternoon and evening going through the dam and the powerhouses, have made boosters of us.* Nobody can visit Boulder Dam itself without getting that World's Fair feeling. It is certainly one of the world's wonders, that sweeping cliff of concrete, those impetuous elevators, the labyrinths of tunnels, the huge power stations. Everything about the dam is marked by the immense smooth efficient beauty that seems peculiarly American. Though no architect designed it and no one mind planned its masses and its details, it has the effect of great art. And the dam itself is only the beginning.

The tamed water of the Colorado is drunk in hundreds of thousands of southern California homes; it irrigates two million acres of desert land; it will generate, at full capacity, nearly six million kilowatt hours of electricity; it makes possible such big-time desert boomtowns as Henderson, be-

---

* The euphoria of 1946 hardly lasts into 1969. In the years between, threats to put dams in Grand and Marble canyons have made us all reconsider the limits of legitimate reclamation; and up-river dams, such as Flaming Gorge and Glen Canyon, have divided the available water with Lake Mead, with a consequent spreading of exposed mud flats. When we came down the Grand Canyon by boat in the summer of 1968, Lake Powell was being bled to keep up the power head in Lake Mead, and neither reservoir was anywhere near full.

tween Boulder City and Las Vegas; it fructifies, instead of flooding, the Imperial, Coachella, Yuma, and Palo Verde valleys. And in addition to this it provides, in Lake Mead and Parker Lake and the clear river between them, a tourist attraction that will certainly draw a thousand times more people into the desert than ever the gold and silver leads did. Otherwise inaccessible country is opened; camping is possible along 550 miles of shoreline without the desert necessity of packing water; the bass fishing is probably not surpassed anywhere, and there is no closed season. It is no wonder that Las Vegas, the nearest supply point, has been on a red-hot boom ever since work began on the dam. It will continue to boom. Perhaps the Reclamation Service's seismological stations will record the enormous shifting weight of tourist travel, and prosperity be measured by the seriousness of the earth tremors.

Wednesday: If Searchlight, on the brink of a boom, depressed us, Las Vegas in the midst of one depresses us worse. In the 1920's, when it was simply a way station on the Los Angeles-Salt Lake highway, Vegas was a pleasant little desert town. But now it has gone Hollywood, gone glitter and glass and chrome. The streets are full of slickers in Tom Mix shirts; every building is a casino, and you cannot walk past any door without a one-armed bandit reaching out to shake hands.

We wander into the Golden Camel, which used to be a cool dark peekhole oasis in prohibition times, but the charm isn't there. The only correct note is a desert rat with a sheep dog. The rat puts a nickel in the juke box and the dog begins to dance, but the proprietor shoulders out of his office and puts dog and prospector out. This is not as it was. Neither is the sign we see as we shake the dust of Las Vegas from our feet. "Restricted Area of Small Ranches," it says. All the spiders are busily spinning webs around this corner of the desert.

Off to our left, as we run for Death Valley Junction, we see the enticing snowfields of Charleston Peak. These too, we know, have been booby-trapped by the spiders, and contain an all-year lodge in the movie manner. It is so hot that we are tempted to turn off, but resist. Our only contact with the snow mountains is a golden eagle we meet in the desert, perhaps a refugee from the Hollywood characters upstairs. He is a very well-grown fowl indeed, as high as a hydrant on his feet, and as big as a Piper Cub when he takes off.

This is a country where distances mean as little to men as to the eagle. The postmaster of Death Valley Junction commutes seventy miles, from Furnace Creek Ranch. He tells us of the Star Route driver who serves Death Valley with mail. This driver covers four hundred miles a day, from Yermo to Stovepipe Wells and back. He puts in a new engine every two months; what he does to renew himself the postmaster does not say. To us he seems somewhat more heroic than the pony express riders, for the country he drives through is blistered under temperatures up to 125 degrees. Down in the valley yesterday it was 110. And it is 95 here today.

Dave and Miriam are already tired of paved roads. We inquire about the road up Greenwater Canyon, but nobody seems to know much about it. The storekeeper guesses it is passable, and at two o'clock we pull out.

There is a line of stones across the entrance to the Greenwater trail, but they merely whet Dave's appetite.

[63]

He assures us that those are probably put there for casual tourists unprepared for desert travel. For several miles we bounce across scrubby flats, past an abandoned borax mine, and on into a shallow canyon. By now the road is definitely not good. In fact, there is no road, but only the flood-washed gravel. There are tire tracks, however, and the wash has nothing alarming about it. We creak and warp and bounce and low-gear our way on and up.

Several times we stick in deep sand and have to dig out. At 11.7 miles from the turn-off we get stuck again, just short of a sharp turn littered with boulders. We stop for twenty minutes to cool the motor, then shove out, swing wide, take the turn at a run, and crash over the bad spot. Nothing is broken, but it is blazing hot in the wash, the wind is behind us, and the radiator is already boiling again. Dave is very happy now, and full of admiration for the beauties of this scrubby little gulch. Everything on a back road always looks spectacular to him.

At 12.1 we meet our first native resident, a three-foot rattler under a mesquite bush. He strikes furiously at the stick I hold out, and when Page tosses gravel over him he goes into a continuous, hysterical rattle. The ladies screech from the car, so we leave the snake coiled in the midst of his own hysteria and go on.

At 12.4 we meet rattler number two, a joker who plays dead in the road so that I stop indecisively, afraid Dave, who is pushing behind, might step on him. He looks dead enough, but I toss gravel to see. He explodes into a tense coil and strikes in my direction. With pieces of greasewood I keep him from sliding up into a crevice, while Dave takes his picture. This is a sidewinder, a smaller snake than the first one, but just as mad. Eventually we let him slide up into his cranny, and go on.

The road now is totally gone. We strain and creak over bare shelf-rock, over ledges, plow with everybody pushing through deep sand. At 13.1 we stick again and stop to let the motor cool. Our map shows 16.2 miles of this road before we hit a summit trail leading to the Dante's View road. Only three miles to go. We start again.

At 14.3 the hot motor vapor-locks, and we stall. To our right a burro trail leads off, and a sign says, "Painted Rocks." We know there are petroglyphs in this canyon, and are tempted, but the road is steep, the temperature well over a hundred. And it is already five o'clock. We have been three hours making fourteen miles. We decide to get through this in daylight, and after long grinding on the starter I get the engine going. Its whole sound and action seem blown and winded. We take a run, get out of the sand, jerk off across the sagebrush to avoid some boulders. My shoulders are tired from wrangling through sand and rocks.

Ahead is a narrow slot between two big boulders, the slot itself deep with sand, and beyond it a high crown grown with rabbit brush. There is nothing to do but hit it. The wheels begin to chatter, the whole body shudders and shakes, the pushers grunt and strain. Then there is that sudden settling that says the bottom has gone out, Dave yells, and I quit feeding her. There we sit, high-centered and dug in to the hubs, and the motor vapor-locks again.

We wait fifteen minutes, a half hour, digging and brushing as we wait. Then I try the starter. Nothing happens. We wait some more and try again. Still nothing. Dave and I uncouple the gas line and blow through it. Bubbles in the gas tank, so the line is all right. I open the line at the carburetor and step on the starter. One feeble spurt, and then no more. Immediately I give up. I have been intimidated by too many mechanics about fuel pumps. Their automatic assumption is that a balky pump should be replaced. It would not occur to me, a baling-wire-and-string mechanic, to try fixing one. Instead I fill a couple of canteens from the butt, get the girls making sandwiches, and prepare for an eighteen-mile walk back to Death Valley Junction.

But less impetuous counsels prevail. If we have to walk, early in the morning would be a better time. And right now, after wrestling the car all afternoon, I am a little bushed. We repair to the giant killer and start making camp. Dave, he of the curious scientific mind, takes out the fuel pump to see what makes it tick. If it will not serve as part of a high-compression engine, it will serve as educational equipment.

Between courses of dinner, he discovers how the pump works, isolates its principles, and concludes that nothing is wrong with this one. We put it on and try the starter. No go. Then I remember my last fuel-pump trouble, and vaguely recall something about length of stroke. This means nothing to me except that I heard the mechanic say it. To Dave it means everything. If the diaphragm isn't burst, then the length of stroke must be all that is wrong. Within five minutes I am cutting little circles of rubber from an old inner tube, and Dave is packing the connection where the pump hooks on to a rod that in turn hooks onto the cam shaft. When we put the packed pump back on,

[66]

we discover a stripped setscrew, and wrap it with thread so it will hold.

Then I step on the starter. Nothing. We prime the carburetor. Before we try it now we take a prayerful pull on the jug. Then I press the button.

The engine practically blows me out of the seat. I grab for chokes and throttles, assuming that something must be pulled way out, but nothing is. In desperation I shut the ignition off. Cautiously, after a couple of minutes, I turn on the ignition again, and instantly, without my touching the starter, the motor almost leaps through the hood. Now it is clear: we have got too muscular a stroke altogether. Take out a couple layers of inner tube and we will be fixed. By eight-thirty we are sitting on the running board, while the motor purrs smoothly, and we drink a nightcap to the Scientific Mind before we roll into the bags.

This night I expect alarms from the girls, because I know that both have read about rattlesnakes that crawl into sleeping bags to get warm, and I have heard, from their screeches this afternoon, how little either likes snakes. I could show them, in the *Desert Magazine* (an authority whose weight is very great and completely deserved), that the danger from warmth-hunting sidewinders is statistically equal to that from falling meteors. I could demonstrate how much more danger we run any hour on any highway. But I remember the indignant reader who wrote in to the editor of *Desert* to say that he had had snakes in his covers three times during his life, and he did not like either the snakes or the people who said snakes never hunted warmth. It seems indiscreet, in the circumstances, to raise the subject. Everyone goes to sleep like an infant.

Quite late, the moon looks over the rim, and then I see it bridging the canyon, and then it is a luminousness over the western rim, and then I awake to find that the luminousness has shifted its ground, and it is morning. As I look around, I do not see any rattlesnakes, either on top of sleeping bags or in them. All I see is the gray, cindery canyon, the gray greasewood, the morning sky already hot with light, and the old station wagon, awkwardly high-centered and with her wheels deep in the sand, fifteen miles up a 16.2-mile canyon.

Thursday: Before breakfast, Dave and I take a walk up the canyon. The further we go the worse it gets. Eventually even Dave admits we had better go back down the way we came.

This is more easily said than done. From eight to nine we dig and brush our way out of the sand we are stuck in. From nine to ten-thirty we turn around. At a quarter of eleven, somewhat fagged, we start back down Greenwater, leaving our ruts full of greasewood brush for the next wayfarer to read.

In Death Valley Junction the mechanic tells us that only two days ago he went up in a towcar for a party stranded in the canyon. The stranded party walked in eighteen miles —exactly what I was going to do last night. What makes us feel better about our retreat from Everest is the mechanic's assertion that to his knowledge no one ever went *up* over the Greenwater road. His client of day before yesterday hadn't even been able to get down.

Friday: Into Rhyolite (pop. 3), most satisfactory of ghost towns. The metabolic rate was highest of all here. Rhyolite grew and matured and died in four years. And if one gets tired of the ghostly refrain among the ruins he can visit Bottle House, made of beer bottles laid in adobe, and buy rock samples or ultraviolet glass. Or he can go to the other intact building, the railroad station, once the grandest in Nevada, which now sits high and dry without rails to serve it. A gentleman named Westmoreland owns it now—bought the whole town at a tax sale—and has made it into the "Ghost Casino," patronized by tourists from the Valley. At eight in the morning it smells glumly of last night's revels. The barkeep is dourly cleaning up. On every square inch of wall photographs of nude ladies simper and coquette, but the hour and the hot morning sun are against them; we leave them for the bartender and the ghosts.

The Titus Canyon road is a steep, narrow succession of switchbacks. Twice, going up, we have occasion to comment on how miraculously a sidewinder can duck a car's wheels, even when he seems asleep. We have seen more than our quota of rattlers on this trip, and we guess that the lack of tourist travel during the war has let them multiply.

The road down loops in tortuous switchbacks through Leadfield, a very dead ghost rotting dryly in the gulch, and on between steep walls that at times pinch in so that we cannot open the car doors when we stop. Speculation on what it would be like to be caught in this slot during a flash flood hustles us out to the gateway. The whole north end of Death Valley opens up, with the unbroken barrier of the Panamints across the west, and Telescope Peak high and snowy. The interlocking alluvial fans of the Panamints are beautiful studies in clean line. Around us too is the patchwork poetry of our place-names. We have had it all the way: the Calicos, the Ivanpahs, the New York Mountains; Black Mountain and the McCullough Range and the El Dorados; Pahrump and the Funeral Range and the Bullfrog Hills; Muddy Mountains, the Grapevines, the Panamints, the Shadow Range. Most of the naming processes that George Stewart speaks of in *Names on the Land* are here.

For a while now we see sights again, winding up at the Hollywood Moorish pile of Scotty's Castle. This Page enjoys in spite of our superior airs. He is not annoyed by the transcribed commercial of the guide, nor by the tapestry which was woven by Don Quixote. He would be willing to buy the dollar postcards—not sold anywhere else—if we did not yank him away.

Except in wet weather, which is notably infrequent, a desert dry lake is the best of all possible roads, and the one we meet at the top of Grapevine Pass is smooth as concrete and hard as rock. Driving on it is like cutting didoes on ice skates. In the middle of the Sarcobatus Flats we meet Highway 95, and roll up over Stonewall Pass in a spattering thunder shower. Then a dusty graded road, and more passes—Lida Pass, through nutpines and drifts of snow, and down again into Fish Lake Valley, and then over Gilbert Pass into Deep Springs Valley. As we top the summit with the sun almost down, there is the Sierra across the west, white and pinnacled and filling the whole horizon. We see why it is called the Sierra Nevada, the snowy range, and when we make camp we pick a wash that will let us see the peaks when their snowfields are washed in rose at sunrise.

Saturday: We spend this morning visiting Deep Springs School, a private prep school conducted by the Telluride Association. Once, fifteen years ago, I was here for a few hours, and once twelve years ago I all but signed up to teach here, so I have a personal curiosity to see how education fares in the desert.

The school has not changed much. Students still work a half day on the ranch. The student body is still held down to about twenty. Masters are not quite as numerous as they used to be, but there is still one for every three or four students. The buildings look older.

Few of the boys are around now. The truck which passed our camp very early this morning contained about eighteen of them, bound on a nine-day trip to Death Valley, Boulder Dam, Grand Canyon, Zion, and Bryce. They make these annual trips unsupervised, packing camp equipment and armed only with letters from Simon Whitney, the director. The three boys who remain behind have voluntarily given up the trip so that the essential work around the ranch will get done.

Deep Springs is a friendly place. But it looks lonelier now than it did when I was twenty-four. The snow lies deep on Westgaard Pass in winter, isolating the valley for days at a time, and the nearest town is Big Pine, twenty-seven miles away. I am sure that the boys who spend three years at Deep Springs get something that they could get nowhere else, but I am just as glad that I am not a master here.

Deep Springs is our last desert port of call. From Big Pine up the Owens Valley and on north along the foot of the Sierra we are on Highway 395, which rolls behind us mile after mile. The passes rise and fall under our wheels:

Sherwin Summit, Deadman's Pass, Devil's Gate. On all of them the snow remains in great drifts, with sometimes whole slopes covered. Skiers' cars are parked along the highway, and the slopes are cross-hatched with tracks. All afternoon we peg north, at times down in the hot valley, at times between drifts ten feet deep. At Carson City we swing sharp left into the main range, hoping that the snow won't be so deep around Tahoe that we can't camp.

But the shores of Tahoe, what is left of them between the cottages, are either buried in snow or soggy with mud and water. We try the public camp at Meyers and find it flooded. It is practically dark; we are all chilled and starving, but we decide to pull over Echo Pass and camp on the west slope, where it will be drier.

On the first steep pitch of the pass the fuel pump gasps twice, coughs, and goes out. By frantic choking I keep the engine alive long enough to turn around, and we coast back into Meyers. Dave is unhappy that we haven't made it all the way home on his cobbled pump, and the rest of us are tired and sore. Only Page profits from this difficulty: he finds a snowbank and gets his hands blue for the first time in two years.

The new pump takes us a half hour. It is almost nine when we top the pass and start down past the ski lodges, through the snow-choked forest. Eventually we find a section of the old highway, marooned when the road was straightened. The wind off the snowbanks chatters our teeth, but wood is plentiful, and on this southern slope above the road it is dry. We fortify ourselves with giant-killer and the quickest food we can think of: soup and chile and bread, and for dessert the napoleons we bought

[72]

at a French bakery in Bishop, away back in the Owens Valley.

Tonight we all hit the bottom of our sleeping bags, and even the sagebrushing Bonners go to bed in all their clothes. I pull my head in and do not come out until morning, either for air or for a look at the moon. By this time the moon is a pretty moth-eaten piece of merchandise anyway.

Sunday: So back home now, the loop almost closed. Down the south fork of the American, past lumber mills and flumes and yards stacked with enough lumber to ease a small housing shortage, past new buildings enough to care for every veteran in the Western states. It seems that every vacant spot of ground in this quarter of the Sierra is being built on. The number of Bide-a-Wees and Shangri Las is due to be doubled shortly. We wonder why the taste of summer cottages in the West is so infallibly bad. It cannot be simply that many people build their own, because some of these we pass are manifestly neither amateur jobs nor inexpensive ones. And many of the people who commit atrocities in these mountains have chaste and impeccable homes in town. There is some madness in brown shingle, some itch for bright color, some suppressed impulse toward cuteness that borders every road through the Sierra with blue-shuttered horrors. Across the canyon we see a Civil War cannon that someone has towed up the pass, derricked across the river, and mounted on the cliff-like hill under a pergola. Why?

We are dangerously close to sounding like Henry Miller, and spitting the taste of this Camp Cozy nightmare from our puckered mouths. But it is healthy to remember John

[73]

Muir, who practically invented the Sierra and who should certainly have been one to mourn the pollution of the clean wilderness. He wasn't. Instead of thinking what men did to the mountains, he kept his mind on what the mountains did to men, and he might not have considered even the wretched and pretentious ugliness along the shores of Tahoe and through the passes and on every Sierra lake too heavy a price for the health, the happiness, and eventually the cleansing of taste, that hundreds of thousands derive from the Snowy Range.

Out of the mountains now, through a half-and-half region of orchards and pines, and out onto the long green spurs that stretch down this side of the range. At Placerville we make our last gesture toward the back roads, turning off on a sub-major highway through the Motherlode country. Here gulches and bars are upended and turned over by a succession of panners, hillsides are crazy with abandoned sluices, riverbeds are full of dredges feeding messily like hippopotamuses on the gravels that even after a hundred years give up gold. Sutter Creek, Mokelumne Hill—the names echo, but what charms us now is not these placer towns with their storefronts reminiscent of '49 and their graveyards full of history, but the dreamy, highspring, New England loveliness of this countryside. Like Tamsen Donner, Mary must botanize. She finds eighteen varieties of wild flowers in a space a yard square, and all around us there are blue hills, yellow swales, lavender and white and pink meadows, and everywhere the ecstatic green of California's brief and furious spring.

With home in sight, Page, who has been caged among grown-ups for ten days, shushed, pushed aside, and ignored, begins to generate unbearable pressures. His vocabulary is that of his third-grade kind—about five cant phrases, generally meaningless, interspersed with sound effects. I give him the long strong doubletalk of a father pretending to be good and annoyed, but I am really remembering a quarter of a century ago, when I sat in the back of a loaded car as this one sits now, surrounded by a Stoll auto tent, folding camp beds, tarpaulins, blankets, suitcases, and all the assorted paraphernalia we thought necessary for touring. We had a food box built onto the right front fender, a luggage carrier on the running board, and a trunk rack on the rear, with a dusty canvas lashed to it. I remember that old car and every item of that equipment and every volt and ampere that went through my squirming young body. I remember places we camped, roads we went over in Montana and Wyoming and Idaho and Utah. There were no back roads then, because everything was a back road. I remember the gumbo near Thermopolis, Wyoming, that stripped the rubber off both our rear tires and plugged it up under the fenders until we stalled. I remember the tire we hung on a tree in West Yellowstone, with its incredible mileage painted on it in white, "6,000 miles and still going!" In those days we counted twenty miles an hour a remarkable average for a hard day's drive. I remember the broken springs and the boiling radiators, the red dust of roads under construction, the waving of hands from every car, back in the days when touring was still only a step from the goggles-and-ulster stage and the roads were the lineal descendants of the Oregon Trail.

When I turn to look at the noisemaking buffoon who is my later duplicate, his eyes are bright as a squirrel's, and through his milk-bottle horn he lets me have it. His ricochet effect bounces off my skull, and I fall back to driving. But

I am plenty content, because we shall hardly be well recovered from this desert trip before we shall be off again, across the continent. We shall not be following our pre-war custom of hitting the Lincoln Highway at sixty-five, driving seven hundred miles a day, and sleeping in motels. We'll be lugging our sleeping bags and jungling up in inner-spring washes. We shall see the Wah-Wah Mountains and the San Rafael Swell, the Goosenecks of the San Juan and Monument Valley, the Four Corners and the sandrock country and the western slope of the Colorado Rockies, and we shall probably stop somewhere on the banks of the Platte and eat lunch among primroses. And we shall meet most of America on the road.

3

Packhorse Paradise

One of the special pleasures about a back road in the West is that it sometimes ends dead against a wonderful and relatively unvisited wilderness. The road from Grand Canyon to Topacoba Hilltop ends dead against a ramshackle shed and a gate that closes the bottom of the gulch. The whole place looks less like a hilltop than anything we can imagine, but our Indian guide is there, along with a half-dozen other Indians, cooking beans over an open fire. He waves his hands, white with flour, and says we shall be ready to go in thirty minutes.

Eating a lunch of oranges and cookies and a thermos of milk, we look out from the end of the gulch to the outer rim of a larger and much deeper canyon—possibly the Grand Canyon itself, possibly some tributary or bay. The heat is intense, and light glares from the rock faces and talus slopes. Ahead of us is a fourteen-mile ride into Havasu

Canyon, the deep-sunk, cliff-walled sanctuary of the Havasupai Indians.

At twelve-thirty the white-handed Indian, a boy of about eighteen, leads up a skinny packhorse and loads on our sleeping bags, tarps, cooking gear, and the small amount of food we are taking for a three-day trip. He is handy at his diamond hitch, but uncommunicative; his hair grows down over his forehead and he wears big blunt spurs. The horses he brings up look to us like dwarfs, unable to carry our weight, but they do not sag when we climb on. My saddle is too small, and the stirrups won't lengthen to within six inches of where I want them; I console myself with the reflection that if I did put them down where they belong they would drag on the ground, the horse is so small.

For a quarter mile we circle the shoulder of a hill, and then, turning the corner, Mary looks back at me as if she can't believe what she has seen. Below us the trail drops in an endless series of switchbacks down an all but vertical cliff. And this is no cleared path, no neat ledge trail built by the Park Service. This trail is specially created for breaking necks. It is full of loose, rolling rocks, boulders as big as water buckets, steep pitches of bare stone, broken corners where the edge has fallen away.

Our guide, whose name turns out to be Hardy Jones, starts down casually, leading the packhorse, and we follow with our seats uneasy in the saddle, ready to leap to safety when the horse slips. We have ridden trail horses and mules before, but never on a trail like this. But it takes us less than a half hour to relax, and to realize that our horses have neither stumbled nor slipped nor hesitated. They know all the time where all their feet are. At bad places, with a thousand-foot drop under them, they calmly gather themselves and jump from foothold to foothold like goats.

As we descend, we learn too how these stunted horses got this way. Far up on the canyon walls, among housesized boulders and broken rockslides, we see wild horses grazing as contentedly as if they were up to their knees in bluegrass in a level pasture. A half dozen of them are in absolutely impossible places, places where no horse could get. But there they are. And there are signs too that surefootedness is not innate: two thirds of the way down we pass a week-old colt dead by the side of the trail at the bottom of a fifty-foot drop. I ask Hardy what happened. "He fall down," Hardy says.

Ahead of us, in the bottom of a wide sandy wash, a wriggly canyon head begins to sink into the red rock. As soon as we enter this deepening ditch, Hardy turns the packhorse loose up ahead to set the pace. He himself dismounts and lies down in the shade with his hat over his eyes. After a half hour he catches and passes us, and after another fifteen minutes we pass him again, snoozing in the shade. I suspect him of all sorts of things, including nursing a bottle on the sly, but I finally conclude I am wronging him. He is simply sleepy. On occasion his yawns can be heard a half mile.

Once or twice he rides up close and starts a conversation. We discover that he is a good roper, and later in the month will ride to Flagstaff to compete in a rodeo. He has three good rope horses of his own, and he has finished the sixth grade in the Havasupai school. I ask him what he'll take for the pony he is riding, a sightly, tiny-footed, ladylike little mare, and he tells me, I am sure inaccurately, fifteen dollars. Then he asks me what I had to pay for the camera slung around my neck, and when I tell him, he looks incredulous and rides on ahead to take another sleep.

The canyon cuts deeper into rock the color of chocolate ice cream. At times the channel is scoured clean, and we ride over the bare cross-bedded stone. The *Grand Canyon Suite* inevitably suggests itself, and we are struck by the quality of the sound produced by hoofs on sandstone. It is in no sense a clashing or clicking sound, but is light, clear, musical, rather brittle, as if the rock were hollow.

The packhorse leads us deeper into the rock, going at a long careful stride down hewn rock stairs, snaking along a strip of ledge, squeezing under an overhang. It is an interminable, hot, baking canyon, but there are aromatic smells from weeds and shrubs. None of the varieties of trees we meet are known to us. One is a small tree like a willow, with trumpet-shaped lavender flowers, another a variety of locust covered with fuzzy yellow catkins. Still another, a formidable one to brush against, is gray-leafed, with dark-blue berries and thorns three inches long. I pick a berry and ask Hardy what it is. "No eat," he says.

2

For three hours we see nothing living except lizards and the occasional wild horses grazing like impossible Side-hill Gazinks on the walls. Then around a turn comes a wild whoop, and a young horse bursts into view, galloping up the bouldery creek bed past us. After him comes an Indian boy swinging a rope, and they vanish with a rush and a clatter up a slope that we have just picked our way down at a careful walk. In ten minutes the new Indian and Hardy come up behind us leading the colt, which has a foot-long cut across its chest as if from barbed wire, and which leaves bloody spots on the trail every time it puts its feet down.

Hardy is pleased at the neatness with which he roped the colt as it tried to burst past him. He breaks into a wild little humming chant, accented by grunts and "hah's," a jerky and exclamatory song like the chant of a Navajo squaw dance. As we ride he practices roping the hind feet of the horse ahead of him. After a while we are somewhat astonished to hear him singing with considerable feeling, "Oh, why did I give her that diamond?"

Now on a high rock we see a painted sign, "Supai." A handful of Indian kids whose horses are tied below sit on the top of the rock and wave and yell. We shift our sore haunches in the saddle and wonder how fourteen miles can be so long. At every turn the tight, enclosed canyon stirs with a breath of freshness, and we look ahead hopefully, but each time the walls close in around a new turn. A canyon comes in from the left, and a little brackish water with it, and there are cottonwoods of a cool and tender green, and willows head-high to a man on a stunted horse. There is a smell, too, sharp and tantalizing, like witch hazel, that comes with the cooler air as we make a right-hand turn between vertical walls.

Then suddenly, swift and quiet and almost stealthy, running a strange milky blue over pebbles like gray jade, Havasu Creek comes out of nowhere across the trail, a stream thirty feet wide and knee-deep. After more than four hours in the baking canyon, it is the most beautiful water we have ever seen; even without the drouthy preparation it would be beautiful. The horses, which have traveled twenty-eight miles today over the worst kind of going, wade into the stream and stand blowing and drinking, pushing the swift water with their noses. The roped colt tries to break away, and for a moment there is a marvelous picture at the ford, the white-toothed laughter of the Indian boys, the horses plunging, the sun coming like a spotlight across the rim and through the trees to light the momentary action in the gray stream between the banks of damp red earth.

That wonderful creek, colored with lime, the pebbles of its bed and even the weeds at its margins coated with gray travertine, is our introduction to Supai. After five minutes we come out above the village and look down upon the green oasis sunk among its cliffs. There are little houses scattered along a mile or so of bottom land, and at the lower end a schoolhouse under big cottonwoods. Men are irrigating fields of corn and squash as we pass, and fig trees are dark and rich at the trailside. At the edge of the village a bunch of men are gambling under a bower of cottonwood branches, and two kids, fooling away the afternoon, gallop their horses in a race down the trail ahead of us.

Both of us have from the beginning had the feeling that we shall probably be disappointed in Havasupai when we reach it. We have been deceived by the superlatives of travelers before, and we have seen how photographs can be made to lie. But this is sure enough the Shangri-la everyone has said it is, this is the valley of Kubla Khan, here is Alph the sacred river, and here are the gardens bright with sinuous rills where blossoms many an incense-bearing tree.

When we mount stiffly again and ride on after registering with Mrs. Guthrie, the wife of the Indian sub-agent, we pass little cabins of stone and logs, orchards of fig and cherry and peach, hurrying little runnels of bright water, a swinging panorama of red-chocolate walls with the tan

[82]

rimrock sharp and high beyond them. Havasu Canyon is flat-floored, and descends by a series of terraces. We camp below the first of these, within fifty feet of where Havasu Creek pours over a fifty-foot ledge into a pool fringed with cress and ferns.

The terrace above our campsite is full of what I take at first to be the twisted roots of dead fig trees, but what turn out to be rootlike lime deposits left by the stream, which used to fall over the ledge here. Probably they were originally grasses and water plants on which the mineral deposit formed a sheath; now they writhe through the terrace, fantastically interwound, some of them six inches in diameter. In the center of each is a round hole, as if a worm had lived there. In these holes and in the rooty crevices is lizard heaven. Geckos and long-tailed Uta lizards flash and dart underfoot by hundreds, as harmless as butterflies.

The same kinds of deposits are being formed under the pouring water of the falls; the whole cliff drips with them. And all down the creek the water has formed semicircular terraces like those at Mammoth Hot Springs in Yellowstone. Each terrace forms a natural weir, and behind each weir the water backs up deep and blue, making clear swimming pools eight to ten feet deep and many yards across. No creek was ever so perfectly formed for the pleasure of tourists. We swim twice before we even eat.

When we crawl into our sleeping bags at dusk, the bats and swallows fill the air above us, flying higher than I have ever seen bats and swallows fly before. It is a moment before I realize that they are flying at the level of the inner canyon walls, catching insects at what seem from the valley floor to be substratospheric heights. For a while we wonder how bats fly so efficiently and dart and shift so sharply without any adequate rudder, but that speculation dwindles off into sleep. Above us the sky is clouded, and in the night, when my face is peppered by a spatter of rain, I awake to see the moon blurry above the rim. For a moment I think a real storm is coming on, until I realize that the noise I hear is Havasu Creek pouring over Navajo Falls and rushing on down through its curving terraces. It is for some reason a wonderful thought that here in paradise the water even after dark is blue—not a reflection of anything but really blue, blue in the cupped hands.

3

Below our camp a quarter of a mile, past a field half overgrown with apparently wild squash vines and the dark green datura, the Western Jimson weed, with its great white trumpet-flowers, Havasu Creek takes a second fall. Apart from its name, Bridal Veil, it is more than satisfactory, for it spreads wide along the ledge and falls in four or five streamers down a hundred-foot cliff clothed in exotic hanging plants and curtains of travertine. The cliff is green and gray and orange, the pool below pure cobalt, and below the pool the creek gathers itself in terraces bordered with green cress.

A little below the fall a teetery suspension footbridge hangs over a deep green pool, dammed by a terrace so smooth that the water pours over it in a shining sheet like milky blue glass. And down another half mile, after a succession of pools each of which leaves us more incredulous, the stream leaps in an arching curve over Mooney Falls, the highest of the three. At its foot are the same tall cottonwoods with dusty red bark, the same emerald basin, the same terraced pools flowing away, and below the pools is another suspension footbridge on which we sit to eat lunch and converse with a friendly tree toad.

It is a long way to the mouth of the canyon, where Havasu Creek falls into the Colorado in the lower end of Grand Canyon. We stop at the abandoned lead and copper mine below Mooney Falls, where we ponder the strength of the compulsion that would drive men to bring heavy machinery piecemeal down into this pocket on the backs of horses, set it up under incredible difficulties, construct an elaborate water system and a cluster of houses and sheds, bore into the solid cliffs for ore, and then tote the ore back out miles to some road where trucks could get it. The very thought gives us packhorse feet, and we make our way back to camp, yielding to temptation at every pool on the creek until we have a feeling that our skins are beginning to harden with a thin sheath of lime. After a day, we are beginning to realize how truly paradisiac the home of the Havasupai is.

There are in the West canyons as colorful and as beautiful as Havasu, with walls as steep and as high, with floors as verdantly fertile. There are canyons more spectacularly narrow and more spectacularly carved. But I know of none, except possibly Oak Creek Canyon south of Flagstaff, which has such bewitching water. In this country the mere presence of water, even water impregnated with red mud, is much. But water in such lavish shining streams, water so extravagantly colorful, water which forms such terraces and pools, water which all along its course nourishes plants that give off that mysterious wonderful smell like witch hazel, water which obliges by forming three falls, each

more beautiful than the last, is more than one has a right
to expect.

4

Yet even Shangri-la has its imperfections, the snake lives
even in Eden. As we are working back from the canyon
walls, where we have been inspecting a small cliff dwelling,
we hear the barking of dogs. Below us is a field surrounded
by fruit trees, and in the middle of the field, staked out in
a line, we find four miserable starving mongrels. Each is
tied by a length of chain to a post; at the top of each post
is a bundle of branches loosely tied on to give a little shade.
Around the neck of each dog is a collar of baling wire
wrapped with rags, and near each a canful of muddied
water is sunk in the sand. Yelps and whines grow frantic
as we cross the field, and out of the bushes at the far end
comes a staggering skeleton with a drooping tail. In the
brush from which she emerged we find four squirming
puppies.

The job of these dogs is obviously to serve as scarecrows,
and they are obviously completely expendable. Clearly they
have not been fed for days, and none of them can live beyond a day or two more.

The usual Indian callousness toward animals is not unknown to us, and we are willing in theory to accept that
cultural difference without blaming the Indians. Perhaps
this Indian thought it a good idea to get rid of some of
his excess dogs, and at the same time protect his fruit. But
our passing through the field has stirred the miserable animals into hopefulness. The tottering skeleton of a mother
dog, dragging her dry teats, tries to follow us to camp;

the others howl and whine and bark until we feel like running.

Our own food is meager, since we underestimated our appetites when we packed the grub bag, and there is nothing to be bought in the canyon. All we have left to serve us for our last two meals is a can of grapefruit juice, two oranges, a can of lamb stew, four slices of bacon, six slices of bread, and a handful of chocolate bars. The oranges and the grapefruit juice will be of no use to the dogs. Chocolate might make their starving stomachs sicker. The bread and bacon and lamb stew are slim pickings for ourselves.

After a half hour of trying not to hear the howling, I go back and clean out all the water cans, refilling them from the irrigation ditch. None of the dogs is interested in the nice clean water. They are all howling louder than ever when Mary and I start a fire and heat the lamb stew, butter half the bread, lay out the oranges and the chocolate bars for dessert. They howl so loud we can't eat; the stew is gravel in our mouths. We end by spreading two slices of bread with all our remaining butter and taking those and half the stew over to the field. What we bring is a pitiful mouthful apiece, gone so quickly that we wince. Hope has leaped so high in the starving mongrels now that Mary gets three chocolate bars and distributes them. Aware that we are absurd, that our humanitarianism is stupid and perhaps immoral, granting that the dogs have to starve to death day after tomorrow anyway, we carefully divide the meal according to size of dog, and give the skeleton mother a double dose of chocolate.

Then we go home and swim and crawl into our bags, but the dismal howling goes on after dark. It has dwindled off to an occasional sick whimpering by the time we get to sleep, and we have wondered seriously if we should not rather have knocked all nine dogs on the head and paid their owner a suitable fee for the loss of his scarecrows. James Russell Lowell to the contrary notwithstanding, it is a wretched thing either to give or to share when you haven't enough to do any good.

To heighten our disenchantment, we are both bitten during the night by the bloodsucking beetles known locally as Hualpai Tigers, which leave an oozing inflammation about twenty times as irritating as a flea or chigger bite. Next time we come down here we will come with a supply of roach powder.

Not an absolutely idyllic paradise, despite its seclusion and peace and its shining blue water. We see other things when we mount Hardy's horses the next morning and start on our way out. Looking with less eager and more critical eyes, we see girls and women and old men lying on couches in the sun outside the little stone and log cabins. Tuberculosis. We notice among the Supai what Dickens noticed among all Americans a hundred years ago—the habit of spitting all the time and everywhere, even into the creek —and we are glad we dipped our drinking water from a spring. We learn from Mrs. Guthrie that the tribe is less numerous than it used to be, and that it barely holds its own now at about two hundred. A year ago a dysentery epidemic carried off more than half the young children in the village, and measles has been deadly among them.

We learn too that some of the young men, especially those few who served in the armed forces, are restless in the static life of the canyon, and want to get out. We see signs of change in the tractor that the Guthries have had packed in, a piece at a time, and which the Indians can rent for a small fee. We hear speculation about the possibilities of an automobile road into Havasu, and of a guest lodge to be owned by the Indians and run by them and for them, with Indian Service assistance. We hear of the need of increasing the income of the tribe, and of the benefit that increased tourist travel might bring. Out at the fence we hear Hardy Jones, sitting and swinging his big spurs far under the belly of his little mare, singing "Oh, why did I give her that diamond?" which he has laboriously and inaccurately transcribed from the radio onto a piece of cardboard.

The problem of what is best for Havasu—the place and the people—is curiously complex and difficult. If one looks at it purely from the standpoint of conserving natural scenery, the conclusion is inevitable that an automobile road and a guest lodge would spoil a spot that is almost unbelievably beautiful, clutter it with too many people, bring the regulation and regimentation that are necessary when crowds come to any scenic area. Fifty people at one time in Havasu would be all the canyon could stand. The present two hundred visitors a year leave no real mark, but five times that many would. If the conservation of the canyon's charm is the principal end—and this is the view of the National Park Service, which does have a voice in the matter since the Havasu reservation lies within the Grand Canyon National Park—the canyon should be left primitive, a packhorse paradise.

5

What of the people, the two hundred Havasupai? Those who work with them and see the need for medical care and education and guidance know how difficult it is to bring the tribe even these minimal things under present

[89]

conditions. Communication is by packhorse and telephone; the mail comes in twice a week, and supplies the same way, on the backs of horses. Though there is a school, Mrs. Guthrie is teaching everyone in it, both primary and advanced pupils, because it is impossible to get another teacher. It is equally impossible to find and keep a doctor and a nurse; when dysentery swept the canyon there was little anyone could do but bury the dead; when the Guthries' own son fell ill last winter he had to be taken out to a doctor by horse litter.

Though at the bare subsistence level the canyon can be nearly self-sufficient, there are considerable and growing needs induced by contact with civilization. There are clothes—because the Havasupai no longer wear the garments of beautifully dressed white deerskin that they used to wear. They wear boots and Levis and shirts and Stetson hats. They like sugar, candy, coffee, radios, dozens of things that take cash; and cash they can now obtain only from two sources: sale of horses or cattle to the outside, or charges at ten dollars a head for packing in tourists. The Guthries are inclined to feel that if the flow of tourists could be increased, and if accommodations could be created for them, the standard of living and health and education of the whole tiny tribe could be raised considerably.

There is no doubt about the truth of that opinion. The canyon could be made a commercial "good thing" with a little promotion, and if the enterprise were carefully watched, the Indians could get the whole benefit. But there is something to be said against this proposal, too. We are morally troubled as we talk about it, for how sure can we be that the loose and indefinable thing called "well-being" will necessarily be promoted by greater prosperity, better education, even better health, when these things may bring with them the dilution or destruction of the safe traditional cultural pattern? Is it better to be well fed, well housed, well educated, and spiritually (which is to say culturally) lost; or is it better to be secure in a pattern of life where decisions and actions are guided by many generations of tradition?

There is a threat that one feels in this paradise. The little tribe with its static life may be at the edge of stagnation, of fatalistic apathy, as some villages of the Hopi are reported to be; it barely holds its own, the dynamics of its life reduced to the simple repetition of a simple routine, its needs few and its speculations uncomplicated. It is easy for that kind of equilibrium to be broken, for that kind of society to be utterly confounded and destroyed by contact with the civilization of white America. It takes intelligence, and patience, and great strength of character, and a long period of time, for any people safely to cross a cultural boundary as these Indians must. Perhaps doubling or trebling the number of tourists in Havasu Canyon each year would not materially increase the danger to the Havasupai. But build a road in, let the gates down on the curious and careless thousands, and the whole tribe would be swept away as the last big flood washed away the orchards of peach trees, introduced by John Doyle Lee when he was hiding from the Federal officers after the Mountain Meadows Massacre.

Yesterday I wanted to take a snapshot of an old Supai packer with bushy hair and prickly thin whiskers. His asking price was a dollar and a half. We finally settled for a half dollar, but even at that price that packer was getting dangerously close to the commercialized status of the Indians who with Sioux feathers in their Mojave or Paiute or Yuman hair wander around in populous tourist spots being picturesque for a fee. There is something to be said for the policy that urges keeping the barrier canyons around this tribe unbridged, for according to the ethnologist Leslie Spier, the Havasupai retain their native culture in purer form than any other American Indians. Other Indians, losing their hold on their native culture, have ceased to exist.

I doubt if there is a clear-cut answer to the problems the Havasupai face. Inevitably there will be more and more intrusion on their isolation, and inevitably they must proceed through the phase of falling between two cultures, of being neither Indian nor white American. If they are lucky, they can make that transition slowly enough so that eventually they can patch up a new order of cultural acceptances taking good things from both the warring cultures of their inheritance. I should say they might learn something from the white man about how to treat animals; they would do ill to lose their own native gentleness in dealing with children. They can borrow the white man's medicine and keep their own simple unspeculative friendliness with the earth. If they are lucky they can do this. If they are not lucky, their paradise might in fifty or a hundred years be like the retreat of old Yosemite, beaten dusty by the feet of tourists, and no trace of the Havasupai except squash vines gone wild in the red earth by a spring, or an occasional goat-wild horse on the talus slopes.

I should not like to be God in this paradise, and make the decisions that will decide its future. But I can hope, looking at Hardy Jones lolling in the saddle, singing, "Oh, why did I give her that diamond?" that on the difficult cultural trail he is traveling no one will crowd him too hard. The trail between his simple civilization and the inconceivably complex world beyond the rims is difficult even for those who can go at their own pace. Hardy has gone part way without apparent demoralization; he listens to his radio and will go to Flagstaff and perhaps win a roping prize. But the smoke-colored colt lying with his neck broken below Topacoba Hilltop is warning of what can happen to the too young and the too inexperienced on that path.

4

~~~~~~

Navajo Rodeo

Out in the Navajo country opportunities for entertainment come seldom. The Indians who live scattered over enormous distances, moving their sheep and goats from winter ranges to the summer grass on Black Mesa or the Lukaichukai Mountains, may get an occasional afternoon of hanging around a trading post hearing the gossip, a squaw dance or a *yehbetzai* at some chance encampment, a little gambling on a blanket outside the hogan, a little horse racing between boys of an afternoon. And that is about all. But in the fall, moved by sound business sense and a genuine liking for their Indian customers, many traders will throw a rodeo, putting up prize money and sacrificing a few steers for a barbecue. And occasionally, at posts near the edges of the reservation, even a paved-road tourist can look on while the Navajos have a good time.

The rodeo, we shall say, is at Art Greene's Marble Canyon Lodge, just above the Navajo Bridge spanning the Colorado River. The day before the shindig you can watch them coming: whole familes in rattling, loose-spoked wagons; groups of young men riding and leading prized running or roping horses; longhairs in tall hats; lean adolescents in Levis and dark glasses; women in red and blue and orange and purple velvet blouses, loaded with the family wealth in silver and turquoise and coral; girls in all their finery, on their feet saddle shoes and bobby sox, and in their grinning mouths wads of bubble gum. The hogans around the post fill up, tents and shelterless camps sprout among the sagebrush, wiggling trails mark the sand where men have dragged firewood poles from the foot of the Vermilion Cliffs. The post is full of pop-drinkers.

Twice during the afternoon, trucks carrying loads of Navajo laborers to pick potatoes in Idaho stop for refreshment. The passengers get wind of the coming rodeo, and bedrolls start coming off the trucks. The drivers swear and plead; they are under contract to deliver the workers, and they have bonuses in view. But in the end they resign themselves and pull their trucks back of the service station and join the little crowd which has gathered to watch a card game being played on a blanket against the station wall. It is a kind of cross between poker and rummy; no white man seems to know how to play it; no amount of watching makes it intelligible. It will go on without pause for two days and nights.

There are perhaps a hundred and fifty Navajos in camp as the sun drops behind the Kaibab Plateau westward and the Vermilion Cliffs darken from pink to purple and the irregularities jut out in relief from the shadowed wall. The smoke of piñon fires is fragrant, and the dust of a band of steers being driven to the corrals for tomorrow's show lies in a pinkish band along the cliff's foot. On the great plain which is the Marble Canyon Platform the last light still shows moving dots: more Indians coming in.

Everything moves slowly, with much standing around. A medicine man, his long hair clubbed under a tall, undented hat, makes a circuit of the tourists touching them for handouts. Within five minutes, having got his stake, he is in the card game, where he stays as long as I watch him. About eleven o'clock, when many of the tourists have gone to bed, a group of Navajo boys lean together under the awning of the post and break into the wild, wavering, heavily-accented chant of the squaw dance. People appear silently and lean against the wall—Navajos, white men, a few squat Paiutes. Art Greene's daughters tag Navajo boys and shuffle off in a circle, Navajo girls with their faces muffled in their blankets lay hands on the coatsleeves of tourists and hang on until their captives sheepishly come along.

There is no conversation—few of the girls speak English. Self-contained, giggling a little, flashing their eyes upward over the edge of the blanket, they accept without words the quarter or half dollar their partners pay when they want to drop out. The dance has no breaks or intermissions, and you can shuffle all night for a quarter if you want to. But when you drop out you are immediately tagged again, sometimes by two girls at once. Sometimes a very small girl, a mere child of ten or so, will come out weeping and grab some white man, and then will sniffle to herself all through the dance, while the mother who sent her to make an honest quarter watches silently from the wall. It is no hardship to get tagged in a squaw dance; Navajo girls are often extremely pretty. But an hour or two of dancing will hold most of us. We slip off to bed sometime after midnight, with the chant still going.

The rodeo next day is a blaze of sun, a stream and flash of color, a fume of dust. Under a canopy of cottonwood boughs, the thing old Mormon traders used to call a "bowery," the girls from the post sell pop and watermelons as fast as they can make change. By now there are half a hundred tourists, and every tourist with a camera. I am curious to see the reaction of the Indians, because few of them like being photographed. Once, when I raised up out of a car in the Canyon de Chelly to snap a Navajo driving a band of sheep up the canyon, he threw up his arm in anger, clapped his heels to his horse, and literally vanished, abandoning his sheep. Out here, however, on the white man's highway, they appear more accustomed to the winking-eye box. Mainly they ignore the tourists snapping on every hand; once in a while an angry old woman will throw her blanket over her head when she sees a cameraman taking aim.

As rodeo performers Navajos are not the best. They work few cattle, and consequently are not good ropers, bull-doggers, calf-throwers. But they can ride with any two-legged creature. To watch one of these slim kids hook his hand in the surcingle of a bawling, helpless steer, then nod a signal for the release and take off through the sagebrush in wild leaps, fanning the steer and spurring him from ears to flanks, is to watch superb skill and nerve. They are quite as good at bareback bronc riding, and horse racing is their daily fare. For this last they strip off to a pair of

Levis, shedding even their boots, and they ride bareback. There are clowns among them, too. The antics of the joker who strips off to his long drawers for the men's footrace bring hoots and catcalls and belly-holding laughter.

Tireless spectators, intense competitors, both men and women go about their pleasure with utter singlemindedness. The squaw race is for blood until the finish line is reached, when the girls fall on each other's necks with giggles and gasps and screams. The squaw tug of war between Navajo and white girls has both sides all but bursting blood vessels until the plain, tough strength of the Indian girls uproots the white girls and drags them over the line. The pride they take in winning this one is almost touching.

There are incidents: in the midst of the wild-cow milking an old range cow which has been roped and thrown and outraged by milkers' hands three or four times stands a little groggy, head down, and then quite suddenly goes berserk. She drops her horns and makes for a crowd of women and children—and a cow is more dangerous than a bull because she hooks with her eyes open. Men swing children up into the cabs of trucks, the beds of wagons. Women run shrieking. The cow chases a photographer around a wagon and in under the endgate, where another card game is going on. Nothing in the whole rodeo has caused such delight as this. The cardplayers lean and scramble, trying to unload the photographer, as the cow hooks left and right between the wheels. Eventually a pick-up rider ropes the cow's hind leg and drags her out of the way, and the photographer crawls gratefully out from the laps and cards and chips. The players kid him, shaking their heads. Down from trucks and wagons come the children, so loaded with jewelry their competing fathers and mothers have hung on them that they can hardly walk.

It is a big day, circus and county fair in one, and much money and some horses have changed hands and much of Art Greene's beef has been roped, ridden, milked, bulldogged, thrown and variously misused. A good deal of it now is being eaten. The Navajos are not a people used to excessive feeding; they make the most of Art's slaughtered steers. The pervasive, mouth-watering smell of roasting meat is over the whole camp, mingled with the smell of piñon smoke.

In the evening, one of the professional photographers puts on a show—colored nature movies from Alaska. The Indians are silent and attentive; only twice do they react. Once, when three-foot salmon are being lifted from a spawning stream that crawls and flashes with fish, there is a kind of sigh, as of wonder. And at another point, when the telephoto lens brings right up into their faces five great Alaskan brown bears feeding across a blueberry bog, there is a startled and unanimous "Hough!" of astonishment, and a quick whispering.

But what ends this show most spectacularly is Art Greene's private variety of fireworks. Truck drivers who haul his supplies bring him all the old tires they find along the road, and these, along with boxes of excelsior and other such rubbish, he saves for occasions like this. Now when night is utter black over the Marble Canyon platform the whole camp, several hundred strong, walks down to where the Navajo Bridge soars above the Colorado. In the darkness the invisible river far below is only a faint sigh, like a tree-top wind.

At first, while Art and his helpers prepare the main fire-works, we amuse ourselves by emptying boxes of kitchen matches over the rail near the north rim. For what seems minutes there is no sign from below, and then the blackness blooms with hundreds of tiny fireflowers as the matches ignite on the rocks below.

Out in the middle of the bridge, where they have been filling a truck tire with gasoline, there is a yell and a flash, and the flaming tire shoots off into space. It howls like a fire siren as it falls, and the sound comes up fainter, farther. The tire falls like a comet, trailing flame and dropping, vanishing almost, as if it were falling utterly off the earth. Then there is a wide splash of fire, the water leaps into flame for rods around, the walls of the canyon light up, the river is visible from shore to shore, light-tipped and swift, and now comes the solid, breath-jolting WHOMP! of the tire hitting the river. All the air between bridge and water is filled with an aftermath of tiny blue stars that hang and float and finally wink out. The tire too floats for a while, a flaming doughnut, until the river swallows it in a gulp of fire. The walls disappear, the blackness rushes together, the sound of the crowd on the bridge is sibilant in the dark.

Three more tires go over, then three quick cartons of excelsior soaked in gasoline. These last fall without the wild howling of the tires, but they stay afloat on the river and the whole outline of the canyon down toward Badger Creek Rapid is lighted. It is more than two miles to the first bend, but two cartons are still glowing when the river carries them out of sight.

Now spilled gasoline flames up on the bridge itself, and people scatter and retreat. The whole center of the bridge is ablaze, so that a truck driver coming in from Cameron stops in consternation. It takes some talking to convince him that as soon as the fire burns out it will be safe to cross.

It is quite safe; in all the bridge and the canyon it spans there is nothing burnable, and pastimes that would be penitentiary offenses elsewhere are forgivable here.

We leave the bridge, stinking of gasoline, and climb the curving highway to where the smell of campfires hangs in the air. In the morning the Navajos will be on the move again—hundreds of miles north of Idaho to pick potatoes, back to hogans along the San Juan, down the valley toward Cameron, in eastward toward Tuba City and Red Lakes and the trading posts of the Painted Desert, perhaps into the Hopi towns to take advantage of Hopi hospitality during autumn ceremonials.

It is a bad life and a hard one, a life dirty, ridden with tuberculosis and trachoma and ringworm, a life always close to the edge of real hunger, a life made ambiguous by the Indian's mixed status as both citizen and government ward. But it is a life with certain compensations, and among these it would be unwise not to mention, in addition to the freedom and the beauty of the sterile land he lives in, the Navajo's enduring and wonderful capacity to enjoy himself. Like a wise man he will postpone anything to have a good time.

5

~~~~~~~~~~~~~~~~~~~~~~~~~~~~~~~~~~~~~

San Juan and
Glen Canyon

To start a trip at Mexican Hat, Utah, is to start off into empty space from the end of the world. The space that surrounds Mexican Hat is filled only with what the natives describe as "a lot of rocks, a lot of sand, more rocks, more sand, and wind enough to blow it away." The nearest rail point is at Thompsons, up north on the Denver and Rio Grande, 175 miles away by road.

This road, the only real road in the area, has an advantage which some of this country's roads do not: it can be traveled both ways. You can come down Highway 160, which links Salt Lake with Mesa Verde and Santa Fe, and follow the diminishing trail through Blanding and Bluff to Mexican Hat. Or you can come up from Grand Canyon across the Hopi and western Navajo reservations by way of Moenkopi, Tonalea, Kayenta, and Monument Valley. Or if you have no mercy on your car, you can come up from Gallup to Shiprock and then take out over the axle-breaking trail to Kayenta by way of Dinnehotso.* Or you can fight your way up from the southern Navajo country over wagon tracks deep in sand. When you reach Mexican Hat you are at the end of the world and the beginning of the San Juan country.

It is useful to know where you are. On a map of Utah notice how the Colorado River cuts across the state from northeast to southwest, blocking off a great triangle in Utah's southeast corner. All but the tip of this triangle is San Juan County. Just a trifle smaller than Massachusetts, a little bigger than Rhode Island, Connecticut, and Delaware combined, the county was formed in 1880 before it had any white population. At the last census its population was still under 5000, and a third of that number were Navajos and Paiutes.

The first automobile crossed the sandy fifty-five miles across Monument Valley between Kayenta and Mexican Hat in 1921. There has been more traffic since, but not too much. This is not real tourist country, irrigated by foreign dollars. This is a scenic dry-farm, the biggest and almost the last. The wilderness stretches out on every side from the San Juan country, a primitive area at least a hundred miles square. But the San Juan country proper, between the Abajo Mountains and Monument Valley, and between the Colorado boundary and Glen Canyon of the Colorado, is the heart of the last great wilderness. Through the middle of it, flowing in a continuous canyon to its junction with the Colorado 133 miles westward, runs the San Juan River, as little known and as little celebrated as the country it drains.

* Now a paved highway, alas.

The dozen of us who gather in Mexican Hat Lodge on the evening of June 5 have a date with the river. We are a motley crowd: a movie photographer and his wife, a pair of engineers, a dentist's assistant, a physical education instructor, a radio technician, a few plain tourists, an old lady of seventy-two, and a little girl of ten. In the morning we will start down the San Juan by boat to Lee's Ferry.

We are not pioneers, explorers, or even adventurers, but simply backroads tourists who have put ourselves in the hands of Norman Nevills, probably the best-known river boatman in the world. Norman has been down the full length of the Green and Colorado more than once; he has run the Grand Canyon more times than any man alive or dead, and will run it again this summer. He has run the Salmon and the Snake in Idaho, and he nurses a secret dream of some day running the Brahmaputra, in India. He is like a broncobuster who cannot bear to leave any horse unridden.* The trip he will take us on starting tomorrow is a milk run for Norman; he has made it two dozen times. But as he gives us a genial briefing with pictures, it does not look like any milk run to us. Even if it isn't dangerous, even if a spry old lady and Norman's ten-year-old daughter can go along, it looks like excitement and it looks like fun. And even the milk run has been made by only a few hundred people at most.

At Mexican Hat the canyon walls are low, but they rise rapidly downstream. When we gather on the beach after breakfast we see the river bowling along, gray-brown with silt, its middle marcelled with two-foot waves. Yesterday

* His luck did not hold. He was killed, along with his wife, Doris, in a crash of his Piper Cub at Mexican Hat a few years after this.

two young men put their homemade boat in the river a
little above here to try it out. They managed to struggle
ashore at the bridge, but they have decided to take Norman's advice and not attempt the river in that boat. We
help them put it back on the roof of their car, and they
stand a little disconsolately with the rest of Mexican Hat's
slim population as the four square-ended semi-cataract boats
of Norman's party shove off. Four of us miss the launching because we are going overland to the Goosenecks to get
pictures as the boats swing into the deep hairpins of the
meander. We will join the others about noon at the foot
of the Honaker Trail.

One after another the boats pull into swift water, swing
sideways to take the waves, and are rushed downstream.
They seem to shrink to half their size as soon as they are
afloat, and they look tiny and frail as they speed down
under the bridge and the cable-hung bucket of the Geo-
logical Survey gauging station and disappear around the
first bend.

We are at the Goosenecks a good while before the boats,
which have to travel sixteen miles in the canyon to reach
here. Below us the gray-brown river has sunk itself 1300
feet into the rock in a perfect double hairpin—what geolo-
gists call an "entrenched meander." The San Juan used to
be a sluggish river running on a level plain, and meandering
like any old-age stream. Then a great plateau was slowly
lifted across its path, so slowly that the river could cling
to its old course and simply dig in. So it still has the
crooked course of a slow river, though it is actually the
fastest major stream in the United States, with a gradient
of almost eight feet to the mile. Just for comparison, the
Mississippi's gradient is eight *inches* to the mile; that of the

Colorado in the Grand Canyon, the most furious water on
the continent, is 7.56 feet to the mile. The San Juan below
us is not furious, but it is undeniably fast; we can see the
speed of it in the glasses, looking down on the throat of
the middle bend, where the canyon comes within a hundred yards of cutting through the ridge before it turns and
makes a three-mile loop westward, to come back barely
a stone's throw from where it started.

For nearly an hour we sit on the hot, barren rim with
the towers of Monument Valley—Agathla's Needle and the
spiry monuments on the Utah side—breaking the southern
horizon. Then the first tiny boat comes in sight down below, and we hear Norm's "river voice" bellowing. We
bellow back, though we know the river noise will prevent
our being heard. The four white twigs rotate in almost
military formation through a little rapid and disappear under the wall at the turn. Then they emerge again going
away from us, on their way around the tedious three-mile
hairpin. After a wait, here they come again. Through the
glasses I can see them buck and leap in the waves, and I
see a combing wave break clear over the bow of the first
boat where Mary sits. I can almost see the expression on
her face, and I envy her the coolness of that ducking.

The four of us on the rim are all of one mind: pictures
or no pictures, we want to get down and get in on the fun.
As soon as the last boat has disappeared we pile in the truck
and are taken by a wretched mesa-top trail out to another
part of the rim, where a rock cairn marks the top of the
Honaker Trail. From here it is 1300 feet to the river; the
way we have to walk, it is three miles.

2

The Honaker Trail has been specially recommended to me by Norm because I am gathering material for a biography of John Wesley Powell, the first navigator of the Colorado. This trail, Norm says, will show me what it means to try to climb out of one of these canyons in case of shipwreck or loss of supplies. It shows me that, certainly, switching along the outcropping ledges, sliding down shaly talus full of fossils, going far out of its way to find a way down to the next ledge. It shows me also, if I needed to be shown, what lengths men will go to for a chance to strike it rich. This trail was built by the Honakers at the turn of the century, and for several years they slaved and sweated trying to get a fortune out of the San Juan gravel bars. Altogether they got about $1500, perhaps a tenth of what it was worth to build the trail. There is nothing on the trail now but a collared lizard with a canary-yellow collar and a marvelous emerald belly, who obligingly poses for color photographs. He is the one lizard in this country, outside the rare and poisonous Gila monster, who will bite you if you fuss with him.

We meet the boats on a sandbar, and after lunch we get our taste of river travel. The river falls two hundred feet in the next twenty-three miles, shooting us through the Honaker Point, Eyemo, John's Canyon, Government, and Slickhorn Rapids, all of them small, with a fall of about four feet apiece, but all exciting enough to amateurs, and good for enough wettings to cool us off.

There is a feeling of continuous rapids on the San Juan, not only because the current boosts us along at an average speed of seven miles an hour but because of the river's peculiar and characteristic "sand waves." These are formed by the piling up of waves of sand on the bottom, which as they accumulate start a series of water waves moving slowly upstream against the current. The waves appear quite suddenly, move upstream growing deeper and more violent, and crest with a roaring noise for a minute or two before they disappear. At this stage of water they average three feet in height, though occasionally we catch one four or even five feet high. They have been measured up to six. Even in their middle sizes, they toss and pound a boat spectacularly, especially if taken head on. Norm takes them the easy way, sideways, and they afford endless fun with their rocking-horse pitching and the occasional boat-load of water they dump on us if we hit them combing.

We are wet and dry all day. At the foot of Slickhorn Rapid, where we pull in to camp after a day's run of forty miles, Paul, our aviation engineer, caps the day by falling off into the rapid's tail wave, clothes, camera, and all. Our camp is among willows and tamarisks on the bar—the tamarisks that not too many years ago were imported from India to combat erosion in desert washes and have now been blown and spread by birds through every gulch in the Southwest.* After dinner (steak) all the ladies go off with Norm to be initiated into the order of Driftwood Burners. They build piles of kindling all around an immense tangled pile of driftwood at least an acre in extent, and at a signal touch them off. Within minutes the inferno drives us clear to the water's edge. The hot glow creeps up the cliffs, gradually revealing the rims a quarter mile

* And become, under the local name of salt cedar, the worst plant pest in the region.

above; it throws leaping red light up Slickhorn Gulch and touches the abandoned oil rig below the toilsome trail where prospectors at the turn of the century fought their way down here to drill among the oil seeps.

Norm tells us stories of the river, Powell, the ill-fated Brown-Stanton expedition, while the flames eat into the driftwood and the whole gorge glows with red light. Full of energy as a grasshopper, he leads an impromptu squaw dance as close to the fire as skin will stand it, and then abruptly heads for bed. The party breaks up and follows him. Hours afterward I wake in the night and feel at two hundred yards the heat of the embers, and see the steady glow on the cliffs. It is pleasant to think that so big and satisfactory a bonfire has only good results: there is no danger from it, and it helps keep Lake Mead from filling up with drift and débris. Through the night the Big Dipper moves down the slot until its handle rests on the rim where the canyon curves left below camp. At the other end of the reach the moon is coming up, shining pale silver on Slickhorn Rapid.

Kent Frost, the boatman-cook, beats on his frying pan at 5:30. During breakfast the sun touches the rims and begins to creep down, but it still has not reached the water when we stop, after an hour's run, to get pictures at the mouth of Grand Gulch. In this red-walled wash, which caused enormous trouble to the Mormon pioneers coming across from Hole-in-the-Rock in 1880, the archaeologist Prudden first clearly isolated the Basket Maker culture as separate from and earlier than the Pueblo. It has, we know, considerable ruins, but we do not stop to explore. Between walls that rise sheer from the water, but lessen in height downstream, we run down to the open valley called

Paiute Farms, beyond the quicksand-sown fjord known as Clay Hills Crossing. Here the river spreads out like the Platte over a channel half a mile wide. We hunt cautiously for channels, and several times we go overboard to push. The second boat grounds so definitely that we do not see it again until just before we stop for the night. But in this open stretch we see the only human beings we are to see, besides ourselves, between Mexican Hat and Lee's Ferry. They are four Navajos tending sheep among the tamarisks on the reservation side of the river. On the north bank Norm shows us the bar where he crash-landed his Piper Cub last February and was marooned for two days before another plane located him.

All through the shallows, in a blazing hot afternoon, we cool ourselves off by going overboard to tow or swim behind the boat. Even here on the flats the current is much too strong to swim against; it can barely be walked against. At noon Mary discovered that she could sit down in the shallow water and be pushed along like a kiddy car. But it is a little disconcerting to go overboard with a yell in sand waves four feet high, with the boat standing on its beam-ends, and find the water only knee-deep. We spend half our time throwing each other overboard until the canyon walls begin to narrow again and the river gathers itself.

3

The canyon of the San Juan is geologically a highly instructive place. In any part of this country one learns to recognize the rock strata and know their profiles and coloring and the peculiarities of their bedding and weathering as one knows the faces of his friends. The San Juan gives us a one-way tour of all the strata we have ever known before, but with characteristic perversity starts in the oldest and flows downward into the highest and youngest.

The gray Hermosa and Rico formations in which we started form terraced cliffs with banded horizontal ledges of harder strata. Below the Honaker Trail these beds disappear under the covering layer of the Cedar Mesa sandstone, red and massive, which forms sheer cliffs like those under which we slept last night. At Clay Hills Crossing and along through Paiute Farms we meet the gray-blue Chinle, which breaks down into badlands slopes, and the thin-bedded red-brown Organrock, which in exposed faces erodes into irregular columns and statuary. And finally these are overtaken by the two most impressive layers of all, the Wingate and Navajo sandstones, both very massive and both very beautiful.

The Wingate, which crops out in bold cliffs clear down into New Mexico, is rich red. It forms marvelously sheer cliffs, straight and hewn as the wall of a building, which often rise straight from the water, though where we first meet this stratum it shows talus slopes of great blocks that cover the Chinle and Organrock underneath. The great planes of cliffs are filigreed with delicate tracery and stained with the shiny, black-brown "desert varnish." We float between great blackboards scrawled with the doodlings of giant children. Once we put in to replenish our water at Nevills Canyon, an alcove full of snake-grass and cane and with a clear sweet spring. The hot run through Paiute Farms has emptied our canteens, and though most of us have sampled river water "just to see what water with real *body* to it tastes like," we prefer our drink without quite so much grit.

As we drift on we see, above the cloven front of the Wingate cliffs, the domes and "baldheads" of the salmon-colored Navajo sandstone which forms the roof of the world here. As the Wingate is a cliff-forming, the Navajo is an arch-forming member. High in the walls amphitheaters a quarter of a mile across open up. Their bottoms are green and lush, and high across their upward curve, just below where the arching roofs begin to overhang, there is a level line of seepage at a joint in the rock. From the seepline, water-stain and fringes of maidenhair fern make a scalloped necklace of green and black and white against the salmon-colored wall.

All around the Great Bend we are in the Wingate capped by Navajo, and caves and alcoves and arched windows appear high in the upper wall, with blackboard cliffs below. At one point where the current sweeps close under an overhanging wall, we catch a glimpse of crosshatched petroglyphs. Across the river from here, on his last trip down, Norm surprised a mountain lion at the water's edge.

4

This second night there is no fire or squaw dance. We have run forty-nine miles and pushed and swum, and we hit the sleeping bags early in a camp among great boulders covered with petroglyphic animals and symbols. The last thing I see as I roll in is Annie and Joan, the oldest and the youngest, braiding each other's hair for bed. The first thing I see in the morning is Al, the movie cameraman, somewhat agitatedly shaking two scorpions out of his sleeping bag.

In quick succession this morning we shoot Express Train

and Paiute Rapids, both pleasantly exciting, but nothing alarming the way Norm runs them. He is at once so careful and so nonchalant that he makes even bad water look easy. I have tried my hand at the oars several times by now, and I know enough to discount Norm when he says that running these rivers depends 90 percent on the boats, 5 percent on luck, and 5 percent on skill. There is much more skill in it than that, though the boats are amazing—clumsy and hard to row, wide in the beam and square at both ends, but they ride rapids like ducks on a pond.

Where the river swings in another northward bend, Norm takes Al up a cliff and over the ridge so he can get pictures of us coming around. For two or three miles I am the boatman, and without Norm in the boat to point out rocks I am a little edgy as I steer down through the riffles around the bend, trying to keep facing my danger but not quite sure what single rock or cliff is most dangerous. We are to land on a short bar above a big rock, and I pull into the eddy with great brilliance, making the tricky landing so professionally that I am goofily proud of myself and eager to be of assistance to lesser men. George is coming in too low down, obviously bound for a collision with the big rock. I jump overboard to grab his line, and disappear. In the scouring eddy the water is six feet instead of six inches deep. As I come up I hear cheers from the cliff, and see Al and Norm waving. In my first piece of movie acting I have stolen the scene.

Being already sodden, I am the natural goat for a rigged quicksand sequence. I am to step off into a patch of quicksand and be rescued in the nick of time. I step off all right, and the quicksand sucks me in all right, and the ropes and the rescuers come flying and I am pulled out all right, but

George, one of the boatmen, who used to be an all-con-
ference halfback at Brigham Young, forgets in his enthusiasm that I am locked in to the waist and that my legs bend
only one way. From this time until the end of the trip I
walk with a cane, but the service we have rendered to
cinematographic art gives us all a deep satisfaction.

Now the next-to-worst rapid on the San Juan, Syncline,
where the boats are lightened and where some of the passengers have to walk around. Mary and I get to ride it
down, thanks to Powell, but it is disappointingly tame,
and we think Norman guilty of building up these riffles
to something worse than they are. But at Thirteen-Foot
Rapid, further along, we see what he means by white water. All the boatmen call this one nasty to run because of
its structure, though it is not in a class with the bad ones
on the Colorado and Green, with Lodore and Disaster Falls
and Badger Creek and the Sockdologer.

Norm wants to stunt this one for the camera. Again
thanks to Powell, I get to go along. We row out into the
broken rock-filled channel and all in an instant the current
grabs us. I have had the oars in my hands enough to know
how this would feel if I were rowing. But Norm half
stands, watching the white water ahead, picking his way
between rocks, driving stern-first toward the end of the
chute where the water rears up on a great rock and then
falls away to the left in a white cascade. A push with one
oar, a pull with the other, a little tense adjustment, a quick
pull away, a swing back to duck a water-covered rock,
and we drive into the roar of the rapids. Norm has men-
tioned the express-train, earth-shaking thunder of bad water; we almost get it here. We are deliberately bow-light
for the stunting, and at the last minute Norm swings so that

our bow climbs the big rock and then falls left down what seems ten sheer feet into a boiling hole, shipping a little water and a lot of spray, and bouncing down into the diminishing tail waves.

The other boats are run through one at a time, two of them smacking solidly into a rock in the deep hole at the rapid's foot, but bouncing off unharmed. We stop for lunch a little below, in Redbud Canyon where there is a sweet-water spring, and after lunch Al and Alma and I go on ahead with Kent, rowing hard to get out in front of the others so we can shoot pictures at the junction with the Colorado.

The last few miles of the San Juan canyon are deep and narrow, beautifully sheer in the Navajo sandstone; the Wingate has slid underneath us. At the junction we float out into a wide, deep, quiet river, moving fast but not as fast as the San Juan, that rounds into a turn to the west. When we land and climb the cliff across the Colorado we can look up Glen Canyon between the salmon-pink walls to a high butte; on every side, across on Wilson's Mesa between the rivers and north and south of us on both sides, the Navajo sandstone is eroded in knobs and domes. Back of us is the knife-edged profile of the Kaiparowits Plateau, high and gloomy, locally called Wild Horse Mesa; and to the south the cool, gray-green mound of Navajo Mountain overlooking the meeting place of the rivers. We are not explorers or pioneers, but we feel a little like explorers here. Not too many people have visited this spot. The distances in very direction are barren of man, the great mountain south of us is a holy place where no Navajo will be caught after dark, there is no sound on our slickrock ridge except the rustle of a small dry wind.

When we hear Norm's river voice, and photograph the boats stringing out into the big river, and Kent scares the boat party by rolling a tub-sized boulder off the cliff with a heart-stopping roar, we turn our backs on the San Juan. But we do it regretfully. It is a fine, friendly, and very beautiful little river, a marvelous roadway into wonder, and we allow ourselves, in this remote spot, to grow exasperated with the Rivers of America series for not including so colorful a stream. Basket Maker, Pueblo, Navajo, Paiute, Spaniard, Mormon, goldseeker, and oil prospector have left their scratches on its walls and their quickly erased footprints at its few passable fjords. Curiously, the Indian has changed this river more than the white man. There is every evidence that in Pueblo times the San Juan country supported a larger population than it does now, and that the town-dwelling Indians grew gardens where now there are barren boulder-strewn washes. With the coming of the herdsman tribes the desert cover was gradually grazed off, the floods grew more disastrous, and the land that used to line the canyons went down the river.

5

In Glen Canyon we are again in the stream of history, on a main road. Near the upper end, at Hole-in-the-Rock, the Mormon pioneers of the San Juan country blasted their way down the cliffs and struggled across on their way to Bluff and the completion of the most appalling wagon trip ever taken anywhere. Down below us, at Padre Creek, Father Escalante lowered his supplies over the wall and swam his mules across to the south bank on his adventurous way back to Santa Fe in 1776. This part of the Colorado canyon has been a blessed interlude of rest for every river expedition since Powell's first one in 1869. In all the miles of Glen Canyon there is not a rapid, hardly a rock, nothing more dangerous than whirlpools and sucks. Regular boat trips come down from Hite and up from Lee's Ferry through scenery that is at once awesome and charming. The sheer cliffs of Navajo sandstone, stained in vertical stripes like a roman-striped ribbon and intricately cross-bedded and etched, lift straight out of the great river. This is the same stone, though here pinker in color, that forms the domes and thrones and temples of Zion and the Capitol Reef. It is surely the handsomest of all the rock strata in this country. The pockets and alcoves and glens and caves which irregular erosion has worn in the walls are lined with incredible greenery, redbud and tamarisk and willow and the hanging delicacy of maidenhair around springs and seeps. Our real voyaging stopped with the San Juan; from here on we loaf, pulling ashore to explore something every mile or two.

Our first camp in Glen Canyon, just below the junction, is almost unimaginably beautiful—a sandstone ledge below two arched caves, with clean cliffs soaring up behind and a long green sandbar across the river. Just below us is the masked entrance of Hidden Passage Canyon, which at sunup glows softly red, its outthrust masking wall throwing a strong shadow against the cliff. Behind this masking wall is the kind of canyon that is almost commonplace here, but that anywhere else would be a wonder. Music Temple, Hidden Passage, Mystery Canyon, Twilight Canyon, Forbidden Canyon, Labyrinth Canyon, we explore a dozen, and there are dozens that we pass by. The most innocent opening, apparently a mere keyhole of an alcove, may be the door to a gorge a quarter of a mile deep and heaven knows how long, sometimes rods wide, sometimes less than a yard. Often the water has cut down irregularly, so that the walls waver and overhang and cut off the sky. Sometimes one has to ascend wading waist-deep in rock-floored pools; sometimes the canyon will jump suddenly up narrow waterfalls, generally dry at this season, or seeping a thin wetness down the discolored rock.

Follow one of these canyons in far enough, and it usually ends either at a fall or in one of the echoing caves and chambers the Navajo sandstone is fond of forming. Music Temple, for instance, is a domed chamber five hundred feet long and two hundred high, with a little eavespout of a creek coming out of a slot in the roof and dropping into a clear pool. Powell, who camped here on both of his river expeditions, and whose men left their names and initials carved into a rock face here, described the creek-slot as a skylight. It is actually more like the slot in an observatory roof. The shadows in a chamber like this, the patterns of light and shadow, are miraculous and utterly unphotographable, and the walls re-echo the slightest sound.

Mystery Canyon ends in the same sort of domed cave, with an even larger pool. Echo Cave Camp, maintained by Rainbow Lodge just above the Rainbow Bridge, is another such chamber. The walls of Twilight Canyon are undercut, first on one side and then on the other, with huge caves, one so immense that the whole Hollywood Bowl could be set back into it, and so perfect acoustically that six- and seven-word echoes pursue us as we walk through. Most bizarre of all the canyons, the spookiest concession in this rock fun-house, is Labyrinth Canyon, which narrows down to less than two feet, and whose walls waver and twist so that anyone groping up this dark, crooked, nightmare cranny in the deep rock has to bend over and twist his body sideways to get through. Floor and walls are pocked with perfectly round pockets like nests, full of the pebbles and rocks that have scoured them. Though we cannot see the sky, we know that the walls go up several hundred feet, and though we scramble back in at least a mile and a half, scaling one dry waterfall, we see no sign of an end. The thought of what it would be like to be caught in here in a rain gives us the fantods, and we come out fast.

The high water tempts us into a number of canyons, for overnight the river has risen from what Norm estimated at 40,000 second-feet to what he is sure is over 60,000, and the doorways of many canyons are flooded so that we can row in as into fjords, winding in and out and once poling through a watery tunnel formed by a fallen slab. Every sandbar is green with tamarisk and redbud; wherever there is an accumulation of soil, cottonwoods have taken hold, to hang on until the next big flood scours the channel clean and the cycle starts over.

Many years ago, reading Powell's account of his explorations, I got the notion that I wanted to come down into Glen Canyon and hole up in an alcove where there was water and a little soil. "Nine bean rows will I have there, and a hive for the honey bee. . . ." Now as I think of what we are likely to see in the papers when we end this river trip in a day or two, I suggest to Norm that I'd still like to hide out here for a while. He is full of enthusiasm at once; he will lend me a boat and help me get in supplies, either by river or by plane. I can sit in my green alcove and watch the river whirl by and write a book.

He doesn't know how close he is to being taken up. I reflect on those scientific friends of mine at M.I.T. and Harvard who are quite seriously stocking their Vermont farms against Armageddon, and it is a temptation to imagine that there might be sanctuary in this remote and beautiful canyon. But that lasts only thirty seconds. Out in the flood-swollen stream, snags and logs and drift go by, rocking in the swift water, circling with corpselike dignity in eddies and whirlpools, and as we watch we see a dead deer or sheep, its four stiff hooves in the air, go floating by in mid-river. We abandon the notion of sanctuary: even here, the world would drive its dead sheep and driftwood by the door.

But we can forget that at least another day, until we hit Lee's Ferry. At the mouth of Forbidden Canyon, after we return from the fourteen-mile hike to the Rainbow Bridge and back, we discover that the catfish will bite on anything or nothing, they will rise and gobble cigarette butts, or eat empty hooks as fast as we can drop them in. This is the way things were when the world was young; we had better enjoy them while we can.

6

~~~~~~~~~~~~~~~~~~~~~~~~~~~~~~~~~~~~~~

Glen Canyon Submersus

Glen Canyon, once the most serenely beautiful of all the canyons of the Colorado River, is now Lake Powell, impounded by the Glen Canyon Dam. It is called a great recreational resource. The Bureau of Reclamation promotes its beauty in an attempt to counter continuing criticisms of the dam itself, and the National Park Service, which manages the Recreation Area, is installing or planning facilities for all the boating, water skiing, fishing, camping, swimming, and plain sightseeing that should now ensue.

But I come back to Lake Powell reluctantly and skeptically, for I remember Glen Canyon as it used to be.

Once the river ran through Glen's two hundred miles in a twisting, many-branched stone trough eight hundred to twelve hundred feet deep, just deep enough to be impressive without being overwhelming. Awe was never Glen Canyon's province. That is for the Grand Canyon. Glen

Canyon was for delight. The river that used to run here cooperated with the scenery by flowing swift and smooth, without a major rapid. Any ordinary boatman could take anyone through it. Boy Scouts made annual pilgrimages on rubber rafts. In 1947 we went through with a party that contained an old lady of seventy and a girl of ten. There was superlative camping anywhere, on sandbars furred with tamarisk and willow, under cliffs that whispered with the sound of flowing water.

Through many of those two hundred idyllic miles the view was shut in by red walls, but down straight reaches or up side canyons there would be glimpses of noble towers and buttes lifting high beyond the canyon rims, and somewhat more than halfway down there was a major confrontation where the Kaiparowits Plateau, seventy-five hundred feet high, thrust its knife-blade cliff above the north rim to face the dome of Navajo Mountain, more than ten thousand feet high, on the south side. Those two uplifts, as strikingly different as if designed to dominate some gigantic world's fair, added magnificence to the intimate colored trough of the river.

Seen from the air, the Glen Canyon country reveals itself as a bare-stone, salmon-pink tableland whose surface is a chaos of domes, knobs, beehives, baldheads, hollows, and potholes, dissected by the deep corkscrew channels of streams. Out of the platform north of the main river rise the gray-green peaks of the Henry Mountains, the last-discovered mountains in the contiguous United States. West of them is the bloody welt of the Waterpocket Fold, whose westward creeks flow into the Escalante, the last-discovered river. Northward rise the cliffs of Utah's high plateaus. South of Glen Canyon, like a great period at the

foot of the fifty-mile exclamation point of the Kaiparowits, is Navajo Mountain, whose slopes apron off on every
side into the stone and sand of the reservation.

When cut by streams, the Navajo sandstone which is the
country rock forms monolithic cliffs with rounded rims.
In straight stretches the cliffs tend to be sheer, on the
curves undercut, especially in the narrow side canyons. I
have measured a six-hundred-foot wall that was undercut
a good five hundred feet—not a cliff at all but a musical shell for the multiplication of echoes. Into these deep
scoured amphitheaters on the outside of bends, the promontories on the inside fit like thighbones into a hip socket.
Often, straightening bends, creeks have cut through promontories to form bridges, as at Rainbow Bridge National
Monument, Gregory Bridge in Fiftymile Canyon, and dozens of other places. And systematically, when a river cleft
has exposed the rock to the lateral thrust of its own weight,
fracturing begins to peel great slabs from the cliff faces.
The slabs are thinner at top than at bottom, and curve
together so that great alcoves form in the walls. If they are
near the rim, they may break through to let a window-
wink of sky down on a canyon traveler, and always they
make panels of fresh pink in weathered and stained and
darkened red walls.

Floating down the river one passed, every mile or two
on right or left, the mouth of some side canyon, narrow,
shadowed, releasing a secret stream into the taffy-colored,
whirlpooled Colorado. Between the mouth of the Dirty
Devil and the dam, which is a few miles above the actual
foot of the Glen Canyon, there are at least three dozen
such gulches on the north side, including the major canyon
of the Escalante; and on the south nearly that many more,

including the major canyon of the San Juan. Every such gulch used to be a little wonder, each with its multiplying branches, each as deep at the mouth as its parent canyon. Hundreds of feet deep, sometimes only a few yards wide, they wove into the rock so sinuously that all sky was shut off. The floors were smooth sand or rounded stone pavement or stone pools linked by stone gutters, and nearly every gulch ran, except in flood season, a thin clear stream. Silt pockets out of reach of flood were gardens of fern and redbud; every talus and rockslide gave footing to cottonwood and willow and single-leafed ash; ponded places were solid with watercress; maidenhair hung from seepage cracks in the cliffs.

Often these canyons, pursued upward, ended in falls, and sometimes the falls came down through a slot or a skylight in the roof of a domed chamber, to trickle down the wall into a plunge pool that made a lyrical dunk bath on a hot day. In such chambers the light was dim, reflected, richly colored. The red rock was stained with the dark manganese exudations called desert varnish, striped black to green to yellow to white along horizontal lines of seepage, patched with the chemical, sunless green of moss. One such grotto was named Music Temple by Major John Wesley Powell on his first exploration, in 1869; another is the so-called Cathedral in the Desert, at the head of Clear Water Canyon off the Escalante.

That was what Glen Canyon was like before the closing of the dam in 1963. What was flooded here was potentially a superb national park. It had its history, too, sparse but significant. Exploring the gulches, one came upon ancient chiseled footholds leading up the slickrock to mortared dwellings or storage cysts of the Basket Makers and Pueblos

who once inhabited these canyons. At the mouth of Padre
Creek a line of chiseled steps marked where Fathers Escalante and Dominguez, groping back toward Santa Fe in
1776, got their animals down to the fjord that was afterward known as the Crossing of the Fathers. In Music Temple men from Powell's two river expeditions had scratched
their names. Here and there on the walls near the river
were names and initials of men from Robert Brewster Stan-
ton's party that surveyed a water-level railroad down the
canyon in 1889–90, and miners from the abortive goldrush
of the 1890's. There were Mormon echoes at Lee's Ferry,
below the dam, and at the slot canyon called Hole-in-the-
Rock, where a Mormon colonizing party got their wagons
down the cliffs on their way to the San Juan in 1880.

Some of this is now under Lake Powell. I am interested
to know how much is gone, how much left. Because I
don't much like the thought of power boats and water
skiers in these canyons, I come in March, before the season
has properly begun, and at a time when the lake (stabilized
they say because of water shortages far downriver at Lake
Mead) is as high as it has ever been, but is still more than
two hundred feet below its capacity level of thirty-seven
hundred feet. Not everything that may eventually be
drowned will be drowned yet, and there will be none of
the stained walls and exposed mudflats that make a drawdown reservoir ugly at low water.

Our boat is the Park Service patrol boat, a thirty-four-
foot diesel workhorse. It has a voice like a bulldozer's. As
we back away from the dock and head out deserted Wahweap Bay, conversing at the tops of our lungs with our
noses a foot apart, we acknowledge that we needn't have
worried about motor noises among the cliffs. We couldn't

have heard a Chriscraft if it had passed us with its throttle wide open.

One thing is comfortingly clear from the moment we back away from the dock at Wahweap and start out between the low walls of what used to be Wahweap Creek toward the main channel. Though they have diminished it, they haven't utterly ruined it. Though these walls are lower and tamer than they used to be, and though the whole sensation is a little like looking at a picture of Miss America that doesn't show her legs, Lake Powell *is* beautiful. It isn't Glen Canyon, but it is something in itself. The contact of deep blue water and uncompromising stone is bizarre and somehow exciting. Enough of the canyon feeling is left so that traveling up-lake one watches with a sense of discovery as every bend rotates into view new colors, new forms, new vistas: a great glowing wall with the sun on it, a slot side canyon buried to the eyes in water and inviting exploration, a half-drowned cave on whose roof dance the little flames of reflected ripples.

Moreover, since we float three hundred feet or more above the old river, the views out are much wider, and where the lake broadens, as at Padre Creek, they are superb. From the river, Navajo Mountain used to be seen only in brief, distant glimpses. From the lake it is often visible for minutes, an hour, at a time—gray-green, snow-streaked, a high mysterious bubble rising above the red world, incontrovertibly the holy mountain. And the broken country around the Crossing of the Fathers was always wild and strange as a moon landscape, but you had to climb out to see it. Now, from the bay that covers the crossing and spreads into the mouths of tributary creeks, we see Gunsight Butte, Tower Butte, and the other fantastic pinnacles of the Entrada formation surging up a sheer thousand feet above the rounding platform of the Navajo. The horizon reels with surrealist forms, dark red at the base, gray from there to rimrock, the profiles rigid and angular and carved, as different as possible from the Navajo's filigreed, ripple-marked sandstone.

We find the larger side canyons, as well as the deeper reaches of the main canyon, almost as impressive as they used to be, especially after we get far enough up-lake so that the water is shallower and the cliffs less reduced in height. Navajo Canyon is splendid despite the flooding of its green bottom that used to provide pasture for the stolen horses of raiders. Forbidden Canyon that leads to Rainbow Bridge is lessened, but still marvelous: it is like going by boat to Petra. Rainbow Bridge itself is still the place of magic that it used to be when we walked the six miles up from the river, and turned a corner to see the great arch framing the dome of Navajo Mountain. The canyon of the Escalante, with all its tortuous side canyons, is one of the stunning scenic experiences of a lifetime, and far easier to reach by lake than it used to be by foot or horseback. And all up and down these canyons, big or little, is the constantly changing, nobly repetitive spectacle of the cliffs with their contrasts of rounding and sheer, their great blackboard faces and their amphitheaters. Streaked with desert varnish, weathered and lichened and shadowed, patched with clean pink fresh-broken stone, they are as magically colored as shot silk.

And there is God's plenty of it. This lake is already a hundred and fifty miles long, with scores of tributaries. If it ever fills—which its critics guess it will not—it will have eighteen hundred miles of shoreline. Its fishing is good and apparently getting better, not only catfish and perch but rainbow trout and largemouth black bass that are periodically sown broadcast from planes. At present its supply and access points are few and far apart—at Wahweap, Hall's Crossing, and Hite—but when floating facilities are anchored in the narrows below Rainbow Bridge and when boat ramps and supply stations are developed at Warm Creek, Hole-in-the-Rock, and Bullfrog Basin, this will draw people. The prediction of a million visitors in 1965 is probably enthusiastic, but there is no question that as developed facilities extend the range of boats and multiply places of access, this will become one of the great water playgrounds.

And yet, vast and beautiful as it is, open now to anyone with a boat or the money to rent one, available soon (one supposes) to the quickie tour by float-plane and hydrofoil, democratically accessible and with its most secret beauties captured on color transparencies at infallible exposures, it strikes me, even in my exhilaration, with the consciousness of loss. In gaining the lovely and the usable, we have given up the incomparable.

The river's altitude at the dam was about 3150 feet. At 3490 we ride on 340 feet of water, and that means that much of the archaeology and most of the history, both of which were concentrated at the river's edge or near it, are as drowned as Lyonesse. We chug two hundred feet over the top of the square masonry tower that used to guard the mouth of Forbidden Canyon. The one small ruin that we see up Navajo Canyon must once have been nearly inaccessible, high in the cliff. Somehow (though we do not see them) we think it ought to have a line of footholds leading down into and under the water toward the bottom where the squash and corn gardens used to grow.

The wildlife that used to live comfortably in Glen Canyon is not there on the main lake. Except at the extreme reach of the water up side canyons, and at infrequent places where the platform of the Navajo sandstone dips down so that the lake spreads in among its hollows and baldheads, this reservoir laps vertical cliffs, and leaves no home for beaver or waterbird. The beaver have been driven up the side canyons, and have toppled whole groves of cottonwoods ahead of the rising water. While the water remains stable, they have a home; if it rises, they move upward; if it falls, the Lord knows what they do, for falling water will leave long mud flats between their water and their food. In the side canyons we see a few mergansers and redheads, and up the Escalante Arm the blue herons are now nesting on the cliffs, but as a future habitat Lake Powell is as unpromising for any of them as for the beaver.

And what has made things difficult for the wildlife makes them difficult for tourists as well. The tamarisk and willow bars are gone, and finding a campsite, or even a safe place to land a boat, is not easy. When the stiff afternoon winds sweep up the lake, small boats stay in shelter, for a swamping could leave a man clawing at a vertical cliff, a mile from any crawling-out place.

Worst of all are the places I remember that are now irretrievably gone. Surging up-lake on the second day I look over my shoulder and recognize the swamped and truncated entrance to Hidden Passage Canyon, on whose bar we camped eighteen years ago when we first came down this canyon on one of Norman Nevills' river trips. The old masked entrance is swallowed up, the water rises almost over the shoulder of the inner cliffs. Once that canyon was a pure delight to walk in; now it is only another slot with water in it, a thing to poke a motorboat into for five minutes and then roar out again. And if that is Hidden Passage, and we are this far out in the channel, then Music Temple is straight down.

The magnificent confrontation of the Kaiparowits and Navajo Mountain is still there, possibly even more magnificent because the lake has lifted us into a wider view. The splendid sweep of stained wall just below the mouth of the San Juan is there, only a little diminished. And Hole-in-the-Rock still notches the north rim, though the cove at the bottom where the Mormons camped before rafting the river and starting across the bare rock-chaos of Wilson Mesa is now a bay, with sunfish swimming among the tops of drowned trees. The last time I was here, three years ago, the river ran in a gorge three hundred feet below where our boat ties up for the night, and the descent from rim to water was a longer, harder way. The lake makes the feat of those Mormons look easier than it was, but even now, no one climbing the thousand feet of cliff to the slot will ever understand how they got their wagons down there.

A mixture of losses, diminishments, occasional gains, precariously maintained by the temporary stabilization of the lake. There are plenty of people willing to bet that there will never be enough water in the Colorado to fill both Lake Mead, now drawn far down, and Lake Powell, still 210 feet below its planned top level, much less the two additional dams proposed for Marble and Bridge canyons,* between these two. If there ever is—even if there is enough

* Since given up, at least temporarily.

to raise Lake Powell fifty or a hundred feet—there will be immediate drastic losses of beauty. Walls now low, but high enough to maintain the canyon feeling, will go under, walls now high will be reduced. The wider the lake spreads, the less character it will have. Another fifty feet of water would submerge the Gregory Natural Bridge and flood the floor of the Cathedral in the Desert; a hundred feet would put both where Music Temple is; two hundred feet would bring water and silt to the very foot of Rainbow Bridge. The promontories that are now the most feasible camping places would go, as the taluses and sandbars have already gone. Then indeed the lake would be a vertical-walled fjord widening in places to a vertical-walled lake, neither as beautiful nor as usable as it still is. And the moment there is even twenty or thirty feet of drawdown, every side canyon is a slimy stinking mudflat and every cliff is defaced at the foot by a band of mud and minerals.

By all odds the best thing that could happen, so far as the recreational charm of Lake Powell is concerned, would be a permanently stabilized lake, but nobody really expects that. People who want to see it in its diminished but still remarkable beauty should go soon. And people who, as we do, remember this country before the canyons were flooded, are driven to dream of ways by which some parts of it may still be saved, or half-saved.

The dream comes on us one evening when we are camped up the Escalante. For three days we have been deafened by the noise of our diesel engines, and even when that has been cut off there has been the steady puttering of the generator that supplies our boat with heat, light, and running water. Though we weakly submit to the comforts, we dislike the smell and noise: we hate to import into this rock-and-water wilderness the very things we have been most eager to escape from. A wilderness that must be approached by power boat is no wilderness any more, it has lost its magic. Now, with the engines cut and the generator broken down, we sit around a campfire's more primitive light and heat and reflect that the best moments of this trip have been those in which the lake and its powerboat necessities were least dominant—eating a quiet lunch on a rock in Navajo Canyon, walking the 1.7 miles of sandy trail to the Rainbow Bridge or the half mile of creek bottom to the Cathedral in the Desert, climbing up the cliff to Hole-in-the-Rock. Sitting on our promontory in the Escalante canyon without sign or sound of the mechanical gadgetry of our civilization, we feel descending on us, as gentle as evening on a blazing day, the remembered canyon silence. It is a stillness like no other I have experienced, for at the very instant of bouncing and echoing every slight noise off cliffs and around bends, the canyons swallow them. It is as if they accentuated them, briefly and with a smile, as if they said, "Wait!" and suddenly all sound has vanished, there is only a hollow ringing in the ears.

We find that whatever others may want, we would hate to come here in the full summer season and be affronted with the constant roar and wake of power boats. We are not, it seems, water-based in our pleasures; we can't get a thrill out of doing in these marvelous canyons what one can do on any resort lake. What we have most liked on this trip has been those times when ears and muscles were involved, when the foot felt sand or stone, when we could talk in low voices, or sit so still that a brilliant collared lizard would come out of a crack to look us over. For us, it is clear, Lake Powell is not a recreational resource, but only a means of access; it is the canyons themselves, or what is left of them, that we respond to.

Six or seven hundred feet above us, spreading grandly from the rim, is the Escalante Desert, a basin of unmitigated stone furrowed by branching canyons as a carving platter is furrowed by gravy channels. It is, as a subsidiary drainage basin, very like the greater basin in whose trough once lay Glen Canyon, now the lake. On the north this desert drains from the Circle Cliffs and the Aquarius Plateau, on the east from the Waterpocket Fold, on the west from the Kaiparowits. In all that waste of stone fifty miles long and twenty to thirty wide there is not a resident human being, not a building except a couple of cowboy shelter shacks, not a road except the washed-out trail that the Mormons of 1880 established from the town of Escalante to Hole-in-the-Rock. The cattle and sheep that used to run on this desert range have ruined it and gone. That ringing stillness around us is a total absence of industrial or civilized decibels.

Why not, we say, sitting in chilly fire-flushed darkness under mica stars, why not throw a boom across the mouth of the Escalante Canyon and hold this one precious arm of Lake Powell for the experiencing of silence? Why not, giving the rest of that enormous water to the motorboats and the waterskiers, keep one limited tributary as a canoe or rowboat wilderness? There is nothing in the way of law or regulation to prevent the National Park Service from managing the Recreation Area in any way it thinks best, nothing that forbids a wilderness or primitive or limited-access area within the larger recreational unit. The Escalante Desert is already federal land, virtually unused. It and its canyons are accessible by packtrain from the town of Escalante, and will be accessible by boat from the facility to be developed at Hole-in-the-Rock. All down the foot of the Kaiparowits, locally called Fiftymile Mountain or Wild Horse Mesa, the old Mormon road offers stupendous views to those who from choice or necessity want only to drive to the edge of the silence and look in.

I have been in most of the side gulches off the Escalante —Coyote Gulch, Hurricane Wash, Davis Canyon, and the rest. All of them have bridges, windows, amphitheaters, grottoes, sudden pockets of green. And some of them, including the superlative Coyote Gulch down which even now it is possible to take a packtrain to the river, will never be drowned even if Lake Powell rises to its planned thirty-seven-hundred-foot level. What might have been done for Glen Canyon as a whole may still be done for the higher tributaries of the Escalante. Why not? In the name of scenery, silence, sanity, why not?

For awe pervades that desert of slashed and channeled stone overlooked by the cliffs of the Kaiparowits and the Aquarius and the distant peaks of the Henrys; and history, effaced through many of the canyons, still shows us its dim marks here: a crude *mano* discarded by an ancient campsite, a mortared wall in a cave, petroglyphs picked into a cliff face, a broken flint point glittering on its tee of sand on some blown mesa, the great rock where the Mormons danced on their way to people Desolation. This is country that does not challenge our identity as creatures, but it lets us shed most of our industrial gadgetry, and it shows us our true size.

Exploring the Escalante basin on a trip in 1961, we probed for the river through a half dozen quicksand gulches and never reached it, and never much cared because the side gulches and the rims gave us all we could hold. We saw not a soul outside our own party, encountered not a vehicle, saw no animals except a handful of cows and one mule that we scared up out of Davis Gulch when we rolled a rock over the rim. From every evening camp, when the sun was gone behind the Kaiparowits rim and the wind hung in suspension like a held breath and the Henrys northeastward and Navajo Mountain southward floated light as bubbles on the distance, we watched the eastern sky flush a pure, cloudless rose, darker at the horizon, paler above; and minute by minute the horizon's darkness defined itself as the blue-domed shadow of the earth cast on the sky, thinning at its upward arc to violet, lavender, pale lilac, but clearly defined, steadily darkening upward until it swallowed all the sky's light and the stars pierced through it. Every night we watched the earth-shadow climb the hollow sky, and every dawn we watched the same blue shadow sink down toward the Kaiparowits, to disappear at the instant when the sun splintered sparks off the rim.

In that country you cannot raise your eyes—unless you're in a canyon—without looking a hundred miles. You can hear coyotes who have somehow escaped the air-dropped poison baits designed to exterminate them. You can see in every sandy pocket the pug tracks of wildcats, and every waterpocket in the rock will give you a look backward into geologic time, for every such hole swarms with triangular crablike creatures locally called tadpoles but actually first cousins to the trilobites who left their fossil skeletons in the Paleozoic.

In the canyons you do not have the sweep of sky, the

long views, the freedom of movement on foot, but you do have the protection of cliffs, the secret places, cool water, arches and bridges and caves, and the sunken canyon stillness into which, musical as water falling into a plunge pool, the canyon wrens pour their showers of notes in the mornings.

Set the Escalante Arm aside for the silence, and the boatmen and the water skiers can have the rest of that lake, which on the serene, warm, sun-smitten trip back seems more beautiful than it seemed coming up. Save this tributary and the desert back from it as wilderness, and there will be something at Lake Powell for everybody. Then it may still be possible to make expeditions as rewarding as the old, motorless river trips through Glen Canyon, and a man can make his choice between forking a horse and riding down Coyote Gulch or renting a houseboat and chugging it up somewhere near the mouth of the Escalante to be anchored and used as a base for excursions into beauty, wonder, and the sort of silence in which you can hear the swish of falling stars.

7

The Land of Enchantment

Once the land opened out westward across pink and tan and alkali-white flats, and the horizon stepped down in cliff and talus from juniper-dotted plateaus. Once the distance went backward from gray to mauve and from mauve to lilac and from lilac to purple, and the highway stretched toward that mysterious, hazy beyond like a pictured path in a fairy tale. At sunset, driving west, a traveler saw the mesas burning at the edges with the fire behind them, and knew what Coronado felt, and the Spanish captains, laboring toward the Seven Cities of Cibola.

This land is still there. The motorist on Highway 66 sees it swim toward him like the blur of a microscope's field sharpening toward focus. At a point between Amarillo and Tucumcari there is a sign: "Entering New Mexico, the Land of Enchantment." Everything is as it was, except that the enchantment has been improved and modernized.

As a social historian of sorts, I am interested in the changing styles of enchantment, and since the change has happened under my eyes, as it were, and within twenty or twenty-five years, I have some notion of how it occurred.

In the beginning there was a little sign, hardly bigger than a man's hand, that rose up on the horizon and said, when one got right on top of it, "GAS 3 MI." This was direct, honest, and useful; it reassured the wearied motorist, limping along on three tires and a rim and with the alkali-clogged radiator of his old car boiling, that there was a haven in this desert and help at hand.

Later there arose another oasis in that desert as the traffic thickened along Highway 66, and competition, which is the soul of trade, and the itching palm, which is the trademark of its oversoul, dictated improvements. The competitor also put up a sign, advertising gas, free air, and ice-cold drinks. Number one then put up a second sign, twice as big, offering complete motor repairs and desert water bags. Number two countered with three notices of Indian curios. About that time the operator of a third trading post, fifty miles west, horned in with a series of fifty signs spaced at mile intervals, and very shortly Harold's Club, in Nevada, a thousand miles west and north, set up a big show-off placard so fancy it made everything else on the road look homemade and seedy, and forced the local boys to renovate and enlarge. This takes only a moment to tell; it took perhaps a decade of hard pioneering work and hard thinking to bring it about.

As infallibly as trees in spring sprout leaves, fence posts in the Land of Enchantment now sprout rectangles of tin or board, and the distances loom with outlines of things as angular and enduring as the mesas.

Today, the keepers of tourist traps on Highway 66 have outgrown their penny-ante beginnings. Some of the newer signs are a good hundred feet long, with letters ten feet high. One I took an inventory of was held up by forty-two telephone poles and a great many two-by-fours, and contained approximately two thousand board feet of one-by-ten pine boards. This was one of twelve signs, six on each side of the trading post they advertised, which in turn was one of four clustered at a source of water. All were about equally well announced along the roadside. The population of those four trading posts could not have exceeded twenty people, but they had impressed themselves upon their environment in a way to excite admiration. It is a pity that this part of the country does not suffer from heavy snows, for thanks to the efforts of these twenty pioneers and a stalwart handful of others like them, the highway from Tucumcari to Gallup is already in such shape that the mere addition of a roof would form a continuous snowshed.

The amount of human determination and labor that has gone into this work is tremendous. Whole groves have been cut down to tell us that beer is available at Alkali Springs. Mesas are denuded and housing projects left lumberless so that we will not be unaware of the Indian pottery at the Red Horse Trading Post. What applies here is the principle that if some is good, more is better. Nowhere else on earth, I think, is that principle so enthusiastically applied.

Here, in addition to the repetition, there is variety. Like the verses of a very slow ballad, nine majestic signs the size of movie screens let a traveler in on one delightful part of the secret at a time: Cactus Candy. Moccasins,

All Sizes. Indian Pottery. Indian Baskets. Indian Jewelry.
Katchina Dolls. Gas and Oil. Cold Drinks. Navajo Rugs.
Into this dignified sequence, like a little dog getting in on
a big dogfight, thrusts up a series of yapping little signs
barking out what you can get at Mag's Good Eats: Ham
and Eggs. Good Coffee. Hot Cakes. Occasionally some
tinhorn outlander tries to muscle in with something about
Auto Parts or Motor Oil; but these signs are coldly ignored
and achieve nothing.

The local imagination is rich and full. It provides not
only grandeur, but also mystery and whimsy. At a certain
point we encounter the black, enigmatic silhouette of a
jackrabbit, mute and somehow threatening. A mile or so
farther on, a bigger version of it crouches at the top of a
rise. Still farther on, an enormous one haunts a blind curve.
What can they mean? Is this the Jack Rabbit Highway,
maybe, like the Lincoln Highway up north? Or are these
black rabbits part of some Indian ritual? As the silhouettes
keep cropping up, mile after mile, it becomes a game to
search for them, and our pointing fingers leap out and
our excited voices cry, "There's one!" or, "There's another!" But nobody comes close to guessing what they
mean. We all have a merry laugh when we roll past a
trading post and gas station with a crowning, gigantic
black rabbit on its ridgepole. The Jack Rabbit Trading
Post, of course.

Often there are even more whimsical treatments of the
same theme—for instance, question marks stuck on posts
for a dozen miles, or signs saying, "Mystery Spot." All
these lend interest and suspense to driving; sometimes it is
hard to wait until the mystery is revealed, and the excite-

ment of solving it takes the mind and eye off the dry, empty country.

But most interesting of all, more interesting than the slow-revelation technique, or the unrolled-like-a-scroll-across-a-mile-of-range technique, or even the guess-what technique, is the see-the-animals technique, which, mainly in the years since the war, has enriched and internationalized our western highways and sold incalculable gallons of gasoline.

This, too, has sprung from small beginnings. I can remember a time about twenty-five years ago when a gas station on Highway 91, between Salt Lake and Los Angeles, kept a pen of desert tortoises for sale as pets to movie stars and others. They were then called Hollywood bedbugs and were quite a fad for a time. But the quarter of a century that has passed since that faraway innocent time has not left us standing still. A Hollywood bedbug would now look about as outdated as a Stutz Bearcat.

First you put a sign at your entrance advertising whatever modest little thing it is that you have captured. "See the Rattlesnake," you suggest. This, like a penicillin tablet, will allay the commercial fever and hoarseness for a time. But soon a man is moved by soul or oversoul to larger things. The competitor down the road sticks up an ignorant, arrogant sign saying, "See the Gila Monster, the World's Only Poisonous Lizard." If you dig up a coyote den and add a mangy cub to your collection and your advertising, he is just as likely to write to a friend in Florida, where rattlesnakes grow to huge size, and import a reptile he advertises as "The World's Largest Rattlesnake." Then, perhaps, your rattlesnake gets loose and bites one of your waitresses, who dies, and you erect a monument to her memory: a really big sign, with big, brilliantly painted letters, that says, "See the Snake That Killed Agnes Littlefield!"

For a time this silences the competition. But before long, as the signs string out along the highway, growing bigger as the immediate roadside is used up and open range has to be utilized, he comes up with a new one: "See the Three-Time Killer!" You suspect that he has fed his torpid Florida snake three pack rats; but his sign is a worry and an exasperation. You wait your chance and the new idea that will use him up, and as a precaution you buy a hundred and sixty acres of the mesa for its timber rights, and during the slow season, you expand your establishment back from the highway a hundred feet or so, adding coops and pens for the stock.

Perhaps, eventually, a circus goes broke and you pick up its boa constrictor at a bargain. Before you have a chance to enjoy your triumph, your competitor comes up with a cobra. So it goes, a seesaw battle. Then you notice that tourists tend to drive by, not seeing your station for the signs. To correct this, you erect a forty-foot tower over the station and invite the customers to visit the free lookout. You have by now hired a sign painter and a snake wrangler, full time. Observing the success of your rival's cobra, you import some, too, and buy a book on herpetology and start a series of "Did You Know" signs aimed at public instruction: "Did You Know That 20,000 People Die of Cobra Bites Every Year?" "Did You Know That the Cobra Is the Deadliest Poisonous Reptile in the World?" Shifting into high, you line yourself up with a zoological supply house, get some brood stock, and begin to wholesale cobras to stations up and down the line.

To a curious foreign visitor, astonished to find exotic fauna so acclimated in the Land of Enchantment, one can point out this entire process as an excellent example of the American's restless will to alter and control his environment. After a moment's thought, he will have to admit that the environment here is controlled, all right, and altered for sure. He will have to admit, too, that a curious law of compensation operates in all the characteristic forms of American exploitation. The exploitation of one natural resource may leave results that critics carp at, but these effects are balanced by the results of other forms of exploitation: What is cut down in Michigan sprouts anew, like the phoenix, in New Mexico. What levels our forest elevates our roadside.

It took some time to find a New Mexican gas station that did not advertise serpents; but when we found it and stopped to fill our tank, we asked the young man how come he felt he didn't need reptiles in his business. He told us he was just starting out, hadn't really got going yet, but did have his eye on some nice specimens. They were part of the stock of the cobra wholesaler down the road, the one whose signs had sheltered us from the wind all the way from Albuquerque. This man had, in the free spirit of trade, supplied cobras and boas, as well as lesser Ophidia, to stations as far away as Kansas. He was a real go-getter and strictly aboveboard, the boy said. If he advertised "See the Deadliest Living Serpent. Alive! Alive! Alive!" and his cobra died that night, he'd be right out there taking his sign down. And not three days later, either. The next morning. Yes, sir, he really had everything he said he had.

The spirit of this is stimulating and restorative. It repeats a spirit and a vision as old as America. Whitman would have responded to it with strong chants. I can imagine the good gray poet, not afoot but definitely lighthearted, taking to the open road down Highway 66, and I can see his eagle eye and his wind-split beard, and hear his words as he squints westward along the vista walled by the work of these latter-day pioneers.

"Oh road," I can hear him shouting,

"You road I enter upon and look around, I believe you are not all that is here,

I believe that much unseen is also here."

It is hard to fool a poet.

8

Coda

Wilderness Letter

Los Altos, Calif.
Dec. 3, 1960

David E. Pesonen
Wildland Research Center
Agricultural Experiment Station
243 Mulford Hall
University of California
Berkeley 4, Calif.

Dear Mr. Pesonen:

I believe that you are working on the wilderness portion of the Outdoor Recreation Resources Review Commission's report. If I may, I should like to urge some arguments for wilderness preservation that involve recreation, as it is ordinarily conceived, hardly at all. Hunting, fishing, hiking, mountain-climbing, camping, photography, and the enjoyment of natural scenery will all, surely, figure in your report. So will the wilderness as a genetic reserve, a scientific yardstick by which we may measure the world in its natural balance against the world in its man-made imbalance. What I want to speak for is not so much the wilderness uses, valuable as those are, but the wilderness *idea*, which is a resource in itself. Being an intangible and spiritual resource, it will seem mystical to the practical-minded—but then anything that cannot be moved by a bulldozer is likely to seem mystical to them.

I want to speak for the wilderness idea as something that has helped form our character and that has certainly shaped our history as a people. It has no more to do with recreation than churches have to do with recreation, or than the strenuousness and optimism and expansiveness of what historians call the "American Dream" have to do with recreation. Nevertheless, since it is only in this recreation survey that the values of wilderness are being compiled, I hope you will permit me to insert this idea between the leaves, as it were, of the recreation report.

Something will have gone out of us as a people if we ever let the remaining wilderness be destroyed; if we permit the last virgin forests to be turned into comic books and plastic cigarette cases; if we drive the few remaining members of the wild species into zoos or to extinction; if we pollute the last clear air and dirty the last clean streams and push our paved roads through the last of the silence, so that never again will Americans be free in their own country from the noise, the exhausts, the stinks of human and automotive waste. And so that never again can we have the chance to see ourselves single, separate, vertical and individual in the world, part of the environment of trees and rocks and soil, brother to the other animals, part of the natural world and competent to belong in it. Without any remaining wilderness we are committed wholly, without chance for even momentary reflection and rest, to a headlong drive into our technological termite-life, the Brave New World of a completely man-controlled environment. We need wilderness preserved—as much of it as is still left, and as many kinds—because it was the challenge against which our character as a people was formed. The reminder and the reassurance that it is still there is good for our spiritual health even if we never once in ten years set foot in it. It is good for us when we are young, because of the incomparable sanity it can bring briefly, as vacation and rest, into our insane lives. It is important to us when we are old simply because it is there—important, that is, simply as idea.

We are a wild species, as Darwin pointed out. Nobody ever tamed or domesticated or scientifically bred us. But for at least three millennia we have been engaged in a cumulative and ambitious race to modify and gain control of our environment, and in the process we have come close to domesticating ourselves. Not many people are likely, any more, to look upon what we call "progress" as an unmixed blessing. Just as surely as it has brought us increased comfort and more material goods, it has brought us spiritual losses, and it threatens now to become the Frankenstein that will destroy us. One means of sanity is to retain a hold on the natural world, to remain, insofar as we can, good animals. Americans still have that chance, more than many peoples; for while we were demonstrating ourselves the most efficient and ruthless environment-busters in history, and slashing and burning and cutting our way through a wilderness continent, the wilderness was working on us. It remains in us as surely as Indian names remain on the land. If the abstract dream of human liberty and human dignity became, in America, something more than an abstract dream, mark it down at least partially to the fact that we were in subtle ways subdued by what we conquered.

The Connecticut Yankee, sending likely candidates from King Arthur's unjust kingdom to his Man Factory for rehabilitation, was over-optimistic, as he later admitted. These things cannot be forced, they have to grow. To make such a man, such a democrat, such a believer in human individual dignity, as Mark Twain himself, the frontier was necessary, Hannibal and the Mississippi and Virginia City, and reaching out from those the wilderness; the wilderness as opportunity and as idea, the thing that has helped to make an American different from and, until we forget it in the roar of our industrial cities, more fortunate than other men. For an American, insofar as he is new and different at all, is a civilized man who has renewed himself in the wild. The American experience has been the confrontation by old peoples and cultures of a world as new as if it had just risen from the sea. That gave us our hope and our excitement, and the hope and excitement can be passed on to newer Americans, Americans who never saw any phase of the frontier. But only so long as we keep the remainder of our wild as a reserve and a promise—a sort of wilderness bank.

As a novelist, I may perhaps be forgiven for taking literature as a reflection, indirect but profoundly true, of our national consciousness. And our literature, as perhaps you are aware, is sick, embittered, losing its mind, losing its faith. Our novelists are the declared enemies of their society. There has hardly been a serious or important novel in this century that did not repudiate in part or in whole American technological culture for its commercialism, its vulgarity, and the way in which it has dirtied a clean continent and a clean dream. I do not expect that the preservation of our remaining wilderness is going to cure this condition. But the mere example that we can as a nation apply some other criteria than commercial and exploitative considerations would be heartening to many Americans, novelists or otherwise. We need to demonstrate our acceptance of the natural world, including ourselves; we need the spiritual refreshment that being natural can produce. And one of the best places for us to get that is in the wilderness where the fun houses, the bulldozers, and the pavements of our civilization are shut out.

Sherwood Anderson, in a letter to Waldo Frank in the 1920's, said it better than I can. "Is it not likely that when the country was new and men were often alone in the fields and the forest they got a sense of bigness outside themselves that has now in some way been lost . . . Mystery whispered in the grass, played in the branches of trees overhead, was caught up and blown across the American line in clouds of dust at evening on the prairies . . . I am old enough to remember tales that strengthen my belief in a deep semi-religious influence that was formerly at work among our people. The flavor of it hangs over the best work of Mark Twain . . . I can remember old fellows in my home town speaking feelingly of an evening spent on the big empty plains. It had taken the shrillness out of them. They had learned the trick of quiet . . ."

We could learn it too, even yet; even our children and grandchildren could learn it. But only if we save, for just such absolutely non-recreational, impractical, and mystical uses as this, all the wild that still remains to us.

It seems to me significant that the distinct downturn in our literature from hope to bitterness took place almost at the precise time when the frontier officially came to an end, in 1890, and when the American way of life had begun to turn strongly urban and industrial. The more urban it has become, and the more frantic with technological change, the sicker and more embittered our literature, and I believe our people, have become. For myself, I grew up on the empty plains of Saskatchewan and Montana and in the mountains of Utah, and I put a very high valuation on what those places gave me. And if I had not been able periodically to renew myself in the mountains and deserts of western America I would be very nearly bughouse. Even when I can't get to the back country, the thought of the colored deserts of southern Utah, or the reassurance that there are still stretches of prairie where the world can be instantaneously perceived as disk and bowl, and where the little but intensely important human being is exposed to the five directions and the thirty-six winds, is a positive consolation. The idea alone can sustain me. But as the wilderness areas are progressively exploited or "improved," as the jeeps and bulldozers of uranium prospectors scar up the deserts and the roads are cut into the alpine timberlands, and as the remnants of the unspoiled and natural world are progressively eroded, every such loss is a little death in me. In us.

Coda

I am not moved by the argument that those wilderness areas which have already been exposed to grazing or mining are already deflowered, and so might as well be "harvested." For mining I cannot say much good except that its operations are generally short-lived. The extractable wealth is taken and the shafts, the tailings, and the ruins left, and in a dry country such as the American West the wounds men make in the earth do not quickly heal. Still, they are only wounds; they aren't absolutely mortal. Better a wounded wilderness than none at all. And as for grazing, if it is strictly controlled so that it does not destroy the ground cover, damage the ecology, or compete with the wildlife it is in itself nothing that need conflict with the wilderness feeling or the validity of the wilderness experience. I have known enough range cattle to recognize them as wild animals; and the people who herd them have, in the wilderness context, the dignity of rareness; they belong on the frontier, moreover, and have a look of rightness. The invasion they make on the virgin country is a sort of invasion that is as old as Neolithic man, and they can, in moderation, even emphasize a man's feeling of belonging to the natural world. Under surveillance, they can belong; under control, they need not deface or mar. I do not believe that in wilderness areas where grazing has never been permitted, it should be permitted; but I do not believe either that an otherwise untouched wilderness should be eliminated from the preservation plan because of limited existing uses such as grazing which are in consonance with the frontier condition and image.

Let me say something on the subject of the kinds of wilderness worth preserving. Most of those areas contemplated are in the national forests and in high mountain country. For all the usual recreational purposes, the alpine and forest wildernesses are obviously the most important, both as genetic banks and as beauty spots. But for the spiritual renewal, the recognition of identity, the birth of awe, other kinds will serve every bit as well. Perhaps, because they are less friendly to life, more abstractly non-human, they will serve even better. On our Saskatchewan prairie, the nearest neighbor was four miles away, and at night we saw only two lights on all the dark rounding earth. The earth was full of animals—field mice, ground squirrels, weasels, ferrets, badgers, coyotes, burrowing owls, snakes. I knew them as my little brothers, as fellow creatures, and I have never been able to look upon animals in any other way since. The sky in that country came clear down to the ground on every side, and it was full of great weathers, and clouds, and winds, and hawks. I hope I learned something from knowing intimately the creatures of the earth; I hope I learned something from looking a long way, from looking up, from being much alone. A prairie like that, one big enough to carry the eye clear to the sinking, rounding horizon, can be as lonely and grand and simple in its forms as the sea. It is as good a place as any for the wilderness experience to happen; the vanishing prairie is as worth preserving for the wilderness idea as the alpine forests.

So are great reaches of our western deserts, scarred somewhat by prospectors but otherwise open, beautiful, waiting, close to whatever God you want to see in them. Just as a sample, let me suggest the Robbers' Roost country in Wayne County, Utah, near the Capitol Reef National Monument. In that desert climate the dozer and jeep tracks will not soon melt back into the earth, but the country has a way of making the scars insignificant. It is a lovely and terrible wilderness, such a wilderness as Christ and the prophets went out into; harshly and beautifully colored, broken and worn until its bones are exposed, its great sky without a smudge or taint from Technocracy, and in hidden corners and pockets under its cliffs the sudden poetry of springs. Save a piece of country like that intact, and it does not matter in the slightest that only a few people every year will go into it. That is precisely its value. Roads would be a desecration, crowds would ruin it. But those who haven't the strength or youth to go into it and live can simply sit and look. They can look two hundred miles, clear into Colorado; and looking down over the cliffs and canyons of the San Rafael Swell and the Robbers' Roost they can also look as deeply into themselves as anywhere I know. And if they can't even get to the places on the Aquarius Plateau where the present roads will carry them, they can simply contemplate the *idea*, take pleasure in the fact that such a timeless and uncontrolled part of earth is still there.

These are some of the things wilderness can do for us. That is the reason we need to put into effect, for its preservation, some other principle than the principles of exploitation or "usefulness" or even recreation. We simply need that wild country available to us, even if we never do more than drive to its edge and look in. For it can be a means of reassuring ourselves of our sanity as creatures, a part of the geography of hope.

Very sincerely yours,

Wallace Stegner

Part II

At Home in
the Fields of the Lord

I have always envied people with a hometown. They always seem to have an attic, and in the attic albums of pictures, spellers used in the third grade, gocarts and Irish mails with the scars of young heels and teeth on them. In the houses of these fortunate ones there is always some casual friend of thirty or forty years' standing, someone who grew up next door, some childhood sweetheart, some inseparable companion from primary days. Some people even live in the houses their fathers and grandfathers used; and no matter how wide they may scatter from the hometown, always behind them is a solid backstop of cousins and grandmothers and relatives once or twice removed, maintaining the solidarity and permanence of the clan.

None of these forms of moss clings to a rolling stone, and I was born rolling. If I met a playmate of forty years ago we would not recognize each other even as

[157]

names. Since I left them (or they me) to move elsewhere, I have never again encountered a single one of the children I knew in any of my various dwelling places. The things that accumulate in others' attics and in their memories, to turn up again in their futures, have been cleaned out of mine five dozen times to simplify moves. Since I was born in Iowa in 1909 (my hometown held me six weeks) I have lived in twenty places in eight different states, besides a couple of places in Canada, and in some of these places we lived in anywhere from two to ten different houses and neighborhoods. This is not quite the same thing as traveling extensively; it involves having no permanent base whatever. Until my wife and I built a house I am sure no member of my family had ever owned one.

The absence of roots has always seemed to me a deprivation both personally and professionally. Personally, I was condemned to friendships that were always being sharply cut off and rarely renewed, so that for a time they tried to live by mail and then lamely dwindled out. Professionally, as a writer, I considered myself unequipped with the enduring relationships from which the deepest understanding of people might have come. I have always thought of myself as a sort of social and literary air plant, without the sustaining roots that luckier people have. And I am always embarrassed when well-meaning people ask where I am from.

That is why I have been astonished, on a couple of recent trips through Salt Lake City, to find a conviction growing in me that I am not as homeless as I had thought. At worst, I had thought myself an Ishmael; at best, a half stranger in the city where I had lived the longest, a Gentile in the New Jerusalem. But a dozen years of absence from Zion, broken only by two or three short revisitings, have taught me different. I am as rich in a hometown as anyone, though I adopted my home as an adolescent and abandoned it as a young man.

A Gentile in the New Jerusalem: certainly I was. Salt Lake City is a divided concept, a complex idea. To the devout it is more than a place; it is a way of life, a corner of the materially realizable heaven; its soil is held together by the roots of the family and the cornerstones of the temple. In this sense Salt Lake City is forever foreign to me, as to any non-Mormon. But in spite of being a Gentile I discover that much of my youth is there, and a surprising lot of my heart. Having blown tumbleweed-fashion around the continent so that I am forced to *select* a hometown, I find myself selecting the City of the Saints, and for what seems to me cause.

It has such a comfortable, old-clothes feel that it is a shock to see again how beautiful this town really is, quite as beautiful as the Chamber of Commerce says it is; how it lies under a bright clarity of light and how its outlines are clean and spacious, how it is dignified with monuments and steeped in sun tempered with shade, and how it lies protected behind its rampart mountains, insulated from the stormy physical and intellectual weather of both coasts. Serenely concerned with itself, it is probably open to criticism as an ostrich city; its serenity may be possible only in a fool's paradise of isolationism and provincialism and smugness. But what is a hometown if it is not a place you feel secure in? I feel secure in Salt Lake City, and I know why. Because I keep meeting so

[159]

many things I know, so many things that have not changed since I first saw the city in 1921.

True, it has grown by at least fifty thousand people since then, new roads have been built and new industries imported, new streets of houses are strung out from the old city limits. But there were people and roads and industries and houses there before; these new ones have not changed the town too much, and seem hardly to have affected its essential feel at all.

It was an amazement to me, returning, to realize how much I know about this city until I remembered that I had lived there off and on for nearly fifteen years; that as a Boy Scout I had made an elaborate and detailed map of its streets in order to pass some test or other; that as a high school student I had solicited advertisements among all its business houses; that while I was in college I had worked afternoons in a store that was always in need of somebody to double as a truck driver, so that I delivered parcels lengthwise and endwise over the city. There is no better way to learn a place; I have known no place in that way since.

Moreover, Salt Lake is an easy town to know. You can see it all. Lying in a great bowl valley, it can be surmounted and comprehended and possessed wholly as few cities can. You can't possibly get lost in it. The Wasatch comes with such noble certitude up from the south and curves so snugly around the "Avenues" that from anywhere in the city you can get your directions and find your way. And man has collaborated with Nature to make sure that you can't got lost. The streets are marked by a system so logical that you can instantly tell not merely where you are but exactly how far you are from anywhere else. And when your mind contains, as I found recently that mine did, not merely this broad plat but a great many of the little lost half streets with names like Elm and Barbara and Pierpont, then you have blocked off one of the great sources of nightmare.

You can't get lost. That is much. And you can always see where you are. That is even more. And you can get clear up above the city and look all the way around and over it, and that is most. Looking into the blank walls of cities or staring up at them from dirty canyon sidewalks breeds things in people that eventually have to be lanced.

Sure and comfortable knowledge is reinforced by association, which often amounts to love and always involves some emotional relationship. Mere familiarity, I suppose, generates an emotional attachment of a kind, but when years of the most emotionally active time of one's life have been spent among certain streets and houses and schools and people and countrysides, the associational emotion is so pervasive that it may be entirely overlooked for years, and comprehended only in retrospect. Nostalgia, the recognition of old familiarity, is the surest way to recognize a hometown.

In a way, my family's very mobility helped to make this town peculiarly mine, for we lived in many neighborhoods. We lived at Fifth South and Fifth East under old cottonwoods behind a mangy lawn; we lived on Seventh East across from Liberty Park so that I knew intimately the rats in the open surplus canal; we lived in a bungalow on Eighth East, an old brick ruin on Twenty-first South and State, a pleasant house on Fifteenth East above the high school I attended. We lived on Ninth East and Fourth South, on Seventh South and Eleventh East, in an apartment on First Avenue, in an ancient adobe down near the heart of town by the post office. I beat my way to school across lots from many different directions, and my memory is tangled in the trees on certain old streets and involved in the paths across many vacant lots and impromptu baseball fields.

The mere act of writing them down amplifies and extends the things that remain with me from having lived deeply and widely in Salt Lake City. I suppose I played tennis on almost every public and private court in town, and I know I hiked over every golf course. For three or four winters, with a club basketball team, I ran myself ragged in the frigid amusement halls of a hundred Mormon ward houses and took icy showers and went home blown and rubber-legged late at night. With a team in the commercial league, or with the freshman squad at the university, I hit all the high school gyms, as well as the old rickety Deseret Gymnasium next door to the Utah Hotel, where cockroaches as big and dangerous as roller skates might be stepped on behind the dark lockers. From games and parties I ran home under dark trees, imagining myself as swift and tireless as Paavo Nurmi, and the smell and taste of that cold, smoky, autumnal air and the way the arc lights blurred in rounded golden blobs at the corners is with me yet. It makes those streets of twenty and twenty-five years ago as real as any I walk now; those are the streets I judge all other city streets by, and perhaps always will.

This, I discover belatedly, is the city of many firsts: the first car, the first dates, the first jobs. No moon has ever swum so beguilingly up over mountains as it used to swim up over the Wasatch; none has ever declined

so serenely as it used to decline sometimes when we came
home at two or three after a date and a twenty-mile
drive out to Taylorsville or Riverton to take our girls
home. No friends have ever so closely and effortlessly
touched the heart. No sandwiches have ever since had
the wonderful smoky flavor that the barbecued beef used
to have at the old Night Owl on Ninth South, by the
ball park. No heroes have ever walked so tall as Willie
Kamm and Tony Lazzeri and Lefty O'Doul and Duffy
Lewis and Paul Strand and Fritz Coumbe of the old Salt
Lake Bees in the Pacific Coast League. The year Tony
Lazzeri hit sixty home runs over the short left field fence
at Bonneville Park I haunted State Street, outside that
fence, and risked death in traffic a hundred times to chase
batting-practice balls and get a free seat in the left field
bleachers. And when Coumbe, who had pitched (I believe) for the Athletics and played against Babe Ruth
(Ruth hit the first ball he threw him over the centerfield
fence) came to live in the other half of a duplex from
us, and brought other heroes home with him, and gave
me a left-handed first base mitt that had belonged to
George Sisler, I grew twelve inches overnight.

Here for the first time I can remember triumphs, or
what seemed triumphs then. In Salt Lake I wrote my
first short story and my first novel. In Salt Lake I fell
in love for the first time and was rudely jilted for the
first time and recovered for the first time. In Salt Lake
I took my first drink and acquired a delightful familiarity
with certain speakeasies that I could find now blindfold
if there were any necessity. I experimented with ether
beer and peach brandy and bathtub gin and survived them
all, as I survived the experience of driving an automobile

at sixteen or seventeen, by hairbreadth but satisfactory margins.

It seems to me now that in the course of one activity or another, driven by that furious and incomprehensible adolescent energy which lies dead somewhere in Salt Lake and which I wish I could bring back as readily as I bring back its memory, I surged up and down and across the New Jerusalem from Murray to Beck's Hot Springs, and from Saltair to Brighton and Pinecrest. And how it was, its weathers and its lights, is very clear to me.

So is the country that surrounds the city and that gives the city so much of its spaciousness and charm and a large part of its nostalgic tug.

Salt Lake lies in the lap of mountains. East of it, within easy reach of any boy, seven canyons lead directly up into another climate, to fishing and hunting and camping and climbing and winter skiing. Those canyons opened out of my back yard, no matter what house I happened to be living in. City Creek and Dry Canyon were immediate and walkable. Parley's could be penetrated by the judicious who hung around on the tracks behind the state penitentiary and hooked onto D&RG freights as they began to labor on the grade. Sometimes we rode a boxcar or a gondola; sometimes an indulgent fireman let us ride on the coal in the tender. Up in the canyon we could drop off anywhere, because even with two engines on, the train would only be going ten or fifteen miles an hour. South of Parley's was Mill Creek, and this we reached on more elaborate expeditions with knapsacks. In spring there were lucerne fields and orchards to go through toward the canyon's mouth, and the lucerne patches could always be counted on to provide a racer snake or two, and the orchards a pocketful of cherries or apricots. On a hot day, after a climb, cherries chilled in the cold water of Mill Creek and cherished, one by one, past teeth and palate and throat, were such cherries as the world has not produced since.

And the other canyons: the little swale of Hughes, where in late April the dogtooth violets were a blanket under the oakbrush; Big Cottonwood, up which ore trucks used to give us a lift to the Maxwell or the Cardiff mine, and where the peaks went in a granite whorl around the lakes and cottages of Brighton; Little Cottonwood, with the ghost town of Alta at its head, since famous for ski slopes; and Bell's, a glacial U with waterfalls and hanging glacial meadows lifting in a long steep south-ward curve toward Long Peak and the point of the mountain, from which we could look down on the narrows where the Jordan River slipped between alluvial gravel slopes toward the dead sea.

Knowing Salt Lake City means knowing its canyons, too, for no city of my acquaintance except possibly Reno breaks off so naturally and easily into fine free country. The line between city and mountains is as clean as the line between a port city and salt water. Up in the Wasatch is another world, distinct and yet contributory, and a Salt Lake boyhood is inevitably colored by it.

There is a limit to the indulgence of recollection, for fear nostalgia should be overcome by total recall. But it is clear to me, now that I have chosen a hometown, that I do not believe unqualifiedly in a "most impression-able age" between five and ten. The lag between experience and the kind of assimilation that can produce nostalgia is considerable, I suppose. In our early maturity we have just come to realize how much our tender minds absorbed in early childhood. But later we may have other realizations. Other recollections brighten as the first ones fade, and the recognition that now makes me all but skinless as I drive down Thirteenth East Street in Salt Lake City is every bit as sharp and indelible as the impressions my blank-page senses took as a child. Not all experience, not even all romantic and nostalgic experience, is equivalent to Wordsworth's.

Any place deeply lived in, any place where the vitality has been high and the emotions freely involved can fill the sensory attic with images enough for a lifetime of nostalgia. Because I believe in the influence of places on personalities, I think it somehow important that certain songs we sang as high school or college students in the twenties still mean particular and personal things. "I'm Looking over a Four Leaf Clover" is all tied up with the late-dusk smell of October on Second South and Twelfth East, and the shine of the arc light on the split street tipping up the Second South hill. "When Day Is Done" has the linseed oil smell of yellow slickers in it, and the feel of the soft corduroy cuffs those slickers had, and the colors of John Held pictures painted on the backs. "Exactly Like You" means the carpet, the mezzanine, the very look and texture and smell, of the Temple Square Hotel.

Salt Lake is not my hometown because my dead are buried there, or because I lived certain years of my youth and the first years of my marriage there, or because my son was born there. Duration alone does not do it. I have since spent half as many years in Cambridge, Massachusetts, without bringing from that residence more than a pitiful handful of associations. I was not living in Cambridge at the pace and with the complete uncritical participation that swept me along in Salt Lake. To recall anything about Cambridge is an effort, almost an act of will—though time may teach me I took more from there, too, than I thought I did. But Salt Lake City, revisited either in fact or in imagination, drowns me in acute recognitions, as if I had not merely sipped from but been doused with Proust's cup of reminding tea.

From its founding, Salt Lake City has been sanctuary: that has been its justification and its function. And it is as sanctuary that it persists even in my Gentile mind and insinuates itself as my veritable hometown. Yet there are darker and more ambiguous associations attached to it, and it is strange to me, returning, to find myself looking upon Salt Lake as the place of my security. It never was at the time I lived there. I suppose no age of a man is less secure than adolescence, and more subject to anguishes, and I think I do not exaggerate in believing that my own adolescence had most of the usual anguishes and some rather special ones besides. Certainly some of the years I lived in Salt Lake City were the most miserable years of my life, with their share of death and violence and more than their share of fear, and I am sure now that off and on and for considerable periods I can hardly have been completely sane.

There are houses and neighborhoods in Salt Lake whose associations are black and unhappy, places where we lived which I thought of at the time as prisons. Yet revisiting the city I am warmed by this flood of recollection, the unhappiness dwindles into proportion or perspective, even unimportance. Or perhaps the unhappiness takes

on a glow in retrospect, and perhaps the feeling of security and well-being which Salt Lake gives me now is
partly satisfaction at having survived here things that
might have destroyed me. Or perhaps it arises from the
pure brute satisfaction of having experienced anything,
even misery, with that much depth and sharpness. Or
perhaps, like the discomforts of a camping trip that become hilarious in the telling, the verbal formulation of
distress has the capacity to cure it. So Emerson, after
flunking a mathematics examination in college, could go
home and triumph over all the arts of numbers by writing
a destructive essay on the subject.

I suppose that may come close to the core of my feeling about Salt Lake. Returning is a satisfactory literary
experience; the present has power to evoke a more or-
derly version of the past. And what is evoked, though
it may be made of unpleasant or unhappy elements, is
satisfactory because it *is* a kind of vicarious thing, a literary product.

Whether it says with the Anglo-Saxon poet, "That
have I borne, this can I bear also," or whether it says,
"There, for a while, I lived life to the hilt, and so let
come what may," my hometown, late discovered, is not
a deprivation or a loss or a yearning backward. I recently had the experience of recognizing, and with pleasure, what the city meant to me, but I was not heartbroken
to leave either it or that youth of mine that it embalms,
and I do not necessarily yearn to return to either. It
does not destroy me with a sense of lost green childhood
or of any intimation of immortality long gone and ir-
recoverable. There is only this solid sense of having had

[168]

or having been or having lived something real and good and satisfying, and the knowledge that having had or been or lived these things I can never lose them again. Home is what you can take away with you.

Born a Square

The thesis of this piece is that the western writer is in a box with booby traps at both ends. By "western writer" I do not mean the writer of Westerns; I mean the writer who has spent his formative years in the West. When I say he is in a box, I mean that he has a hard time discovering what is in him wanting to be said, and that when he does discover it he has difficulty getting a hearing. His box is booby-trapped at one end by an inadequate artistic and intellectual tradition, and at the other end by the coercive dominance of attitudes, beliefs, and intellectual fads and manners destructive of his own. The fact that these attitudes control both the publishing media and large portions of the critical establishment is more important than the fact that publishing is concentrated in another region. This is not a complaint against Leviathan. It is only an extension of the observation that, since any writer must write from what he knows and believes, a writer from the West finds himself so unfashionable as to be practically voiceless.

For this Westerner—any Westerner, except those who come from a few large cities—is the product of a world still nascent, and therefore hopeful. And though each of the several Wests has developed its own kinds of vulgarity, ugliness, and social injustice, none of these is yet rank enough to stink out the scent of prairie flowers and sagebrush in which we began. The fact is, most western writers don't feel at home in a literary generation that appears to specialize in despair, hostility, hypersexuality, and disgust. If only because of their youth, the several Wests continue to represent some degree of the traditional American innocence. They breed more meliorists than nihilists, and they encourage booster clubs, culture clubs, and reform movements more commonly than the despair, decadence, masochism, sadism, self-pity, anger, and the hopeless prick of conscience that are compulsive in many contemporary novelists. If Westerners learn these things, and some do, they learn them in exile and often harbor them in uneasy alliance with a great yearning nostalgia for the health they left behind them. For many, the whole process of intellectual and literary growth is a movement, not through or beyond, but away from the people and society they know best, the faiths they still at bottom accept, the little raw provincial world for which they keep an apologetic affection.

Let us imagine some native-white-Protestant second- or third-generation-immigrant kind of boy who grows up in Corvallis or Ogden or Great Falls, eating well and getting plenty of air and exercise and being a reasonably healthy animal in an essentially pre-industrial, pre-urban society: in short, born lucky. School, the Army, college, travel, sooner or later give him the taste of a wider life, and it is usually much more exciting to him than home ever was. Still, he retains his loyalty to his homeplace, he brags about it *in absentia*, he is not easily poisoned against it. What is more likely to poison his loyalty is books which reveal something different, more bitter, less naïve, more knowing, outside.

Assume that at home he has been one of the local group of artists and intellectuals and that he has satisfied the hungers of his spirit as he could and has written a novel. Until a few years ago, this was nearly certain to be about his family or his boyhood, or an epic about how his corner of the continent was peopled and brought into the civilized world. Or maybe he has only written a story in a magazine and got a letter from a literary agent asking if he has a novel. Upon such an invitation from the great world, he will get to work on one: about his family or his boyhood or how his corner of the continent was peopled. This is all to the good.

But even the smallest success makes his world too small for him. Opportunity does not lie here. He heads for the nearest Rome, as the talented provincial always has and always will. He goes off to some university to learn or to teach, or he goes to join the literary world in San Francisco, Chicago, New York, Paris, veritable Rome. And as he listens to the people around him it slowly dawns on him that his book and the stance from which he wrote it were both embarrassing mistakes. For his novel had a hero, or at least a respect for the heroic virtues—fortitude, resolution, magnanimity. Where it was angry, it was angry at things like incubus bankers and octopus railroads, things remote or irrelevant from the point of view of the contemporary malaise; and where it dealt in the tears of things, its tears were bucolic and unsophisticated, shed for a mother's death or a father's failure or the collapse of a strenuous dream. Though they may have lived in a howling wilderness, his characters were incredibly blind to the paralyzing loneliness that both psychiatry and literature say is incurable, and they ignorantly escaped the lovelessness that the same authorities insist is standard. Their story did not question or deplore life's difficult struggle, but celebrated it.

Our Westerner, writing what he knew, or thought he knew, had filled his book with a lot of naïve belief and health and effort, had made callow assumptions about the perfectibility of the social order and the fact of individual responsibility. He had taken monogamy for granted, at least as a norm; he had kept a stiff upper lip; he had been so concerned with a simple but difficult Becoming that he had taken no thought of Being.

He had had only a little to say about sex, which in his innocence he had confused with love, but until now he had thought that little was definitely good stuff; one big scene had made it quite exciting. He sees now that he should have had some call-house madam of a philosophical turn of mind convey the message that sex is the only thing that makes a rotten world bearable, the only possible means of human contact, and pretty grubby at that, closer to hostility than to affection. He might have handled sex as theme and variations: nobody yet has seized the opportunity of showing wife-trading in a log cabin, or communal sex in the village schoolhouse as the logical end of a box supper. He regrets all those perversions that he neglected, including those that end, as in Tennessee Williams, in cannibalism. He has thrown away his chances at paternal pimps, jolly Peeping Toms, friendly neighborhood pederasts, and misunderstood boys who, thought queer by their fellows, are revealed in the end to be on their way to sainthood through emulation of the greatest of modern saints, the Marquis de Sade.

These are things our Westerner learns among the literary, who are schooled in the torments, isolations, emptiness, and weary kicks of life. Expatriates, beats, faggots, junkies, Southerners committed to Gothic guilts and erratic violences, Negroes remembering three hundred years of labeled or *de facto* slavery, Jews remembering a thousand years of ghettos and pogroms—they are all terribly unfamiliar to his rustic eye, and they all speak with appalling certainty and casualness of things he hardly even dares imagine. Sometimes he wonders if the characteristic American novelist of the 1960's won't turn out to be a Negro of the Jewish faith, born in Alabama and reared in Harlem and expatriated to Paris, where he picks up a living as a hustler in a homosexual joint, wearing beard and Jesus sandals and taking it in the vein and making a devout effort to look, sound, act, and write like something by Norman Mailer out of Djuna Barnes.

It is going to occur to our naïf that he doesn't feel as alienated as he knows he should, and yet to demur at this literary model is to be a square, and who wouldn't rather have his sex torn out with red-hot pincers than to be one of those? He is ashamed of his naïve inheritance, but he cannot quite accept the alternatives. Even

if Mailer suggests he become a white Negro, he doesn't
need James Baldwin to tell him he can't. Imagine as he
may how he might feel if he were a Jew, he knows he
is no Jew, doesn't think like one and can't feel like one,
has neither the cultural stamina nor the special humor
nor the special masochism. His experience with most kinds
of despair and social injustice is academic and synthetic,
and if he has the intelligence I think he has, he knows
too much to try to repair his lacks with a notebook.

He can't share southern guilt or southern pride or
southern loyalty, he can't quite believe in himself as
either Victim or Victimizer, he is outside that terrible
grapple of love and hate. Homosexuality he has been
brought up to understand as an unfortunate illness, not
something to be conscientiously acquired or tried out in
the spirit of research. And however hard he attempts to
be beat, he gives himself away by washing his ankles.
He is hopelessly middle-class, parochial, dewy-cheeked,
born a square; and when he tries to write like people
who are admired for their "honest" and "compassionate"
demoralization, he hears the snickers from the wings. The
society in which he got his conditioning has known no
such demoralization, real or faked.

The world he most feels—and he feels it even while
he repudiates it—offers him only frontier heroics or the
smugness of middle-class provincialism, and those two
things, as he now recognizes, have been the subject matter of nearly every western novel. So, outgrow this
western limitation? Keep constantly in mind that Mary
McCarthy came from Seattle? It is the effort he most
consistently makes, and yet it is a doomed effort. The
literature that seems important, the literature that gave

his crowd in Boise or Spokane its wicked thrill of being Inside with the Outsiders, now shuts him out. It is being written mainly by members of minority groups either wronged by his sort of middle-class world or angrily at odds with it, contemptuous of its limitations. But he himself, God help him, is a sort of majority product, and a belated and provincial one at that, formed by majority attitudes and faiths. In a time of repudiation, absurdity, guilt, and despair, he still half believes in the American Dream.

He is forced to see everyone except himself fulfilled. Southerners, expatriates, beats, Jews, Negroes, homosexuals, junkies can all achieve the status of Man as Victim. But our Westerner stands unwanted, ashamed, still a rank outsider, and he knows that, incorrigibly wholesome and life-acceptant as he is, he deserves no better, because an artist is by definition a victim, a martyr, a loser, a self-loather, a life-hater.

A whole series of questions arises the moment one begins considering western writers as a species. Why, for instance, hasn't the standard organic process of regional maturation produced in the West a recognizable school, as it did in New England, the Midwest, and the South? Why, when so much of our literature (for example, Hemingway) strikes us as dealing with a present which has no past, should western books so often strike us as dealing with a past which has no present? Why haven't Westerners ever managed to get beyond the celebration of the heroic and mythic frontier? Why haven't they been able to find in their own time, place, and tradition the characters, situations, problems, quarrels, threats, and injustices out of which literature is made? Why in particular do we find in them as a class little of the iron sense of enduring evil and pain that in Hawthorne, Melville, Faulkner, even Twain, counterbalances the complacent innocence of the New World? Are Westerners so stupid that they don't believe in evil? Or so smug that they have no personal hells to descend into?

California, it should be said at once, is not part of the West. It is about as much the West as Florida is the South; it is less a region than an extension of the main line. Editors and publishers who come ivory-hunting in these productive jungles know they are coming to another country, and some have the feeling they are coming to a madhouse, and some may even think they are coming to Eden, but they don't feel that they are coming to the sticks. Their map of the United States is shaped like a dumbbell: New York at one end, California at the other, and the United Airlines in between. California is a nation of in-migrants, and its writers are in-migrants too, either writing about the places they came from or frantically scratching around and reading *Sunset* to find specifically Californian patterns to which to conform. It is the sticks I mean when I speak of the West—the last of the sticks—the subregions between the ninety-eighth meridian and the Sierra-Cascades, where patterns of local habit and belief have developed in some isolation, where they are clearer, more innocent, less diluted by outside influences, where they are bred into native sons who later, as writers, find them limited, unusable, or embarrassing.

Anyone who wishes to understand what the West has amounted to in a literary way will have to study, among

[177]

others, Willa Cather, Mari Sandoz, Bernard DeVoto, H. L. Davis, Vardis Fisher, A. B. Guthrie, Paul Horgan, and Walter Van Tilburg Clark. They are good writers, of varying kinds; when I am feeling especially confident I put myself in their company. We have all written books that deal with the settlement and the mythic past, the confrontation between empty land and imported populations, which is the salient historical fact about the West, as about America at large. We have all found it difficult or impossible to make anything of the contemporary West except as articles for *Holiday*, and when we have finished our most personal books, we have all taken refuge in history, fictionalized or straight.

At the very heart of a novelist's feeling life must be an awareness of struggle, the sense of a conflict that is real, dangerous, and present. But for complicated reasons the Lord has not seen fit to give us in the West a common conscience, a common guilt, a shared sense of wrong, a Lost Cause, a regional Weltschmerz, but only a common impotence when we step outside our own myth, or outside the history that has been suspended ever since our boyhood. We cannot find, apparently, a present and living society that is truly ours and that contains the materials of a deep commitment, even the commitment of rebellion and anger that binds, say, James Baldwin to Harlem. Instead, we must live in exile and write of anguishes not our own, or content ourselves with the bland troubles, the remembered violences, the already endured hardships, of a regional success story without an aftermath.

I know of no Western writer except Wright Morris who has come even close to dealing with his own contemporary regional life, and Morris' Nebraska gets all its tension from the bleak contrast between mythic past and vulgar present; it is an antisuccess story more devastating than Garland's or Ed Howe's. As for history, its questions are all answered, and fiction which asks only the questions it can answer is not good enough. Until some Westerner manages to do for his part of the West what Faulkner did for Mississippi, and discovers a usable continuity between past and present, western literature is going to stay mired in the past.

Vulgarity and complacency are plentiful enough, and some Westerners have made novels of their hatred of them; but vulgarity and complacency are tepid antagonists. We need some of the passion that animates the best Negro novelists, especially Baldwin and Ralph Ellison. We could examine western life for the estrangement and isolation that afflict Saul Bellow's dangling or seizing or wanting anti-heroes. If only we could discover some way in which western society and the western individual were entangled, we could even benefit from the study and transplantation of the hermetic grotesques of Eudora Welty and Carson McCullers and Flannery O'Connor. It may well turn out that more than any other region the West abounds in that characteristic American figure, the symbolic orphan, but he remains to be discovered and recognized. Perhaps, eventually, we shall agree that the Wests share a common guilt for crimes against the land that is only less bitter than the guilt of the nation for crimes against the black race, but this too is still to be discovered.

In these directions, or others, western writers will have to look. Meantime there is the temptation to imitate, to borrow the wrongs and hostilities and despairs of others, and that temptation is fatal. For one thing, by no means all of the disenchantment and spitting in the eye of the moral universe that we find in contemporary novels is as legitimate as it may seem. Or let us say that it is legitimate only for those to whom it is compulsive, an honest reflection of their deepest experience; for others it is only a fashion. No one in his senses would try to deny to any writer the materials and the methods he finds compelling, yet I am pretty sure that some part of our most advertised recent fiction is sick, out of its mind, and out of the moral world, worshipful of Moloch, in love with decay and death. Another part is simply the corrupt answer to a corrupt demand, which is in turn cynically promoted. I do not mean "dirty" words or forthright scenes, sexual or otherwise; I speak of a necrophilic playing with despair, which is nothing to be played with.

This last sort of book is often described in its blurbs as "savagely funny," or praised for its "venomous" tone. Here is a representative sample:

> This collection of stories marks the emergence of a vigorous and highly distinctive new talent. . . . In them, a young . . . writer explores man's will to self-destruction in many guises. In the title story, he tells of a macabre family of sisters living a desolate life on a ruined estate in South Africa, spilling their melancholy and venom on one another, until the eldest slips matter-of-factly into the river to die.
>
> Suicide is again the theme in an allegory of modern Germany, which sketches a strange German woman who,

with a young British lover in tow, wanders through the British Isles in search of some sort of Lebensraum, until she destroys herself in the sea. Not so allegorical, but written with venomous savagery, is the story of a Nazi profiteer who drowns himself in animal lust. And, in the closing story . . . a frustrated antique dealer flings himself one night on his servant's flesh, "a brown bay into which he was about to cast himself and be drowned forever."

Clearly the reader's response to this jacket copy is supposed to emulate the antique dealer's—he is supposed to fling himself upon these stories and be happily drowned. I find myself, instead, desperately treading water. Though any single situation in them is, I imagine, possible, the whole lot of them together are a symptom of disease, and their enthusiastic promotion entirely in terms of their sickness is a sign of cynicism in their publisher.

The usual justification for much literary demoralization, whether it involves the death wish or social disintegration or the transformation of love into an irritable twitch, is either honesty or compassion—what Edmund Fuller calls "the New Compassion." But indiscriminate compassion, which has been a shibboleth in literature at least since Zola, can end by dissolving all moral discrimination. Pitying others indiscriminately, we are pitying ourselves, and there is no more romantic and dangerous kind of moral obfuscation than pity, or self-pity, gone out of hand. To understand all had better not mean to forgive all, or we shall find ourselves remembering poor Eichmann, or even poor Hitler, with tears in our eyes.

As with compassion for the victim and the victimizer, so with other aspects of the novels which purport to interpret life's underworlds to the upper air. It would be the ultimate in priggishness as well as stupidity to deny that many are victimized, that we all need compassion and understanding, that life for nearly everyone is more dark than light, and for some nearly unrelieved dark. But let us keep our criteria; let us not, either as writers or as readers, make easy identifications between some unfortunate individual and Modern Man. Zoo animals, we are told, develop in captivity exacerbated sex impulses and an inordinate hostility. They are not very different from Modern Man as some of our novels present him. But Modern Man lives in the upperworld as well as in the underworld, and sometimes he is a reasonably healthy animal and not an animal in an urban zoo. There is no reason to turn misery, perversion, oversexed hostility, and hatred of life into a rule of the universe, the norm of human experience. These are only a part of it. The rest is what keeps us alive.

Our western naïf, born as lucky as he was born square, probably understands that. He would do well to hang on to his basic hopefulness, instead of giving it up for a fashionable disgust; and he would do well to remind himself that for all the beating they take in literary circles, the conventions of his middle-class society have something to do with making hopefulness possible. Anarchy is its own punishment; despair, like evil, is self-corrective, self-destroying; and disgust, no matter how total, must have in it some seed of the reforming impulse which puts it on the side of the culture clubs and the do-gooders. Working itself out of its own agonized kinks, our serious literature of angst and guilt will have to come straggling back from its bleak outposts, and when it does, it will both disfranchise its shoddy imitators and help make possible the hope that it once thought impossible.

And our Westerner—does he then sing his smiling sunny song and tell his Pollyanna stories about noble pioneers and win book awards with them? Hardly. I have already said that he needs a present to come home to, even if his present is only his identity as an orphan with an inadequate tradition. But he must discover that the full range of doubt, magnanimity, pettiness, the abrasive grind of class and caste struggle, the generation of all the sorts of power needed to run the future, even the full measure of alienation and a fuller-than-average measure of hope, are as native to Salt Lake City or Idaho Falls or Minot as to Saul Bellow's Chicago or Baldwin's Harlem or Camus's Oran or Faulkner's Oxford. The western writer should go away and get his eyes opened, and then look back.

But not back into history. The West does not need to explore its myths much further; it has already relied on them too long. It has no future in exploiting its setting either, for too consistently it has tried to substitute scenery for a society. All it has to do is to be itself at the most responsible pitch, to take a hard look at itself and acknowledge some things that the myths have consistently obscured—been *used* to obscure. The West is politically reactionary and exploitative: admit it, instead of pretending to be the last brave home of American freedom. The West as a whole is guilty of inexpiable crimes against the land: admit that, too. The West is rootless, culturally half-baked. So be it. To deny weaknesses is to be victimized by them and caught in lies forever. But while the West is admitting its inadequacy, let it remember its strength: it is the New World's last chance to be something better, the only American society still malleable enough to be formed.

The West's own problems are likely to be more to the western writer's purpose than any that he can borrow, especially when in borrowing he must deny his gods. In a pluralist country we are bound to be of many kinds. Hemingway preaches the stiff upper lip, Saul Bellow specifically and angrily and repeatedly repudiates it. But the frontier American tradition of stoicism neither invalidates nor is invalidated by the Russian-Jewish tradition of emotional volatility. With the highest respect for Bellow, I have to throw in with Hemingway, at least on this issue, because I grew up in stiff-upper-lip country. We have the obligation to be ourselves even when it seems we are squares.

This western naïveté of strenuousness, pragmatism, meliorism, optimism, and the stiff upper lip is our tradition, such as it is. Any western writer may ultimately be grateful to his western upbringing for convincing him, beyond all chance of conversion, that man, even Modern Man, has some dignity if he will assume it, and that most lives are worth living even when they are lives of quiet desperation. The point is to do the best one can in the circumstances, not the worst. From the western writer's square, naïve point of view, the trouble with Modern Man, as he reads about him in fiction, is that Modern Man has quit.

Just possibly, if our Westerner lived and wrote his convictions, he could show the hopeless where hope comes from, like Aesop's frog which, drowning in a bowl of milk, in the destructive element immersed, swam so desperately that it churned up a little pad of butter on which to sit.

This is not exhortation, neither is it prophecy. It is only, since I am from the West and incorrigible, hope.

3

~~~~~~

History, Myth, and
the Western Writer

It is not quite true, as some have complained, that the critics have ignored western writing. We learned to appraise the mythic figures of western literature from Henry Nash Smith's seminal study, *Virgin Land* (1950). There have been two full-length studies of the western film: W. K. Everson's *The Western* (1962) and K. C. Lahue's *Continued Next Week* (1964). Dozens of people have written on cowboy fiction and western folklore, and all of the major writers of western origin have had plenty of biographical and critical attention. One promising study we missed: at the time of his death, Bernard DeVoto was writing a book about western reality and western myth, but he published only one chapter of it, an essay on *The Virginian*. But now within a few months have appeared James K. Folsom's *The American Western Novel* and Robert Edson Lee's *From West to East:*

Studies in the Literature of the American West, and in 1966, at Colorado State University, there was established a quarterly with the stoutly regional title of *Western American Literature*.

The Western, horse opera, has actually been studied in considerable detail, though it must be admitted that critics rarely approach it from the near, or literary side. They mount it from the right, like Indians, and ride it hard as myth, as folklore, as a part of the history of ideas, or as a demonstration of Freudian or Jungian psychology. I don't recall ever seeing a Western discussed for its original social or psychological insights, for the complexity or depth of its characters, for its poetic evocativeness, for its narrative techniques, or for its prose style. It wouldn't pay to do it, for a Western is not a unique performance but a representative one. Its characters are not individuals but archetypes or stereotypes, and its themes are less interesting for their freshness or their truth to history than for their demonstration of a set of mythic patterns.

I do not intend to get caught in the argument about whether the Western is, or can be, literature on the highest level. I only want to establish its relation to another kind of western story-telling which is not mythic but literary. This literature is western with a small *w*, and only the fact that it all takes place west of the 100th meridian permits us to put it under one rubric, or to put this class of writing beside the Western. Variety is, at least superficially, one of its marked characteristics. As a westerner, I would love to believe that there is some spirit, attitude, faith, experience, tone, something, that binds all small-*w* western stories together as manifestations of a coherent regional culture. And yet I confess I have doubts: in order to get an *unum* out of our *pluribus*, do all of us define "West" and "western" too narrowly, forgetting what does not fill our bill?

It is not exactly classified information that there are many Wests. Neither is it unknown that they have certain things in common—aridity above all else, and the special clarity of light, the colors, the flora and fauna, and the human adjustments that have resulted from aridity. Most of the Wests have been touched by the magic figure of the horseman, and so almost any of them may be a legitimate home for horse opera. And all the Wests are late, large, and new. Those are the basic resemblances. Otherwise, there are almost as many divergent as convergent lines.

Is it legitimate to speak of western literature, except in reference to the Western? Can one find a relation between a story by Willa Cather and one by Steinbeck, Mary Austin, or Walter Van Tilburg Clark? One is fairly sure about such a novel as *Horseman, Pass By*, by Larry McMurtry, because it is an affectionate requiem to the old-time Texas cattleman, whatever they did to it when they made it into the movie *Hud*. But what of McMurtry's latest, *The Last Picture Show*, a sort of small-town *Studs Lonigan?* It is laid in west Texas; is it a "western" novel? Is Bernard Malamud's *A New Life* a western novel? Its setting is Oregon State College in Corvallis. Is Nathanael West's *The Day of the Locust* a western novel? It takes place in Los Angeles. Are Eugene Burdick's *The Ninth Wave* and George Stewart's *Storm* western novels? Both are laid in the San Francisco Bay Area, which was held to be the West when Bret Harte wrote about it.

Literature is one of the things that emerge as by-products when you throw people of an advanced civilization into an unrecorded, history-less, art-less new country. Western writing is only the last stage of what occurred on every American frontier. West Virginia was once as west as west Texas; the literary development of the two should have been approximately the same. According to the organic theory that dominated our cultural self-examination from the Connecticut Wits through Emerson and Whitman to Hamlin Garland and the local colorists, each new part of the continent should have a seedtime of a generation or two, and then reap a harvest. Once it had set its roots, it should develop some variety of that "rocky, continental quality" that Emerson thought he felt in the Mississippi Valley, and start speaking out in its own native voice.

The process took place in New England, it took place in the middle Atlantic states, it occurred like realized prophecy in the Midwest, where literary nativism spread in a series of waves from Indiana to the Dakotas. It began to happen in Gold Rush California and in the cowboy Southwest: it put out belated shoots in the Pacific Northwest and in Mormon country. But I think it cannot be said to have happened plainly all over the West.

Despite large individual differences, midwestern writers from Eggleston to Dreiser and Lewis have tended to be earthy, plain, and realistic. Southern fiction from Poe to Faulkner has had strong infusions of the gothic, the grotesque, the highly colored, the "tall," and it has had its consistent and repetitive themes: color, the lost cause, the persistence of the family fabric and tradition. But when one asks if there are comparable likenesses among western writers, one hedges. Well, probably not. And then again, perhaps yes. Or perhaps only maybe.

I believe that a number of things happened to inhibit, interrupt, and in places block the organic cultural growth the West had a right, from the experience of the rest of America, to expect. One inhibiting factor was simply the West's variety. Climate, physiographic features, resources, characteristic occupations, ethnic mixtures were so various that they began to produce a Plains tradition, a desert tradition, a lumberwoods tradition, a Californian or Mormon or Mexican border tradition, and it is at least open to question whether these have enough in common to be recognizable components of a western tradition.

Moreover, the "fiction factories" that first took hold of the most colorful western themes and characters swiftly petrified them into the large, simple formulas of myth. First the Beadles with their dime novels, then the Wild West Shows, then Street and Smith and the pulp magazines, then the movies, and now television, have found those formulas to be all but foolproof, as good now as they were a hundred years ago. As a result, they do not change; they are only reassembled from interchangeable parts. They remain predictable, serene, and timeless, fantasies of self-reliance and aggression, sexually symbolic or curiously asexual, depending on which critic you read, apparently good for another century and perhaps forever.

This one area of western writing has been so calcified that it escapes the organic imperative: it is not necessary to be homegrown in order to write it. Some of the most persuasive horse operas, as witness Jack Schaefer's *Shane*, have been written by people not native to cow country, to horse, or to gun. When *Shane* came in as a manuscript to Houghton Mifflin, I happened to be in the office, and Dorothy de Santillana asked me to read it. She said she couldn't make up her mind whether it was the best Western ever written, or a parody of a Western. I couldn't tell either, but I certainly advocated its publication.

Variety, dispersion, and constant immigration on the one hand and mythic petrifaction on the other had the effect of producing either stories with little family resemblance, or stories with altogether too much. And history intervened to break up many forming regional patterns. Those patterns develop best in rural isolation; but time and change have often been so syncopated in the West that there has been no time for a native character to form and find its voice.

Settlement in the West was not only late, it was irregular. The mining West, and to a degree the timber, the grazing, and the homestead Wests, were raided, not settled; and sometimes raided for one resource after another, by different breeds of raiders. Despite their colorful history, there has hardly been a *continuous* community life in an Aspen or a Telluride; and when oilfields are superimposed on cattle country in Texas, or subdivisions superimposed on orchards in California, something disruptive has happened in the life of both people and towns. Folklore, more often than not an improvisation on an occupational theme—logging, riverboating, railroading, cowboying—is *only* an improvisation, and though it may be curiously lasting, it lasts as the Western lasts: it is cut loose like a balloon from the actual and continuing lives of men and women.

Few western places can show, even during their short

life, the uninterrupted life of a Maine fishing village or a county seat in Indiana or Iowa or a southern town clustered around the courthouse square. Western people have been notably migrant, and much of the West has happened during the age of swift communication, since the invention of the telegraph. Moreover, urbanization, which is as culturally shattering an experience as the frontier itself, has often followed so hot upon settlement that the only constant in western life has been change. Regional patterns that would have developed in isolation were effaced or blurred, half-formed. The living past, having little apparent relevance to the present, became a dead past, sometimes a pool of nostalgia. To the natural let-down of the second and third generation cheated of the hardships and dangers that kept their parents busy has been added the strangeness and unfriendliness and dissatisfaction of ways that have more in common with New York, London, Paris, Vienna, or Prague than with the brief and strenuous annals of the West.

What I have been saying is of course true to some degree of almost the whole of America, but it is particularly true west of the Missouri. Fearing the loss of what little tradition we have, we cling to it hard; we are hooked on history. If the Western continues to exist in a timeless West, carefully landscaped, around Sedona, Arizona and Kanab, Utah—country suitable for "cutting them off at the pass"—western literature of the small-*w* kind is generally scrupulous in sticking to real places and real experience. But it is a literature almost without a Present.

Western writers of fiction have shown a disinclination, perhaps an emotional inability, to write about the contemporary; and when they occasionally do, we are not inclined to think of their books as western. Not one critic in five hundred would designate *Storm* or *A Shooting Star* "western" novels, but *The Oxbow Incident* would make it because it includes cowboys, and *The City of Trembling Leaves* might make it because, though contemporary and urban (Reno) it exploits the scenery of the Sierra and the Nevada desert, and makes a thematic point of its western-ness.

I shall have more to say about the amputated Present in western writing. For the moment, I only want to emphasize that we do save the term "western"—small-*w*—for fiction of a certain kind, a kind not so petrified as the Western, but related to it. It is almost by definition historical and rural, or at least limited to the life characteristic of the periods of raid and settlement, the beginnings of a new civilization. Its actions do cluster around certain large and recurrent themes; its characters, however individually conceived, do illustrate certain tribal qualities and virtues, and so may be said to emphasize a type. Limited as I have limited it—which I think is the way most of us limit it—western literature does have elements of a large, loose cohesiveness.

Themes recur: nostalgia, for instance, the elegiac tone. Henry Nash Smith, Folsom, and other critics have pointed out the debt that much western writing owes to Fenimore Cooper, and in nothing is the debt more apparent than in this lament for the noble and lost, the last of a race or a breed or a kind. Chingachgook, the last of the Mohicans, has a thousand descendants. Some, like Noel Loomis's "Grandfather out of the Past," are as authentically native as Chingachgook himself. But the "last survivor" figures are various. The old prospector in Walter Van Tilburg Clark's "The Wind and the Snow of Winter," the cowhands and hispaños in Eugene Manlove Rhodes' "Pasó por Aquí," badman Scratchy Wilson in Stephen Crane's "The Bride Comes to Yellow Sky," Captain Forrester in Willa Cather's *A Lost Lady*, the wilderness in Guthrie's *The Big Sky*, the sea of grass in Conrad Richter's novel of the same name, all are touched with the tone of nostalgic regret. It is a tone that may seem odd in a new country, and yet it may express something quintessentially American: our sadness at what our civilization does to the natural, free, and beautiful, to the noble, the self-reliant, the brave. Many of the virtues of the typical western hero are virtues seen as defeated, gone by, no longer honored.

The regret, in fact, seems almost as compulsive as our need to "break" the wilderness and plant our civilization. Like many other American attitudes, it seems accentuated in the West, perhaps because the West *was* the last home of frontier freedom and largeness, perhaps because as horsemen's country it always had more glamor than clodhopper country, perhaps because in spite of its virile tradition the West itself is fragile—it does not heal readily, the ugliness we create stays visible, bare, and glaring. In a way it is a more honest region than most.

Whenever western fiction does approach the contemporary, the theme of ugliness and vulgarity is likely to show. Willa Cather, in love with the frontier's spaciousness and health, revolted from the villages and towns it had bred: compare *O Pioneers!* with *A Lost Lady* or *One of Ours*. Mari Sandoz, another Nebraskan who always struck me as wishing she had been born a Sioux, did her native state bleakly in *Capitol City*, a very different

Nebraska from the Niobrara frontier of *Old Jules*. Bernard DeVoto, putting his hometown of Ogden into *The Crooked Mile* and other novels, could find nothing good to say of it, though that same country, when it was prowled by Utes and mountain men, heated his imagination to incandescence. And those are not isolated instances. The typical western writer loves the past, despises the present, of his native region.

In a way, the dichotomy between the past and present is a product of two forces frequently encountered in both western fiction and the Western: the freedom-loving, roving man and the civilizing woman. Given the circumstances of western settlement and the legitimate inclinations of the sexes, it was natural that the West should find this theme strong in its history, and make it into something pervasive in its literature. The bride comes to Yellow Sky and the old male freedom slouches off, defeated, with its bootheels punching funnel-shaped holes in the sand. The schoolmarm comes to Wyoming, and after a suitable interval of male skylarking and lynching, the Virginian wears a collar. An eastern young lady in New Mexico is the person to whom the hispaño speaks of the desert rock on which old passersby have scribbled their elegiac greeting and farewell, "Pasó por Aquí." It is inescapable. Long before I had heard this theme stated, and before I knew enough western literature to state it myself, I had put it into Bo and Elsa Mason in *The Big Rock Candy Mountain*. Almost every writer who has dealt with family stresses on the frontier has found it in his hands, because he probably grew up with it in his own family. Male freedom and aspiration versus female domesticity, wilderness versus civilization, violence and danger versus the safe and tamed.

It is in *The Big Sky*, in *Giants in the Earth*, in Vardis Fisher's *Toilers of the Hills*, in a cartridge-belt full of indistinguishable Westerns. Done in almost diagrammatic mythic terms or done as realistic fiction, it is as inextricable from western writing as the theme of color is inextricable from the literature of the South.

Allied to it—all these major themes nest and interlock—is the conflict between law as stated in the books and enforced by sheriffs and right as defined by private judgment and enforced by gun, fist, or rope. In practice, the dispute is often but not invariably between fallible book law and the higher moral law. Like the conflict between man-wilderness and woman-civilization, the law theme has an impeccably historical basis, though it is more prominent in stories of mining camps or cowtowns than in those that chronicle the homesteader or sodhouse frontier. The sodhouse frontier was more likely to get its drama out of the location of the county seat or a dispute between landholders—conflicts essentially *within* the structure of established law—than out of lynching bees or walkdowns. Often the woman theme is intertwined with the law theme, as in that source-book *The Virginian*, in Guthrie's *These Thousand Hills*, in Richter's *Sea of Grass*, in the movie *High Noon*. Sometimes the mythic and lawless patterns are turned upside down, as in *The Oxbow Incident*, where private judgment turns out wrong and innocents are hanged, or in Oakley Hall's *Warlock*, which attempts some corrections in the traditional drawing of gunmen and marshals.

The correctives are needed, for one result of condoning handmade personal justice is to encourage vigilantism; and it is true, as DeVoto pointed out in that essay on Wister, that the Johnson County War looks far more innocent in *The Virginian* than it does to the eye of history. If one assumes that fantasy has no social consequences, then one can take all Westerns and some western literature as harmless ways of discharging the aggressive ego. If one assumes otherwise, then most Westerns and some western books are unconsciously immoral, and perhaps dangerous, in the terms of the civilization that has replaced the frontier.

Immoral or upright, dangerous or merely self-reliant, the protagonist of either kind of western story has heroic virtues, horseback virtues—and that goes whether he is the Virginian or Per Hansa with his feet in a Dakota furrow. Often the structure of a story is created by the testing of the hero, sometimes in one of those walkdown situations between rival gunfighters, sometimes in moral crises where book law has presumably broken down and personal justice must be administered, sometimes in the simple risks and endurances that tell a boy he is a man or reassure a man that he is still one.

Of this last kind are two stories that I like as well as any ever written about the West: H. L. Davis' "Open Winter" and Paul Horgan's "To the Mountains." I have done much the same sort of thing in my story "Genesis," included in *Wolf Willow,* and have discovered something in the process of writing it. Very often this testing of the hero has the quality of an ordeal, and in consequence these stories are generally longer than short stories, shorter than novels: the ordeal must go on a good while to be a true ordeal, but it cannot go on too long or it becomes excruciating. One of the classical examples is the section called "The Crawl," in Frederick Manfred's story of old

Hugh Glass, called *Lord Grizzly*. In special and modified terms, Walter Clark's "Hook" is another of those testings of the indomitable spirit, and H. L. Davis' "Homestead Orchard" shows us another boy becoming a man.

The virtues required to survive all these testings are the "manly" virtues of tenacity, courage, the ability to bear pain and hardship, an assured self-trust, generosity, a certain magnanimity of spirit. They do not differ much from the virtues that collectively make up Hemingway's "grace under pressure"; and as Malcolm Cowley has pointed out, Hemingway's virtues are essentially Indian virtues. Western writing is full of them; myth or literature, it is heroic to a degree, and even when fine and honest writers take a hard look at the myths, as Clark does in *The Oxbow Incident* or Milton Lott does in *The Last Hunt*, or A. B. Guthrie does in *The Big Sky*, they do not ever question the validity of heroism.

And that is one of the biggest reasons why to some modern critics the literature we call western seems remote, unreal, uncontemporary, anachronistic, belated. For heroism does not survive into modern literature, or seems not to, and writing which deals with the heroic and the rural seems to have little to say to people whose lives are fully urban and whose minds have grown skeptical or scornful of heroes. At least since Chekhov and Dostoevsky, the main streams of European and American literature have dealt increasingly with victims, not heroes. Look for victims among western stories and you may find them occasionally, as in Crane's "Blue Hotel." "Blue Hotel," beautiful and right as it is, is more "modern" than "western."

The difference in attitude was dramatized by Leslie Fiedler in an essay in which he told of getting off the train at Missoula, Montana, an easterner fresh from the *Partisan Review* offices, and seeing a large, grave, booted, tall-hatted man pass by. The man's face was serene, weathered, and to Fiedler vacant, bemused by an unquestioning faith in what to Fiedler were romantic and untenable fictions. Fiedler records his impression in one line: "'Healthy!' I thought in contempt."*

I want to suggest neither that this "Montana face" was indeed noble and that Fiedler was a diseased New York intellectual, nor that Fiedler was right and the Montana face was the product of a pathetic illusion. I want only to underscore the point I made earlier about the absence of a present in western literature and in the whole tradition we call western. It remains rooted in the historic, the rural, the heroic; it does not take account of time and change. That means that it has no future either, except to come closer and closer to the stereotypes of the mythic, unless it can expand its vision of itself and include things like a Leslie Fiedler lecturing to classes of undergraduates at the University of Montana.

Nostalgia, however tempting, is not enough. Disgust for the shoddy present is not enough. And forgetting the past entirely is a dehumanizing error. One of the lacks, through all the newly swarming regions of the West, is that millions of westerners, old and new, have no sense of a personal and *possessed* past, no sense of any continuity between the real western past which has been mythicized almost out of recognizability and a real western present that seems as cut-off and pointless as a ride on a merry-go-round that can't be stopped. The heroism of a forming civilization has become a thing to smile at, the civilization

* I quote from memory.

a thing to be savagely repudiated. The strenuousness of a hundred western years can be dissolved in strobe lights to the pounding of folk rock that has plenty to do with rock but little to do with folk. You can make the Haight-Ashbury scene in San Francisco, or be a teenage disturber of the peace on the Sunset Strip, you can work in an office in Denver or Dallas, and hear only the strident present, and be persuaded that the past does not exist, that Ford was right when he said history is bunk. But if you are any part of an artist, and a lot of people are some part of one, if you have any desire to understand, and thus to help steer, a civilization that seems to have got away from us, then I think you don't choose between the past and the present; you try to find the connections, you try to make the one serve the other.

No western writer that I know has managed to do it, unless it be Wright Morris in his sequence of novels about Nebraska, and they have a tendency to be hard on both past *and* present. Nobody has quite made a western Yoknapatawpha County or discovered a historical continuity comparable to that which Faulkner traced from Ikkemotubbe the Chickasaw to Montgomery Ward Snopes. Maybe it isn't possible, but I wish someone would try. I might even try myself.

God knows what happens in a future menaced by our incontinent fertility as a species and our incontinent willingness to accept a merely "bearable" world with none of the old western space and elbow room and self-reliance in it. God knows what happens to the heroic virtues when organization and programming have rendered them no longer viable. Maybe we will all sit and watch Westerns on TV, testing ourselves only in fantasy and by standards

[200]

we no longer think applicable to our real lives. Maybe we will all revolt away from everything we mean and into some "other culture." But I hope we will find ways of recognizing at least parts of ourselves in the literature and history the past has left us, and I hope we will find ways of bringing some of the historic self-reliance and some of the heroic virtues back into our world, which in its way is more dangerous than Comanche country ever was.

I share the nostalgia that I have attributed to most writers of the West. I share their frequent distaste for the uglified and over-engineered and small-spirited civilization that threatens to turn us into one gigantic anthill. But I do not think we can forget the one or turn away from the other. In the old days, in blizzardy weather, we used to tie a string of lariats from house to barn so as to make it from shelter to responsibility and back again. With personal, family, and cultural chores to do, I think we had better rig up such a line between past and present. If we do, the term "western literature" will be enlarged beyond its ordinary limitations, and its accomplishments not so easily overlooked.

4

On the Writing
of History

One without valid membership in the community of historians is not entitled to opinions about the profession, but he may have impressions. It is my impression that too many trained professionals consider narrative history, history rendered as story, to be something faintly disreputable, the proper playground of lady novelists.

Recently I asked a doctoral candidate who was embarking on a history of Berlin since World War II if he intended to dramatize the personalities and events of those twenty years. Was he going to write an analysis or a story? How would his book be affected if, as he uncovered his material, he came upon people who played protagonist and antagonist, embodying in themselves significant forces of the cold war? How would he handle the challenges and confrontations, the suspense, the climactic scenes? Clearly he would encounter such things, for how could he overlook Adenauer, Willi Brandt, Walter Ulbricht, the jockeyings for political advantage, the tie-ups on the Autobahn, the airlift, the mass flight, the Wall? But when I asked my question he looked at me, and so did some of the eminent historians on his committee, with a slight quizzical smile. I was thinking like a journalist or a novelist, not like a historian. He had not studied, and they had not trained him, to approach his dissertation in any such mood as that. They had trained him to probe for cause and consequence, to exhaust sources, to analyze, to generalize from tested facts. Pretty obviously they considered the analytical approach the only intellectually respectable one. Obviously they thought that treating those explosive two decades as drama would endanger the dependability of the result. They did not want him producing something like Leon Uris' *Armageddon.*

In holding him to an intellectually rigorous method they were, beyond all question, sound. But I think they dismissed too lightly an approach that would have been, for that particular segment of history, the most proper one. The postwar history of Berlin will not be properly written until it is narrated. A *good* book on Berlin may be a pastiche of communiques, conferences, policies, ultimatums, and abstract forces. The *great* book on Berlin is going to be a sort of Iliad, a story that dramatizes a power struggle in terms of the men who waged it. Which does not mean at all that it will be intellectually deficient.

History's truth is truth to fact, to what happened. "If you take truth from History," says Polybius, "what is left but an improfitable tale?" And what is an improfitable tale but fiction, whose truth is not truth to fact but truth to plausibility? Yet it is not the presence of dramatic narrative that makes false history false. Falseness derives from inadequate or inaccurate information, faulty research, neglected sources, bias, bad judgment, misleading implication, and these afflict the expository among us about as often as they afflict the narrative. It is true that the excitement of story-telling, like the excitement of phrase-making, often tempts a writer into misrepresentation. But the excitement of analysis, the excitement of generalization, can do the same; and the laudable lust for absolute accuracy can lead to dullness, can cause a man to proffer a set of notes instead of a finished book, as if one did not write history, but collected it.

Any method has its dangers. The solution is not to repudiate both generalization and dramatization, both the accurate and the vivid, and sit inert in the middle of one's virtue. Neither is anything gained by pretending that all narrative historians write better than expository historians, for clearly some narrative historians write badly and many expository historians write extremely well. Speaking as an amateur, I should guess that the trick is to make the twin cutting tools of sound research and a sense of the dramatic work together like scissor blades.

I have heard of a university history department which was offered a visiting historian noted for his grace of style. The idea of the donor was to let him have a salutary effect on the quality of the local historical prose. The department refused him, saying in effect, Thank you, no, we'll haggle along with our own dull saw. If they had taken him, he might have taught them that well-written history does not have to be inaccurate, and he might have learned from them that not all dull history is dependable. Maybe both would have learned that the dramatizing of legitimately dramatic true events does not necessarily falsify them, nor need it leave their meaning ambiguous.

Dramatic narrative is simply one means by which a historian can make a point vividly. To imagine historiography without this possibility is like imagining Christ without His parables, or Abraham Lincoln without his anecdotes.

Calliope and Clio are not identical twins, but they *are* sisters. History, a fable agreed on, is not a science but a branch of literature, an artifact made by artificers and sometimes by artists. Like fiction, it has only persons, places, and events to work with, and like fiction it may present them either in summary or in dramatic scene. Conversely, fiction, even fantastic fiction, reflects so much of the society that produces it that it may have an almost-historical value as record. Objective and sociological novels come very close to history, the difference being principally that history reports the actual, fiction the typical. Thus *An American Tragedy*, working out what Dreiser felt to be a characteristic American fate, was built on the extensive study of real murder trials, and in its text—transporting them bodily from real to make-believe—it incorporates many details and several documents from the case of Chester Gillette, who was convicted and executed for the murder of his girl in upstate New York in 1906.

That transposition of the actual into the fictional is only one instance of a common process. There is a whole middle ground between fiction and history. So-called historical fiction, which transposes the fictional into the actual, may have every degree of historical authenticity up to the highest, while things called history and biography may be treated with so little of the historian's responsibility to fact that they amount to frauds. There are respectable books all across the spectrum, but it is important that they be called what they are, and do not pretend to be what they are not.

I defend the middle ground as one who has strayed there several times—in *The Preacher and the Slave, Beyond the Hundredth Meridian, The Gathering of Zion,* and *Wolf Willow*. I doubt that any of those books fuses fiction and history with total success, but each has shown me a different possibility. Any librarian would catalogue the first as a novel, the second as a biography, the third as history. The fourth might give her classificatory heartburn. But at least in the matter of method and approach I am prepared to defend them all.

The Preacher and the Slave, an account of the life and death of the IWW martyr Joe Hill, is a novel: it has a novel's intentions and takes a novel's liberties. As necessary, I invented characters, scenes, motivations, dialogue, and though Hill's execution gave me an inescapable ending, I bent the approach to that conclusion as seemed to me needful. But the bending that seemed needful was also imposed on me, in a way, for I had spent four or five years collecting documentary and other evidence on both Joe Hill and the IWW, had hunted down seven or eight people who had known the elusive Joe Hill in life, had studied the trial transcript and many newspaper files, had talked with the family of the two men Hill was accused of murdering, and with the sheriff who conducted the execution by firing squad, with the Wobbly editor who arranged Hill's public funeral in Chicago, and with ballad-

eers who had written Joe Hill songs. I had attended
IWW martyr meetings. I had gotten the warden of the
Utah State Penitentiary to walk me through a mock execution so that I would know imaginatively how a condemned and blindfolded man might feel in the very soles
of his feet his progress toward death down iron stairs,
across paved courtyard, into cindered alley to the chair
with the bullet-battered backstop.

That is, I took every bit as much pains as I would
have taken if I had intended to write a history, and I
think that when I started to write I knew as much
IWW history as anybody in the world and could judge
its passions and its ambiguities almost as impartially. Also,
I blended the fictional and the documentary as Dreiser
had done. The last section utilizes actual letters to and
from Joe Hill, some of the trial records, some of the
record of a hearing before the pardon board, some of Joe
Hill's songs written in prison. A pretty historical book,
in its way. Nevertheless, I took pains in a foreword to
label it "an act of the imagination," which is what I
wanted it to be.

In *Beyond the Hundredth Meridian* I had no such fictional aim. The book is a biography of Major John Wesley
Powell, which incorporates much of the history of the
western surveys and of the formation of several Washington bureaus. Much of it is as expository as it could well
be. But all the expository history rests upon an opening
section that is nearly pure narrative, pure adventure story:
the account of Powell's first expedition down the Green
and Colorado rivers in 1869. In giving that narrative
nearly a third of the book, I may have been warping some
abstract and ideal proportion, but I invented nothing, not

even the feelings of the men I was following. I only exploited what their journals and letters offered me, and tried to imagine my way into their situation through my own knowledge of the canyons. Unlike the novelist, a historian cannot invent drama but can only take advantage of it when he finds it. In this book I wanted to be a historian.

Invention was not a possibility in *The Gathering of Zion*, either, since my intention was to write the history of the Mormon migration in the terms of the people who made it. Admittedly the aim was selective, since it left out much doctrinal, hierarchic, and political material, but within its limitations I wanted it to be as accurate as I could make it. I was much less interested in the doctrinal and political causes of this march than in the march itself, and in what faith did to the people who held it. In *The Preacher and the Slave* I had been after the personality of a rebel. I had started out by getting interested in *songs* that men had died to. Here on the Mormon Trail was a *faith* that people had died for.

My intention in *The Gathering of Zion* was clearly novelistic in its emphasis on human interest, but historical in that I wanted to be faithful to fact and record. Because I was after visceral history, I gave myself an extensive Parkmanesque exposure to the geography and weather of the trail; and I stuck close to the dust and storms and exhaustion and trials of faith reflected in the letters and journals of a wide range of people. Because this subject had been treated too often by partisans full of the zeal of attack or defense, I tried to exhaust these journal sources and not to stray from them. It is obvious from the amount of space I gave to the hegira from Nauvoo, the pioneer trip to Salt Lake Valley, and the tragic handcart episode that I was seizing every chance to dramatize—seizing, in fact, the same events that the Mormon imagination had already built into myths. Where the events of the migration were not especially dramatic, I told them in summary. So except for a few chapters, this is essentially narrative history. But it *is* history, if I understand the term.

My own opinion is that *Wolf Willow* ought to be called history too, though it is nearly a third reminiscence and more than a third fiction. The publishers solved the problem by subtitling it, "A History, a Story, and a Memory." But I hope that it is one thing, not three, and its dominant impulse was historical. Having grown up literally without history, in a place where human actions had not been formally remembered and recorded, I developed long after I left there the ambition to write at least the beginning of the history of those hills in southern Saskatchewan where the buffalo and the Plains Indians came to their end as a culture and a force. I wanted to be the Herodotus of the Cypress Hills. Like that other father of history, I found the documentation thin—a scrap or two in the *Jesuit Relations*, a bit in *Le Métis Canadien*, a few Hudson's Bay records and reminiscences, some newspaper accounts of the Cypress Hills Massacre and its aftermath, something about Sitting Bull, something about the Mounted Police, some recollections of old-timers, one continuous local newspaper file beginning in 1914. But I had lived in the hills myself, and my memories were sharp. It seemed legitimate, as a means of realizing the country for readers, to put my remembering senses into the book, and my own family's experiences. And when I came to write about the open-range cattle industry, I was irresistibly driven to write it as fiction, as a typical story rather than as an expository summary. I thought I could get more truth into a slightly fictionized story of the winter that killed the cattle industry on the northern plains than I could into any summary. So I wrote that section as three connected stories, a sort of broken novel. Later I took out the middle one, a yarn called "The Wolfer," for entirely literary reasons: it was told in the first person by a Mounted Policeman, and it intruded a disturbingly subjective "voice" into a book that was already discontinuous enough. Unlike fiction, history can have only one voice, the historian's.

Those are only four of many possible combinations that lie between the poles of history and fiction. Whatever the combination, I am positive that the novelist's skill with scene, character, and symbol may be used, not to cheapen history but to enhance it. One way of understanding something is to see it recreated—a playback. The great romantic historians, Bancroft, Motley, Prescott, and Parkman, freely used such skills, and they gravitated naturally toward the heroic subjects that permitted heroic treatment. Their histories are not to be understood out of the context that includes Sir Walter Scott. As David Levin has pointed out, their histories are not so much record as romantic art. Obviously there is every justification for the kind of history that preserves and records, but history as romantic art—or realistic art, for that matter—is not entirely the province of lesser lady novelists and popularizers. As a modern instance of the meeting of a great subject and a great talent I cite you Bernard DeVoto.

It would have frustrated DeVoto, who tried long and hard to be a novelist, to know that his essays and especially his histories would outlast his novels. But it is true that the talents which labor and overheat in the novels run smooth and cool in the histories. They are story-telling talents, but they work better on historical characters and events than on imagined ones. For one thing, the American West gave DeVoto a greater story and more colorful people than any he could possibly have invented. There is nobody in his novels who belongs in the same gallery with his Narcissa Whitman, Tamsen Donner, Susan Magoffin, Jim Clyman, or that large, empty figure John Charles Frémont, whom DeVoto calls "Captain Jinks of the Horse Marines."

For another thing, fiction demands a ventriloquist, and DeVoto spoke best in his own voice.

Modern fiction has complexities and subtleties of point of view unknown to history. Even the word *objective* has different meanings in the two arts. In history it means *impartial;* in fiction it means *invisible.* The fictional author can make himself invisible either by being a camera or by burying himself in the subjective consciousness of one of his characters, as Camus buried himself in Mersault in *The Stranger.* We may make what we will of Mersault; Camus does not explain him, he only presents him or rather, permits him to present himself. Internal as that novel is, Camus was correct in calling it an exercise in objectivity.

Whatever the point of view, modern fiction rarely utilizes the old omniscience that used to be the stance of both fiction and history and is still the stance of history. Instead of being present as judge and commentator, the novelist now is barely more than a shadow or half-heard whisper, what Wayne Booth calls the "suggested author." However the problem of point of view is handled, it is the first thing a man sitting down to write a novel must settle. A historian never has to raise the question. The novelist works tentatively, hesitantly, like a man releasing a slipping clutch on a hill, and sometimes he may share E. B. White's nostalgia for the old Model T, on whose pedal one used to step down with complete positiveness, as he might kick open a door. I am fairly sure that Bernard DeVoto came to history with a certain mental relief, precisely because history still works with the Model T's epicycloidal clutch. DeVoto did not want to be off somewhere like the God of creation, indifferent, paring his fingernails. He was a positive man with positive opinions, and he must have liked the sense that as historian he had no need to hide or disguise either his attitudes or his personal gift of language. He did not, in history, have to write down to some undereducated or inarticulate or hysterical character; he could write always up to his own level. Once he knew his facts he could be bold, with a novelist's eye for drama and a historian's godlike assumption that he speaks not merely to posterity, but for it.

It is a question whether he ever fully understood how much more at home he was in history than in fiction: his natural impulse was to curse the historian's trade picturesquely, but the curses must be discounted. In the DeVoto papers in the Stanford University Library there is a file of correspondence between DeVoto and Garrett Mattingly, his friend and mentor, himself a historian of very great distinction. The two criticized each other's work, bucked one another up, lamented serially and in unison, and read one another lectures, and in the course of twenty-two years managed to discuss most of the problems of historiography. It is a fascinating file. Two men of very different temperament approach history from opposite ends, both working toward that transformation of fact by the imagination that both thought the highest reach of the historian's art. DeVoto was a man whom Mattingly wholeheartedly and all but uncritically admired; Mattingly was a man on whom DeVoto depended as his historical and scholarly conscience. They made a good team, without rivalry. Mattingly, a Renaissance scholar, pretended to know nothing about the American West; DeVoto, a writer, pretended to know nothing about history, though on occasion he thought historians did not know much about it either.

The pretense of incompetence begins early in the DeVoto letters and is never entirely given up. "I can't ever become a historian," he wrote Mattingly in 1933, "for I hate detail and can't spare the time for original research. I'm a journalist, my boy. Besides, the historians being the only group in America who approve of me, it would be a pity to alienate them as I certainly would if I announced I'd forfeited my present immunity as a mere literary gent. . . ." A historian? Me? But in that same letter he was already outlining the book that later would appear as *The Year of Decision: 1846.*

Both that book and *Across the Wide Missouri*, which followed it, were composed as braided narratives following the actions of groups of characters, a complex epic of disparate people all engaged in a single action, the opening of the West, and all revealed through quotation and paraphrase of their letters and journals. This was the sort of history DeVoto found stimulating; if there are complaints about the muse of history in the letters of that time, they are meant jokingly, and they are matched by explosions of enthusiasm, such as the one that reported his discovery of James Clyman as the "culture hero" he needed for a unifying principle. He would not invent, but how happily he discovered in his materials the dramatic and the symbolic! Halley's comet fell into his lap like a shower of pure gold.

But with *The Course of Empire*, which he began writing in the late 1940's, the agonies of history bore down on him. This book, he wrote Mattingly, "is a different *kind* of stuff from its predecessors and I don't enjoy the dilemma, for if this one is history the other isn't, and who am I?" As Mattingly said to DeVoto's friend and assistant, Helen Everitt, when the book was finished,

> Every historian has to grapple with the problem that any significant action occurs in a frame of space, and that the more significant the action the more it is implicated with other actions, antecedent, contemporary and subsequent. . . . Tackling anything like the Lewis and Clark expedition in these terms (something I had no idea Benny meant to do when he started) is a pretty heroic enterprise.

To DeVoto himself, the year before, when DeVoto was nearly frantic with the complexity of what he was trying to do, Mattingly had written encouragement:

> This is a different kind of history from anything you have written so far, but it's been implicit . . . in practically everything you've ever written, and you'd got to the point where it had to be explicit. For your temperament, or mine for that matter, striding across the centuries, hitting the high spots isn't nearly so satisfactory as concentration on a shorter time span. Hard as it is for anyone to know even a very little about North America in 1846 or Western Europe in 1588, it isn't downright impossible; but nobody can cover a line of development over two or

three centuries . . . without feeling oppressed by the weight of his own ignorance. . . .

Oppressed he most certainly was. He lamented his own incapacity:

I am not going to join you any longer in the pretense that I have the kind of mind that can write history . . . I am quite incapable of determining facts, recognizing facts, appraising facts, putting facts into relation to one another, confining myself to facts, guiding myself by facts, or even recording facts. My mind is an instrument superbly designed for inaccuracy. . . .

He lamented the errors of the authorities he wanted to depend on:

I'm getting fed up with historians. Yes, & editors of texts too. I worked two weeks trying to find out why my hero Verendrye thought that the same river flowed both north and south in the same stretch. When I finally followed it back to the original text I found that Mr. Burpee, one of your colleagues, had just inserted a comma.

He lamented the endlessness of historical research:

This was supposed to be about Sacajawea, wasn't it? I figure I can clean up the predecessors of L&C in 30 years more, oh, easy. I figure I can do the empires and the wars in less than 10 years more and the trans-Allegheny U.S., the state of scientific thought, symmetrical geography, the diplomatics and American politics in another 10, and maybe in 5 years I can get Napoleon and La. straightened out. . . . Well, God damn it, twice now you've been able to tell me what book I was writing on the basis of the first draft. . . . You damn well better tell me pretty soon what book I'm working toward now or I'll get buried under it. What's in my mind? . . . What book am I aiming at?

To that blast, Mattingly responded soothingly:

You've just got a light case of *regressus historicus*. I've seen some lulus. Thirty years ago [one of my colleagues] decided that he couldn't write about the 16th century German Sacramentarians without a little background of medieval heresies. Now he despairs of really knowing anything about the Albigenses without exploring the 11th century Bogomils and the 9th century Paulicians, and behind them, he knows, are Yezedees and Manichaeans and dark little twisty passageways leading off into Persia and Assyria and Egypt. Meanwhile he works away doggedly at the connection between Peter Waldo and the Humiliati, at Catherine and Potarini, half a continent and five hundred years from his starting point, which he has practically forgotten.

Buried in multiplying and proliferating sources, cursing his ignorance and his lack of education ("I can't dig out the background of the background of the background. How the hell do I learn historical geography?") DeVoto yearned for some sort of "instant history":

Did anybody ever write a history of the Seven Years War, in one volume, that I could keep on my desk for reference and could rely on? If the answer is the *Cambridge Modern History*, be so good as to include a teaspoonful of strychnine with your bibliographical note.

He groaned when Mattingly, supplying bibliography like a thesis director, sent him to *Le Métis Canadien* at the suggestion of his colleague John Brebner.

Please drop in on Brebner and shoot him. *Le Métis Canadien* has 1293 royal octavo pages. You know my other historical weakness: I have to read all of a book.

Actually he was a glutton for work—twelve to fifteen hours a day seven days a week—and he was also incomparably lucky, for in Mattingly he had the constant assistance and encouragement of a beautifully trained and learned professional. God send all amateur historians such a friend. He steered DeVoto to the right books, he distinguished between reliable and unreliable authorities, he criticized drafts, he bucked up morale, he wrung out crying towels, he summarized peripheral historical matters that DeVoto wanted to know about, such as the Mesta in Spain and the background of Spanish exploration and settlement in the Southwest. He even, humbly, disparaged his own indispensable usefulness, in order to encourage the literary friend whom he considered more brilliant than himself. To hell, he said, with the self-constituted experts to whom DeVoto thought he must pay attention.

> The function of specialists in the historians' economy is to mine and smelt the ore out of which better men write history. I've done that kind of coolie work for years, and have the callouses on my bottom to prove it. . . .

But if he thought that coolie work was all he was doing for DeVoto, he badly underestimated himself. Every once in a while one of his casual remarks touched DeVoto off like a rocket. One instance will illustrate. On November 1, 1945, DeVoto wrote Mattingly in the same mood with which earlier he had described his discovery of Jim Clyman as the culture hero who in his own person had lived the whole West of his time. Now DeVoto was responding to a remark Mattingly had made a few days earlier.

"American history," says you, with the confidence of a man who boasts that he knows nothing about it, "American history is History in transition from an Atlantic to a Pacific phase." If you didn't say it in that way, don't revise it now, for that's the way I want it. As I say, there is a literary ethics: I will steal what I need as I need it, but not from my friends. And I think I'll begin my book, or end it, or both, with those great words, like the couriers that are stayed not on the frieze. Do you want to be accredited in the text or in a footnote?

Accreditation was in order, for crystallizing a major theme and for other services, including the sort of literary criticism that Mattingly should not theoretically have been needed for. The novelist as historian should at least know how to write. In the face of his mountain of facts, blown by all the thirty-two winds of confusion, DeVoto lost his confidence even in that aspect of the writing of history, and faced the prospect gloomily.

I still know as little as ever and I'm oppressed by it. But also I'm suddenly oppressed by how much I know, at least how much information I have, and how hard it's going to be to impose form on it and make it readable. I suppose there is a structure; I know it's going to be hell to find it. . . .

Chapter by chapter Mattingly helped him find it, or more often corroborated the fact that he *had* found it. And he bent his ear, perhaps not unwillingly, when DeVoto blew up at the woes of composition. He was writing, DeVoto said,

the dullest broth of watery, uremic, and flatulent prose
ever compounded, of which there is not only no end but
not even a middle. Middle? Hell, there is not even an
approach, there is not even a beginning. It takes me thirty
thousand words to draw even with where I was when I
began them. To begin a chapter is enough to make sure
that I will be farther from the end of the book when I
finish it—farther by twice as many words and God knows
how many years. I run furiously, at the extremity of
(waning) strength, and the sweat that pours off me is all
words, words, words, words, words by the galley, words
by the thousand, words by the dictionary, and I sink
forever deeper in them, I don't get any farther forward,
I only drift back and disappear under them. And Jesus
Christ, what words, shapeless, colorless, without sound
or substance or taste or perfume or indeed existence,
words of immense viscosity and no energy or lumines-
cense whatsoever, words out of a lawyer's brief or out of
a New Critic's essay on Truman Capote or the ghost who
writes MacArthur's communiques, words of unbaked
dough, of glucose thinned with bilge, words less than a
serum and somewhat more than an exudation, and in all
the mess and mass of them not a God damned thought.
. . . With thirteen million words written or by our lady
two score million, we have now accounted for 229 years
that do not enter at all into my book and have only forty
more years to go, or say an even million words, if in the
meantime I can learn something about concentration . . .
before we reach the beginning of my book and, with a
sigh of infinite satisfaction and a suffusing glow of happy
realization that only ten million words lie ahead, take up
a blank, virgin sheet of paper and write on the top of it
Page One.

Any writer will recognize the symptoms, as Mattingly did. This is a man trying to force shape and eloquence upon a resistant and complex body of historical fact. And doing, as Mattingly pointed out, a great deal better than he admitted. Much of the difficulty of this last volume of the western trilogy arose from the fact that it was much less narrative than the others. The generalizer and synthesizer was constantly called on, the novelist had less chance to shine, and he struggled.

Nevertheless, he retained his fictional license, and wherever he could, in brief brilliant flashes, he rendered the explorations of Mackenzie, Frazer, Thompson, Peter Pond, as story; and he made of the Lewis and Clark expedition a symbolic journey to the end of what Columbus had begun, the full achievement of the Northwest Passage to history's Pacific phase. And he didn't fail to heed, even when his materials were recalcitrant, the advice he had given Mattingly years before, in 1938. If there was one thing wrong with Mattingly's writing, he had said then, it was "forgetfulness, or momentary disbelief, that the reader is in there working too. In narrative fewest is best and you don't have to tell everything, for if anyone is with you at all, he is half a yard ahead of you . . . you're probably giving him more than he needs."

Here is the touch not of a recorder but of an artist: being possessed of mountains of material, restrain yourself, don't dump it all on the reader. Let him come climbing eagerly in discovery. And some other advice he had given, touching on the uses of the dramatic:

> I think you lean over a little backward—I think you refuse to let yourself utilize all the emotional possibilities, sometimes, on the unconscious theory that you'd be populariz-

ing if you did. . . . It's almost as if you pulled up at second base because no scholar ought to knock a home run. Whereas for the dignity of scholarship every scholar who can write, which is damned few, ought to write his head off. . . . When you get a scene, play it. I'd even sacrifice all the dispensable detail in order to get room for drama. You know I'm not arguing that you should leave out anything that ought to be in, or that you ought to pump up a scene that hasn't got enough stuff in itself, or in any other way falsify or cheapen the material or the trade. But I am saying that a man who can write as well as you can ought to take advantage of his opportunities.

That is essentially the historical method that both De-Voto and Mattingly aspired to, coming at it from opposite sides. It is a long way from the meticulously pedestrian. It is also as far as possible from the sort of lady-novelist, best-seller history that an editor once urged on Mattingly: "He offers me," Mattingly wrote DeVoto in a rage, "a bewildering choice of subject, from Richard the Lion Hearted to Prince Henry the Navigator ('now there's a great story that's never been told!') to John Hancock, or how about Maria Theresa. He waves away all possible scholarly doubts. 'If you make it part fiction, or just don't put [in] any footnotes,' he says shrewdly, 'nobody but you will know how much you are making up.'"

The editor has since taken up the pen himself and sold hundreds of thousands of copies of doctored and doped "history." In the process he has done harm to the good name of narrative history, and it is perhaps his kind of books which have created prejudice among the professionals. But one does not judge Thucydides by the practice of an untutored local amateur, and one should not judge narrative history by the people who prostitute it. DeVoto and Mattingly, temperamentally different but alike in their distaste for either the tawdry or the dull, have set far sounder standards of how to tell the stories that history provides, without either missing the drama or leaving out the footnotes.

5

~~~~~~

Three Samples

a. The West Synthetic:
Bret Harte

There are some writers who, no matter how great their living reputations, reveal themselves after their deaths—sometimes long after—to have been greater than their contemporaries thought them. New meanings come pushing up through them like stones pushed upward by the frost; or to take a figure from the Gold Rush, readers panning the tailings and gravel heaps of these old literary placers sometimes find more gold than the original Argonauts found. Bret Harte, it must be said at once, does not seem to be one of these writers. Though the critics have been out in Chinese hordes panning the worked-over gravels of American literature, no critic has made a new strike in him. The consensus on Harte is approximately what it was at the time of his death: that he was a skillful but not profound writer who made a lucky strike in subject matter and for a few heady months enjoyed a fabulous popularity; that once the artifice, narrowness, and shallowness of his work began to be perceived, he fell out of public favor; and that through the last twenty-four years of his life, while he lived abroad, he went on tiredly repeating himself in potboiler after potboiler, turning over his own tailings in a pathetic attempt to recapture what had first made him.

That estimate is not true in all its details or in all its implications, but it is broadly true. Harte *was* lucky, he *was* limited, he *did* swiftly lose his popularity in America, he *did* go on repeating himself. Of the scores of stories that he wrote during his years in Germany, Scotland, and England, all but a small handful return to the picturesque gulches of the Sierra foothills from which, in one blazing strike, he had extracted the nugget of his reputation. Now, no critic takes him very seriously; he is read principally by children and students. And yet he cannot be dismissed. More than a hundred years after his first sketches and poems began to appear in *The Golden Era* in the late 1850's, he remains embedded in the American literary tradition, and it looks as if he will stay. It is worth trying to discover what is keeping him there.

Whatever virtues he had, they were not the virtues of realism. His observation of Gold Rush country, character, and society was neither very accurate nor very penetrating; neither was much of it firsthand. Despite persistent legends of Harte's mining experiences, his Indian fighting, and his stint as a Wells-Fargo gun guard, George Stewart and others have demonstrated that his actual experience in the mines was probably limited to a season of schoolteaching near La Grange, plus a brief "picnic," as Harte called it, in the diggings, plus a later tour with Anton Roman in frank search of literary material. The literary tourists who make pilgrimages to the "Bret Harte country" are seeing it nearly as intimately as Harte did. He was a city man, a bit of a dandy, literary from a precocious age (he published his first poem at the age of eleven), and though he arrived in California as early as 1854, at the age of eighteen, and thereafter lived in the swirling fringe of the Gold Rush and the Comstock silver rush, he managed to get into his writing just about as much Irving and Dickens and Dumas as authentic Jackass Hill.

His geography sounds authentic, but when one attempts to pin it down to locality it swims and fades into the outlines of Never-Never Land. Harte had no such personal familiarity with the Sierra as his contemporaries Clarence King and John Muir had, and no such scientific accuracy of observation. There are a hundred firsthand accounts that give a more faithful picture of life in the mines than his stories do. Some of them, in fact, he used: the *Shirley Letters*, finest of all Gold Rush books, gave him two of the best touches his stories provide: the birth of a child in an unregenerate camp on the Feather River, used as the basis for "The Luck of Roaring Camp," and the silent mounding of snow on the shoulders of a man hanged by vigilantes, an image used to soften the death of Piney and the Duchess in "The Outcasts of Poker Flat." But he did not always have an observer as acute as Louise Amelia Knapp Smith Clappe to draw on, and not all his situations and effects are that good.

He did not have, as the great fiction writers have, the faculty of realizing real characters on the page in terms more vivid than reality. His practice was to select occupations and turn them into types; and though individual models were sometimes present, as in the case of the gambler-duelist prototype of Jack Hamlin, the gamblers, schoolmarms, stage drivers, and miners of the stories are usually predictable. Harte dealt many times with the character of the "Pike," the "Anglo-Saxon reverted to barbarism" who was one of the stand-by's of California literature, but even that type character he did not do as well as Clarence King did him in "The Newtys of Pike" —and as for Mark Twain's definitive portrait in Pap Finn, that is of another and higher order of literature entirely.

Harte was at a disadvantage. He could not draw, as Mark Twain could, on a rich and various experience as smalltown frontier boy, jour printer, river pilot, territorial secretary, reporter, and pocket miner. He could not say of almost any eccentric character, "I know him—knew him on the river." Unlike Mark Twain's human swarm, Harte's characters do not strike us with their lifelikeness. They are self-consistent, they have clear outlines and logical coherence, and they speak a lingo that sounds suitably rough and crude. Yet they look *made*, and they are.

These are, in fact, early forms of some of our most venerable literary stereotypes. Since Harte it has been next to impossible for a writer to present a western gambler who has not some of the self-contained poise, readiness, and chivalry of Jack Hamlin and John Oakhurst. Even Stephen Crane, in his superb short story "The Blue Hotel," succumbed to the pattern that Harte had laid down. Since Harte showed the world how, every horse-opera stage driver has driven with the picturesque recklessness and profanity of Yuba Bill. The schoolmarms of our movie and television westerns owe about as much to Harte's Miss Mary, in "The Idyl of Red Gulch," as to Molly Wood in Owen Wister's *The Virginian*—and it should be noted, in Harte's favor, that "The Idyl of Red Gulch" came thirty-two years before *The Virginian*.

Harte's geography seems vague because he did not know the real geography of the Sierra well, and didn't feel that he needed to. His characters seem made because they *were* made, according to a formula learned from Dickens: the trick of bundling together apparently incompatible qualities to produce a striking paradox. Thus Harte's gamblers, though Lotharios with ladies of easy virtue, are chivalry itself when Innocence makes its call on them, as in "A Protégée of Jack Hamlin's." Thus the virulent Mother Shipton starves herself to death to give her rations to Piney in "The Outcasts." Thus the best shots have only one eye, the strongest men only three fingers, the most dangerous men the gentlest manner, the roughest men the softest center, the most pompous men the most forthright bravery at twenty paces. Characters are not only built to a pattern, but they repeat. Having developed the limited perfection of Jack Hamlin in "Brown of Calaveras," Harte was tempted into re-using him in twenty different stories. Colonel Starbottle accounts for another twenty, Yuba Bill appears in sixteen, John Oakhurst in four. The effect, repetitious as it is, is to emphasize the clear outlines of the little artificial world of Harte's creation—to make it, however artificial, indelible.

The world of the Gold Rush proper, that first blooming of mushroom camps in the gulches, where every man worked his own claim with pan, rocker, or sluice box, where a hotel was canvas over a frame, and a saloon a keg and a tin cup under a tree, was of course gone before Harte began writing of it. Many camps were ghosts within a year or two of their establishment, and the whole first phase of the mines lasted only from the Sutter's Mill strike of 1848 to the Comstock strike ten years later that stampeded all the loose miners over the Sierra and left behind mainly the big mines, the monitors, and the quartz leads. But when Harte's first mining camp stories appeared there were still plenty of people around who had "seen the elephant," and who did not wholeheartedly respond to the fictional variety. Harte's popularity, as a matter of fact, was always greatest in direct proportion to the reader's distance from and ignorance of the mines. By a happy chance of lagging factual reports, his stories reached Eastern readers when they were still titillated by rumor but unsatisfied in detail. As in the Currier and Ives prints about the buffalo plains, art passed for fact until fact overtook it, whereupon it began to lose its currency even as art. Then, after his popularity had dwindled on the Eastern seaboard, Harte found still another audience, even more remote from the Mother Lode, in England, and that audience stuck loyally with him until his death and after. In a way, it was the worst thing that could have happened to him, for it helped keep him from becoming anything more than the writer he already was.

The writer that he was was a product of a long and diligent apprenticeship, a lucky accident, and the publishing acuteness of Anton Roman, who had hired him as editor of the new *Overland Monthly* and had enthusiastically talked up the mines as literary material. With char-

acteristic dilatoriness, Harte missed the first issue, but publication of "The Luck of Roaring Camp" in the second,
in August, 1868, demonstrated Roman's foresight and
Harte's gift. Though there were local objections to a
story written about a prostitute's baby, as well as to such
language as Kentuck's admiring "the d—d little cuss!",
the response from the East, when it came, was one long
joyous outcry. By the end of two years, Harte had published and collected in a book seven stories under the title
The Luck of Roaring Camp, and Other Sketches, and
in September, 1870, he slipped into the *Overland* almost
casually, as filler, the dialect poem called "Plain Language from Truthful James," generally known as "The
Heathen Chinee." That went off in the public's face like
a firecracker; it shook men down in laughter all across
the country, was reprinted in numberless newspapers,
pasted in barbership windows, committed to memory. It
has been seriously suggested that no single work ever
made a writer so famous. And when Harte decided in
1871 to follow his popularity eastward, his progress was
like the passage of a public hero or a president.

Probably the sudden elevation to fame, the familiarity
with the literary great, the universal admiration, went to
his head. He appears to have fallen somewhat short of the
twelve stories and poems he agreed to supply the *Atlantic,*
for a fee of $10,000, during the year. Though he charmed
many people—Mark Twain called him the most charming of men, also the least charming—he disappointed others by not turning out to be a hairy man in boots and a
blue flannel shirt. His popularity began to wane. He went
on three separate lecture tours, at considerable cost in
fatigue and with diminishing financial return. His hopes of

writing assignments and editorial posts came to nothing; he sold less, and to less profitable journals. The play *Ah Sin*, a collaboration with Mark Twain dramatizing "The Heathen Chinee," was only a modest success. Burdened with debts, grabbing at any straw, he accepted an appointment as consular assistant in the silk town of Crefeld, Germany, near Düsseldorf, and in 1878 left behind him his family, his country, and his collapsing reputation. None of them was ever restored to him.

Bret Harte represented two very common American literary phenomena. For one thing he was victimized, as many of our writers have been, by the boom-and-bust freakishness of public favor. For another, he was that American type, the local writer whom fame has drawn away from the local, and who now has a choice between developing new themes and a literary manner more suitable for a sophisticated audience, or repeating from exile, with increasing thinness and unreality, the localism he has left behind.

The very perfection of Harte's little world of the local picturesque made it all but impossible for him to break out of it. Mark Twain, who had never been so typed or so limited, was freed by the variety of his own life and by the vitality with which he welcomed new experience; he escaped into travel literature, into history, into causes, into his rich nostalgia for boyhood and the river. But Harte was imprisoned in his own creation. Pressed for money as he always was, he dared not vary locale or tone. He was bound to his desk by poverty, illnesses, the monthly draft—usually late but never evaded—to his family. Temperamentally, too, he was incapable of mean living, shabby dressing, the avoidance of expensive friends. "I grind out the old tunes on the old organ and gather up the coppers," he wrote his wife in 1879, "but I never know whether my audience behind the window blinds are wishing me to 'move on' or not."

It was the American audience on which he could no longer depend. In 1885 he wrote, "Unfortunately, while my stuff is held at a premium here, it is falling off in America. Dana gives *less than half* what he gave me at first; my publishers, Houghton, Mifflin and Company, scarcely anything." Quite apart from his ambiguous relations with his wife, he could hardly have returned to America if he had wanted to. "As far as I can judge hastily, my chances, for the present at least, are better *here*. I have never stood so well in regard to the *market value* of my works in any other country as here; with all my patriotism I am forced to confess that I do not stand as high in my own country . . . I was told that Mr. Sargent, of California, while Minister to Germany, intimated . . . that he was surprised at my German reputation, as I was completely 'played out' in America."

And so, from necessity, timidity, incapacity, or whatever, Harte made hardly a gesture toward discovering new sources of stories. He did now and then turn to poetry, but "only as a change to my monotonous romances. Perhaps it is very *little change*, for my poetry, I fear, is coming from the same spring as my prose, only the tap is nearer the fountain—and filtered." He also tried several plays, hoping for a success that would relieve his constant financial anxiety ("I am quite content if the papers abuse the play so long as the audience like it, and the thing pays"); but the only half-successful one, *Sue*, never made enough to give him the independence he wanted. And it is doubtful that by 1896, when that play was produced, he could have altered his writing habits in the slightest. He could go on working painfully hard against many handicaps; he could hike his daily production from 600 to 1000 words, "Sundays and holidays, sick or well"; he could retain a rather pathetic professional pride in not doing shoddy work; but he knew better than to respect most of what he wrote, and he had no other sort of thing to write.

Or thought he hadn't. Yet in the *Letters* there is a more personal Bret Harte, one who makes us realize almost with a shock how little Harte's personality shows in the stories. There he is as scrupulously aloof and "indifferent," as "refined out of existence," as the most rigorous dramatic ideal could ask. His characters, whatever else they are, are never made in Harte's image, but are themselves, creations, clean of any taint of their creator. Like the perfect little world of picturesque localism and romantic paradox that they inhabit, they eventually controlled their creator as much as he controlled them; they were a thing he hid behind.

Reading the *Letters*, one wishes that Harte had let himself be revealed more: he is himself more interesting than his gallery of types. For one thing, the letters give evidence that if he had chosen to, he might have become a lively, biased, and outrageous travel reporter in the jingoist tradition of Mark Twain. "The Californian mountains and Coast ranges are vastly superior to these famous Alps—in every respect. As the Rhine is inferior to the Hudson, so is Switzerland to California, and even to the Catskills in New York. The snow peaks visible

[232]

from my window are fine, but I have seen finer views
from a wayside hotel in California country."

That tone alone might have restored him his American
audience, always happy to come out ahead in comparisons
with Europe. And the mingling of complaint with humor, the casting of criticism into exaggerated form, was
in the best vein of the bumptious American visiting the
old home. As with Switzerland, so with the Swiss, "with
their sham sentiments, their sham liberty, their sham
chamois (an ugly cross between a goat and a jackass),
their sham jödel—that awful falsetto as musical as a cat's
serenade; and nothing real about them but their hideous
goiters." Or consider Glasgow, where Harte was un-
happily consul from 1880 to 1885: "I cannot help feeling that I am living by gaslight in a damp cellar with an
occasional whiff from a drain, from a coal heap, from
a moldy potato bin, and from dirty washtubs."

As nostalgic and unhappy as that, yet he never went
back. Lonely as his letters show him to have been, he
neither sent for his family nor returned to them, and
when, twenty years after their separation, they visited
England, he did not live with them. It is probable that
intimate passages have been edited out of Harte's letters
to his wife. Certainly what remains is so cool, so oddly
confiding and courteous and responsible, yet so trans-
parently determined that circumstances will not permit a
reunion, that one itches to know more. Harte was his
own best paradox. In his self-imposed exile he enjoyed
at once the consolations of poverty, hard work, and self-
pity, and the companionship of lords, ladies, and interna-
tional celebrities. This driven hack was one of the most
honored of expatriate American writers. Max Nordau

called him "the Columbus of American fiction"; he was invited to respond to the toast to literature at the Royal Academy; he influenced Kipling and delighted young Chesterton; his life fluctuated between hard hours at his desk and luxurious holidays with the Marquess of North-ampton or the Duchess of St. Albans.

It is one of the great unwritten books—the revelation of what lay behind that self-indulgent and laborious, that miserable and sycophantic, that lonely and cherished, exile. Harte wrote not a word of it, and all we know of his desolation we read between the lines of the *Letters*. That is enough to make us regret that temperament and cir-cumstances kept him away from a more personal sort of writing and held him to the controlled play-acting of Red Dog and Poker Flat. Almost until his death of throat cancer on May 5, 1902, Harte went on producing diffuse variants of the laconic and startling stories that had made his reputation more than thirty years before.

The stories, ultimately, are all he has to be judged by; if anything tangible is keeping him in the textbooks, they are.

Admitting that there is in them little honest observa-tion of people or of nature, no real character, no accurate picture of a society however fleeting, no true ear for the lingo, no symbolic depth, no valid commentary upon the human condition, no inadvertent self-revelation, and no real weight of mind, there is still something. There is humor—pervasive, unprudish, often still fresh and natural. There is good prose, and this is nearly unfailing. He was master of a flexible instrument, and if his language was rather more literary than native, if he leaned toward the King's English and never made of his dialect much more than a sort of decoration, he can hardly be blamed. Of all his contemporaries, only Mark Twain managed to make the vernacular do everything a true literary language has to do. Harte's prose was sometimes inflated and self-conscious, but more often it was markedly clean and direct. He was capable of a notable economy, passages and sometimes whole stories of a striking nervous compactness in which character, situation, and realized place come off the page instantly visual. Try the opening of "A Protégée of Jack Hamlin's," a story written as late as 1893.

Economy and a formal precision were part of both his temperament and his training. In *Condensed Novels*, a series of parodies written during the sixties, he had learned to boil whole novelists down to a few pages of essence. But it was his adaptation of the short story to Californian materials that created something like a revolution. His example emancipated writers in every region, confirming them in their subject matter and confirming them in their preference for the short story form. So great was Harte's influence upon the whole local color school that in 1894 he modestly felt compelled to deny, in an article for *Cornhill*, that he had invented the short story itself. Invent it he did not, but no historian of the short story can overlook his shaping influence upon it or his enormous influence in popularizing it through the expanding magazines.

Humor, economy, mastery of a prose instrument and a compact fictional form, a trick of paradox and color, a chosen (later compulsive) subject matter full of romantic glamor, a faculty for creating types that have become the stock in trade of a whole entertainment industry—these are surely enough to account for Harte's lasting. But there is something more. He made a world.

Admittedly it was a world insufficiently rooted in fact to have realistic validity, and even such facts as it contained were mainly anachronisms already outlived. Yet it was plausible, cohesive, self-contained; and it is peopled by creatures of a simple and enduring kind. The pilgrims who visit the "Bret Harte country," and the chambers of commerce along Highway 49 who set their traps for them, have a surer instinct than the critics; they recognize valid myths when they see them.

For Harte succeeded more than some better writers at creating American archetypes. In his Yuba Bills and Jack Hamlins he made trial syntheses of the American character in local western terms. Despite gross simplifications and despite a failure of superficial realism, his creations have lasted and become stereotypes precisely because they *do* approximate myths. They are all of them—rough but sentimental miners, dishonest but loyal partners, wicked but chivalrous gamblers, virtuous but tender schoolmarms, unvirtuous but tender prostitutes—shapes of the essential American Innocence that Mark Twain, James, Howells, and many more have asserted and personified. With all their faults upon them, the inhabitants of Red Dog and Poker Flat belong somewhere in the same literary tradition with Leatherstocking and Huckleberry Finn.

b. The West Authentic:
Willa Cather

If, as is often said, every novelist is born to write one thing, then the one thing that Willa Cather was born to write was first fully realized in *My Antonia* (1918). In that novel the people are the Bohemian and Swedish immigrants she had known in her childhood on the Nebraska plains; the prose is the prose of her maturity—flexible, evocative, already tending to a fastidious bareness but not yet gone pale and cool; the novelistic skill is of the highest, the structure at once free and intricately articulated; the characters stretch into symbolic suggestiveness as naturally as trees cast shadows in the long light of a prairie evening; the theme is the fully-exposed, complexly-understood theme of the American orphan or exile, struggling to find a place between an old world left behind and a new world not yet created.

But to say that Willa Cather found her subject and her manner and her theme in *My Antonia* is not to say that she found them easily. When *My Antonia* appeared, Miss Cather was 45 years old. She had already had one career as a teacher and another as an editor, and she had published a good many short stories and three other novels.

The first of these, *Alexander's Bridge* (1911), was a nearly-total mistake—a novel laid in London and dealing with the attenuated characters and fragile ethical problems of the genteel tradition. In writing it, Miss Cather later remarked, she was trying to sing a song that did not lie in her voice. Urged by her friend Sarah Orne Jewett to try something closer to her own experience, she revived her western memories with a trip to Arizona and New Mexico, and after her return to Pittsburgh

> began to write a story entirely for myself; a story about some Scandinavians and Bohemians who had been neighbours of ours when I lived on a ranch in Nebraska, when I was eight or nine years old. I found it a much more absorbing occupation than writing *Alexander's Bridge;* a different process altogether. Here there was no arranging or "inventing"; everything was spontaneous and took its own place. . . . This was like taking a ride through familiar country on a horse that knew the way, on a fine morning when you felt like riding.

As she herself instantly recognized, that second book, *O Pioneers!* (1913), came close to being the tune that "lay in her voice." She wrote it spontaneously because she was tapping both memory and affection. She thought of the subject matter as a considerable innovation, because no American writer had yet used Swedish immigrants for any but comic purposes, and nobody had ever written about Nebraska, considered in literary circles the absolute home of the clodhopper.

Actually, there was nothing so revolutionary about the subject matter—it was merely one further extension of the local color curiosity about little-known places and picturesque local types. Hamlin Garland had done German and Norwegian immigrants very like these, on Wisconsin and Iowa farms very like Miss Cather's Nebraska farms, in *Main-Travelled Roads* (1891). *O Pioneers!* was new in its particulars, but not new in type, and it was not Willa Cather's fully-trained voice that was heard in it.

In its method, the book is orthodox; the heroine, Alexandra Bergson, is a type of earth goddess; the theme is
the theme of the conquest of a hard country that had
dominated novels of the American settlement ever since
James Fenimore Cooper's *The Pioneers* in 1823. Miss
Cather's novel, in fact, is considerably slighter and sim-
pler than Cooper's of similar title.

In her third book, *The Song of the Lark* (1915), we
can see Miss Cather systematically and consciously working for the enlargement and complication of her theme.
The locale, at least in the beginning, is again Nebraska,
though she calls it Colorado; the chief character is again
a local girl of immigrant parentage, great promise, and
few advantages. But the antagonist here is not the earth,
and triumph is nothing so simple as the hewing of a farm
out of a hard country. To the problem of survival has
been added the problem of culture. Here the struggle
is involved with the training of Thea Kronborg's fine
voice; the effort of the novel is to explore how a talent
may find expression even when it appears in a crude little
railroad town on the plains, and how a frontier American
may lift himself from his traditionless, artless environment
to full stature as an artist and an individual.

Here we see developing the dynamism between old
world and new that occurs strongly again not only in *My
Antonia* but in *One of Ours* (1922), *The Professor's
House* (1925), *Death Comes for the Archbishop* (1927),
Shadows on the Rock (1931), and several of the short
stories such as "Neighbor Rosicki." It is as if Miss Cather
conceived the settlement of her country as a marriage between a simple, fresh, hopeful young girl and a charming,
worldly, but older man. Thea Kronborg's German music

teacher, Herr Wunsch, is the first of those cultivated and unhappy Europeans who people Miss Cather's fictions —exiles who though doomed themselves, pass on sources of life and art to the eager young of a new land. Thea, like Alexandra Bergson before her and Ántonia Shimerda later, is that best sort of second-generation American who learns or retains some of the intellectual and artistic tradition of Europe without losing the American freshness and without falling into the common trap of a commercial and limited "practicality." These are all success stories of sorts, and all reflect a very American groping toward a secure identity.

But even *The Song of the Lark* was not the precise song that lay in Willa Cather's voice. Or rather, it was the right tune, but she sang it imperfectly. The story of Thea Kronborg's struggle to become an opera singer is told with a realism so detailed that it is exhausting; and it ended by offending its author nearly as much as the pretentiousness of *Alexander's Bridge*. "Too much detail," she concluded later, "is apt, like any form of extravagance, to become slightly vulgar." She never tried a second time the "full-blooded" method: When the next book came along, "quite of itself, and with no direction from me, it took the road of *O Pioneers!*—not the road of *The Song of the Lark*."

The next one was, of course, *My Ántonia*. But the road it took was not quite exactly that of *O Pioneers!* For though the place is still Nebraska and the protagonist is still an immigrant girl contending with the handicaps of a physical and emotional transplanting, *My Ántonia* is a major novel where the earlier ones were trial efforts. *O Pioneers!* was truly simple; *My Ántonia* only looks simple. *The Song of the Lark* was cluttered in its attempt to deal with complexity; *My Ántonia* gives complexity the clean lines and suggestive subtlety of fine architecture.

One technical device which is fundamental to the greater concentration and suggestiveness of *My Ántonia* is the point of view from which it is told. Both of the earlier "Nebraska novels" had been reported over the protagonist's shoulder, with omniscient intrusions by the author. Here the whole story is told by a narrator, Jim Burden, a boyhood friend of Ántonia, later a lawyer representing the railroads. The use of the narrative mask permits Miss Cather to exercise her sensibility without obvious self-indulgence: Burden becomes an instrument of the selectivity that she worked for. He also permits the easy condensation and syncopation of time—an indispensable technical tool in a novel that covers more than 30 years and deals in a complex way with a theme of development. Finally, Jim Burden is used constantly as a suggestive parallel to Ántonia: he is himself an orphan and has been himself transplanted and is himself groping for an identity and an affiliation. In the process of understanding and commemorating Ántonia, he locates himself; we see the essential theme from two points, and the space between those points serves as a base line for triangulation.

The parallel is stressed from the beginning, when Jim, an orphan of ten, arrives in Black Hawk, Nebraska, on his way to live with his grandparents, and sees the immigrant Shimerda family huddling in bewilderment on the station platform, speaking their strange lost tongue. As he is driven to the ranch under a great unfamiliar sky, across a land that planes off mysteriously into darkness—"not a country, but the material out of which countries are made"—Jim feels so lost and strange and uprooted that he cannot even say the prayers that have been taught him back in Virginia. "Between that earth and sky I felt erased, blotted out."

For Jim, protected by his relatives, the strangeness soon wears away. For the Shimerdas, who have none of the tools or skills of farmers, no friends, no English, and who discover that the land they have been sold is bad and their house a sod cave, transplanting is a harsher trial, and harder on the old than on the young, and on the sensitive than on the dull. With the help of their neighbors the Burdens, the Shimerdas make a beginning, but before their first Christmas in the new land Papa Shimerda, gentle, helpless, homesick for the old life in Prague, has killed himself with a shotgun. Survival, which Miss Cather presents as a process of inevitable brutalization, is best managed by the grasping Mama Shimerda and her sullen son, Ambroz. The 14-year-old girl, Ántonia, pretty and intelligent and her father's darling, must put off any hope of schooling and become one of the breadwinners for her miserably poor family. The deprivation is symbolic; this is the deculturation enforced on the frontier. The one thing beautiful in her life, the thing she shares with Jim, is the land itself, the great sea of grass, the wild roses in the fence corners of spring, the mighty weathers, and the tiny things—insects and flowers and little animals—that the eye notices because on the plains there is so little else to take the attention.

Ántonia and Jim as children share a kind of Eden, but they are going toward different futures. At the end of the first long section, which is divided between the presentation of the hardships of an immigrant family and Miss Cather's delicate nostalgic evocation of the freedom and beauty of the untamed land, Jim and Ántonia are lying together on top of the Burdens' chickenhouse while a great electrical storm comes on, and "the felty beat of raindrops" begins in the dust. Why, Jim asks her, can't she always be "nice, like this?" Why must she all the time try to be like her brother Ambroz? "If I live here like you," Ántonia says, "that is different. Things will be easy for you. But they will be hard for us."

There are gradations in the penalties of exile; the most violently uprooted have the least chance. Section Two of the novel reinforces this idea by moving the action from the half-idyllic country to the limited and restricting little town of Black Hawk. In pages that forecast some of the attitudes of Sinclair Lewis' *Main Street* (1920), Miss Cather reveals the pettiness and snobbery, the vulgar commercialism, the cultural starvation, the forming class distinctions, the pathetic pleasures of a typical prairie town just beyond the pioneering stage. Ántonia, Lena Lingard, Tiny Soderball, and other Bohemian, Norwegian, and Swedish immigrant girls work as servants in the houses of the so-called "better families," and though they are snubbed by the town girls, they demonstrate in their vitality and health something sturdier and more admirable than the more advantaged can show. Those for whom "things are easy" develop less character than these girls deprived of school, forced to work at menial jobs, dedicating their wages to help their families back on the farm. They do not even know that Black Hawk is a deprived little hole, but throw themselves wholeheartedly into the town dances and into any pleasure and excitement their world affords. Miss Cather sums up both desire and deprivation in a brief winter scene:

> In the winter bleakness a hunger for colour came over people, like the Laplander's craving for fats and sugar. Without knowing why, we used to linger on the sidewalk outside the church when the lamps were lighted early for choir practice or prayermeeting, shivering and talking until our feet were like lumps of ice. The crude reds and greens and blues of that coloured glass held us there.

It is Jim Burden speaking, but he speaks even more for the "hired girls" than for himself, for he is not confined within Black Hawk's limitations as they are. For him there is more than crude colored glass; opportunity opens outward to the state university in the city of Lincoln. For Ántonia and the others there is only housework, the amorous advances of people like Wick Cutter, the town money lender, and the probability that eventually they will marry some farmer of their own immigrant background, who will work them like farm horses.

Part Three of *My Ántonia* has been objected to as a structural mistake, because it turns away from Ántonia and focuses on the university and city life of Jim Burden —on the opening of his mind, the passionate response he makes to books and ideas under the tutelage of a favorite professor, the quiet affair he has with Lena Lingard, who has set up in the city as a dressmaker. But the criticism seems based on too simplistic a view of the novel's intention. Though the title suggests that Ántonia is the focus of the book, the development from the symbolic beginning scene is traced through both Ántonia and Jim, and a good part of that theme of development is concerned with the possible responses to deprivation and to opportunity. We leave Ántonia in Book Three in order to return to her with more understanding later.

A high point of Jim's life in Lincoln is a performance of *Camille* that he and Lena Lingard attend. Like so many of Miss Cather's scenes, it expands effortlessly out of the particular and into the symbolic. The performance is shabby, the actors are broken-down, but to Jim the play is magic. Its bright illusion concentrates for him everything that he hopes for as he starts east to Harvard to continue his studies, going farther from his country, back toward the intellectual and artistic things that his own country has left behind or has only in second-rate and vulgarized forms. It is worth observing that Jim Burden leaves Nebraska on a note of illusion.

Section Four returns us to Ántonia and to Black Hawk. Back after two years at Harvard, Jim hears that in his absence Ántonia has eloped with a railroad conductor and that after being deceived and abandoned she has returned to her brother Ambroz's farm to bear her child and work in the fields like a man. The contrast between her pitiful failure and Jim's growing opportunities is deliberate; so is the trick of letting Jim come back to Ántonia little by little, first through the stories told of her by townspeople and only later in person. When he does finally go to the farm to see her, the deliberate structural split that began with Book Three is finally mended. Their lives will continue to run in different channels, but they have rediscovered the "old times" that they have in common, the things that by now Ántonia could not bear to leave. "I like to be where I know every stack and tree, and where all the ground is friendly," she says. Her bond is with the land—

she all but *is* the land—while Jim will go on to law school and to occupations and associations unimaginable to her. Again Miss Cather catches a significant moment in a reverberating image, to show both the difference and the intimate relationship between these two:

As we walked homeward across the fields, the sun dropped and lay like a great golden globe in the low west. While it hung there, the moon rose in the east, as big as a cart-wheel, pale silver and streaked with rose colour, thin as a bubble or a ghost-moon. For five, perhaps ten minutes, the two luminaries confronted each other across the level land, resting on opposite edges of the world.

"I'll come back," Jim says, leaving Ántonia, and she replies, "Perhaps you will. But even if you don't, you're here, like my father." Because we must give scenes like these more than realistic value, we recognize here an insistence not only on the shared beauty of childhood in the new land, but on the other tradition that is going to go on operating in Ántonia's life, the gift of her father with his gentleness and his taste. In Ántonia, new world and old world, nature and nurture, meet as they meet in Jim, but in different proportions and with different emphasis.

That union of two worlds is made explicit in Book Five, when 20 years later Jim Burden returns to Nebraska again and finds Ántonia married to an amiable, half-successful Bohemian farmer, with a brood of healthy boys. She is no longer an eager girl, but a worn woman. But the same warmth of spirit still glows in her, and her life that had been half wrecked has been put back together. In most ways, hers is an American family; but within the family they speak only Czech, and thus something of Papa Shimerda, something of Bohemia, is kept—something related to those strangenesses that Jim Burden had noted as a small boy: the dry brown chips he saw the Shimerdas nibbling, that were dried mushrooms picked in some far-off Bohemian forest; and the way Mama Shimerda, given title to a cow by Jim's grandfather, seized his hand in a totally un-American gesture and kissed it. A partly-remembered but valued tradition and an empty land have fused and begun to be something new.

As for Jim Burden, we understand at last that the name Willa Cather chose for him was not picked by accident. For Jim not only, as narrator, carries the "burden" or tune of the novel; he carries also the cultural burden that Willa Cather herself carried, the quintessentially American burden of remaking in the terms of a new place everything that makes life graceful and civilized. To become a European or an easterner is only to reverse and double the exile. The education that lured Jim Burden away from Nebraska had divided him against himself, as Willa Cather was divided. Like people, the education that comes from elsewhere must be modified to fit a new environment. In becoming a man of the world, Jim Burden discovers that he has almost forgotten to be a man from Nebraska. It is Ántonia, who now achieves some of that quality of earth goddess that Alexandra Bergson had had in *O Pioneers!*, who reminds him that no matter where his mind has been, his heart has always been here.

Jim Burden at the end of the novel is in the same position that Willa Cather was in when she finally found the people and themes and country that she was "born to write." The final paragraph is like the closing of a door, shutting in things that until now have been exposed or scattered. As Jim walks through the country he stumbles upon a stretch of the old pioneer wagon road of his childhood:

> This was the road over which Ántonia and I came on the night when we got off the train at Black Hawk and were bedded down in the straw, wondering children, being taken we knew not whither. I had only to close my eyes to hear the rumbling of the wagons in the dark, and to be again overcome by that obliterating strangeness. The feelings of that night were so near that I could reach out and touch them with my hand. I had the sense of coming home to myself, and of having found out what a little circle man's experience is. For Ántonia and for me, this had been the road of Destiny; had taken us to those early accidents of fortune which predetermined for us all that we can ever be. Now I understood that the same road was to bring us together again. Whatever we had missed, we possessed together the precious, the incommunicable past.

It is difficult not to hear in that the voice of Willa Cather, who like Jim left raw Nebraska to become a citizen of the world, and like him was drawn back. Jim Burden is more than a narrative device: he is an essential part of the theme, a demonstration of how such an American may reconcile the two halves of himself. And Ántonia is more than a woman and a character. Jim describes her toward the end as "a rich mine of life, like the founders of early races."

Miss Cather, who did not believe in laboring a point any more than she believed in over-furnishing a novel, clearly wanted us to take away that image of Ántonia. A mine of life, the mother of races, a new thing forming itself in hardship and hope, but clinging to fragments of the well-loved old. Hence *My* Ántonia—any American's Ántonia, Willa Cather's Ántonia. No writer ever posed that essential aspect of the American experience more warmly, with more nostalgic lyricism, or with a surer understanding of what it means.

c. The West Emphatic:
Bernard DeVoto

If I had any temptation to turn this memoir into a testimonial, the memory of Benny DeVoto's round, brown, goggled, sardonic eye would be enough to strike the impulse dead. Being from Utah, he knew about testimonial meetings. It is better simply to record a little about him and try to understand him; praise and blame came to roost in Benny's loft so constantly that from his earliest youth he must have heard them quarreling at his eaves. He earned the one and risked the other, and I do not need to add to either. And if I address myself somewhat personally to the pleasure of talking about him, I do not apologize, for though in November 1960 he is five years dead, he is still personal to me.

Begin at the beginning of my knowledge of him. One morning in 1926, when I was a freshman at the University of Utah, I came into the English building just as a professor yanked open his office door and hurled a magazine into the hall. The offensive journal was *The American Mercury*, about which even I, and even in Salt Lake City, had heard, and the obviously offending part of it was an article entitled "Utah," by Bernard DeVoto. It was a calculated piece of mayhem that out-Menckened Mencken. Though I have not looked at it for thirty-five years, I have a vivid recollection that it said dreadful things about the state where I lived. Apparently we were the ultimate, final and definitive home of the Boob. We were owned by

Boston banks and the Copper Trust, and bamboozled by the Church of Jesus Christ of Latter-day Saints, an institution whose beliefs would bring a baboon to incredulous laughter but whose business acuteness had made it a director of a hundred corporations. This Utah occupied the fairest mountains and valleys on the footstool and grew the best peaches ever grown and had a history of dedication and heroism, in however dubious a cause. But it lived now, as in its founding years, by fantasy, myth, and wishful thinking, and it demonstrated all too faithfully the frontier curve from piety through property to vulgarity. It was conventional, stuffy, provincial, hypocritical, deluded; it had never produced a writer, sculptor, painter, statesman, soldier, scholar, or distinguished man of any sort, it was terrified of any expression of mind, there were not fifteen people in the whole state for whom signing their own names were not an effort.

And so on, a considerable mouthful, spit out with a vigor and venom that only the twenties or Bernard DeVoto, or the two in combination, could have generated. I did not then know anything about the Village Virus or any of the robust literary antibiotics that were being used against it; nor did I know any of the personal reasons that made Mr. DeVoto so angry at Utah and especially his home city of Ogden. I simply let myself be swept up in the happy vehemence of his rhetoric, though even then I suppose I must have understood that a lot of what he said was exaggerated and unjust. If he got a few innocent bystanders, I was willing to sacrifice them for the pleasure of looking upon the more deserving corpses.

As an introduction to DeVoto, that article could have been improved upon, and DeVoto himself never thought enough of it to include it in any of his collections of essays. Nevertheless it expressed him. It had his chosen and almost compulsive subject, the West. It had his habit of challenge and overstatement set off from a launching pad of fact. It had his frequent mixture of the lyrical (when dealing with scenery, say, or peaches, or the beauty of Utah girls) and the vituperative (when dealing with most aspects of society, education, institutions, interests, delusions, or public characters). It had also his incomparable knack of infuriating people. But learn one trick, which most of his readers and all of his friends learned quickly enough: learn to discount him ten to twenty percent for showmanship, indignation, and the inevitable warping power of his gift for language, and there remained one of the sanest, most acute, most rooted-in-the-ground observers of American life that we have had. He wrote dozens of essays out of indignation or with short-term objectives; these he seldom collected, but let them die. The ones that were close to his considered convictions he kept, and often revised. When he caught himself in exaggeration or error, as he did when he came to collect some of his early essays on education, he cheerfully ate crow. For despite a reputation as a wild man or an ogre, he was open always to the persuasion of facts. He seldom dealt in the outrageous merely for the sake of outraging, though he knew the dramatizing value of shock, and used it. His exaggerations were likely to be extensions of observed truth; and when he was wrong, as he surely sometimes was, he was wrong in the right directions. If he said, in effect, that American civilization was sleeping with every bum in town, there was almost certainly *someone* in her bed.

He had a gift for indignation—which means only that

he believed some things passionately and could not contain himself when he saw them endangered by knaves or fools; and however ironic and detached he tried to be, he could become a Galahad in a cause that enlisted as much of him as did the conservation and public lands fights of the late 1940's and 1950's. He began and remained an unfriendly critic of Mormonism, but his half-Mormon heritage and background had bred a good deal of Mormon moralizing into him. Even his peculiar brand of eloquence, at once biblical, orotund, and salty, is related to the eloquence of some celebrated Mormon preachers such as J. Golden Kimball. Like Kimball, Benny could thunder colloquially. Once at Bread Loaf, Vermont, I heard him deliver a sort of lay sermon—let us say it was on the necessity of acknowledging what is under our noses, one of his recurrent themes—and in the course of his talk he got so worked up he brought on a terrible electrical storm that knocked the lights out. No one was in the least surprised; it seemed the most natural thing in the world, the anticipable consequence of the pulpit oratory that went on thundering out of the dark.

But that was much later, a full quarter century after that angry boy, talented and educated beyond his native environment, had fled Ogden with the manuscript of his first novel under his arm. When he wrote his diatribe against Utah, and by extension the whole Rocky Mountain West, he was a young instructor at Northwestern, the author of two novels, beginning to be known as a writer for the magazines, an angry young man full of the heady rebellions of the twenties, with talents that he knew were notable, and with fears of himself that sucked him down into spells of despair and darkness. He was as hot with aspira-

tion as a turpentined mule, an ardent, extravagant, romantic, idealistic, indignant young man with a future. And despite his fears about himself and his fits of depression, he
had some notion what that future would involve.

Among the DeVoto Papers at Stanford University is a
letter to Melville Smith dated October 22, 1920. In it
young DeVoto's natural ebullience is compounded by the
fact that when he wrote it he was recovering from a dis-
appointment in love and from a perhaps consequent nervous illness. Nevertheless it may be taken seriously. It was
Benny's lifetime habit to bounce high when he was thrown
hard, and to fall farther the higher he bounced. "I burst,"
he said:

> I burst with creative criticism of America—I have at last
> found a kind of national self-consciousness. Not the
> mighty anvil-on-which-is-hammered-out-the-future-of-the
> world. Still less the damned-bastard-parvenu-among-the-
> nations. But I have begun to see American history with
> some unity, with some perspective, with some meaning
> . . . to dare to think from cause to effect, from the past
> to the present and future, always with this curious new
> sense of yea-saying youth.
>
> I do not commit the historic folly, from Washington
> Irving to Van Wyck Brooks, of hearing fiddles tuning up
> all over America . . . But I have dared at last to believe
> that the Nation begins to emerge from adolescence into
> young manhood, that hereafter the colossal strength may
> begin to count for the better, as well as for the worse.
> That indeed we have come to say yea, at last.
>
> And in the facts which alone can show whether we take
> the turn, or in the study of them, I shall, I think, spend my
> vigorous years . . . I believe I have found something into

which I may pour that arresting, God-awful emulsion that is I.

Even the friendliest reader will find both self-dramatizing and turgidity in that manifesto, and Benny is surely a figure of the twenties as he says yea to America with one side of his mouth while saying nay to Ogden, the Village, with the other. The earnestness, however, is real, the dedication is real, the repudiation of certain effusive ideas is real (even a favorite whipping boy is anticipated), and the impulse toward history, toward the study of cause and effect in the making of American civilization, is significant. Young Milton impatiently strengthening his wings for broader flights, hypnotized by the novel that was the mirror of his emotional turmoil (its title was "Cock Crow," and the manuscript is among his papers at Stanford), he countered emotional strain by dreaming of an effort more stringently intellectual than fiction. Constitutionally a believer and a yea-sayer, but already suspicious of literary criticism and other forms of "beautiful thinking," he had even at twenty-three a faith in knowledge, in facts; but there were some facts that he did not yet know, one of them being that it was the West, which he scorned, that he most wanted to say yea to. During the next thirty-five years, the "vigorous years" of his dedication, he would be many things—novelist, professor, editor, historian, pamphleteer, critic, and under a half dozen aliases, hack writer —with such range and in such profusion that no neat classification can hold him. Visible in his God-awful emulsion along with the scissors and snails and puppy dogs' tails, as real an ingredient as the irritable idealism and the scorn and the skinless self-doubt, would be a belligerent professionalism. He would pride himself on being a pro, would wear the discipline of deadlines and editorial specifications like a hair shirt, because he despised literary phonies, narcissistic artists, public confessors, gushers, long-hairs, and writers of deathless prose; and he would despise these because he feared them in himself. All through Benny's life, a submerged romantic, a literary Harvard boy from Copey's class, would send up embarrassing bubbles of gas, and one way to cover these moments would be the overt belch of professionalism. Professionalism would lead him, too, to take on many kinds of literary jobs—articles, introductions, magazine stories and serials, political speech-writing, reviews—and he would work himself punishingly. In self-defense he would affect to mistrust the imagination and value the hard head, hard work, hard facts; but certain things would not change, he would retain his contradictions.

His repudiation of his western birthright would not stick; the West would not let him go so casually. He would have to come back and worry its complacent provincials and its Two-Gun Desmonds, deflate its myths, expose its economics and its politics, and tell its story in half a hundred essays, half a dozen novels, several works of criticism, and a monumental series of histories. Debunking or correcting western myths, scorning the things the West had become, he would continue to love, to the point of passion, western openness, freedom, air, scenery, violence; and would accept some of the myths as eagerly as the most illiterate cowhand reading *Western Stories* in the shade of the cookhouse. In all his literary jobs he would be a wholly competent workman; in some, as in his hymn to alcohol called *The Hour,* he would be delightful; in many, as in his pamphleteering essays, he would be splendid. But when he wrote history, when he brought together the whole story of the West as frontier, as dream and discovery, exploration and confrontation, he would be magnificent.

The variety of DeVoto's literary work reflects intellectual and physical vitality, not a groping. Though he did many things on the side, he found his field early, worked at it steadily, and brought it to a triumphant bumper crop in his trilogy of histories. But in thus fulfilling the somewhat incoherent program he had set for himself in 1920, he did not quite comprehend all America as cause and effect, promise and payoff. Not even his appetite for work could accomplish so much—and nostalgia, moreover, is a local emotion. Nostalgia, the release of dammed images, memories, feelings, would be necessary for his imaginative re-creation of the frontier. Whenever Benny's mind and emotions could be brought into phase, when Cambridge could bridge time and space back to Weber Canyon, he wrote as he was manifestly born to write, and produced what a continued residence in the West would have made difficult, but what exile made inevitable.

Without committing the error of imagining an Ordeal of Benny DeVoto, one must insist on the importance of alienation and exile. He was born on a frontier as the frontier was passing, when there was no future for frontiersmen, and division and doubt were in him from birth, for his mother was the daughter of a pioneer Mormon farmer (see "The Life of Jonathan Dyer") and his father, the son of an Italian cavalry officer, was an intellectual, a Catholic, "a man of great brilliance and completely paralyzed will," a total outsider. To go to a Catholic school in a Mormon community, to be the only boy in a roomful of girls, to be brilliant and bookish where brilliance and bookishness had (he came to think) neither audience nor function nor reward—these were only aggravations of a dislocation already begun. Of the seven children of his grandfather, not one stayed on the farm or in the Mormon Church; of all the children and grandchildren, "only the novelist, a romantic," ever revisited the home place after the death of the man who had grubbed it out of the sage-brush and irrigated it into fertility.

A divided inheritance can give a boy parallax, he has a base for triangulation and judgment, but he will never be quite at home in his home. And brilliance, especially when associated with insecurity and assertiveness, can isolate a child as effectively as if the disapproving community had shut him in the closet of his mind. It was in his mind that he lived, there and in the canyons of the Wasatch that let him play at independence, freedom, and self-reliance. The limitations and frustrations of Ogden could be transcended on lonely expeditions, by the practice of partly imaginary survival skills, by feats that tested him where there was no chance of being seen and humiliated, by the comfort of wilderness, by the whistle of marmots in mountain meadows, by the eternal sound of mountain water always passing and always there. The most lyrical of his 1920 letters to Melville Smith describes just such a healing expedition. Many years later, in Cambridge, I used sometimes to get desperate telephone calls from Benny: "Come on and walk me around Fresh Pond!" And when we were spending summers in Vermont there would come letters: "Is there anywhere on your place where a man can walk—walk a long way, off the roads, in the woods? Is there any place where a man can shoot a .22?"

It is entirely possible that like many lonely children young Bernard DeVoto didn't recognize his trouble as loneliness, but I am sure it was. That shooting, for instance. Shooting was his favorite boyhood sport—and there is no lonelier sport unless it is rowing. But where rowing is mindless, subduing body and mind to a rhythm, lulling identity to sleep, shooting is another thing. Marksmanship can not only fill empty time, it can feed fantasy, for you can put any face you want on the black dot of the bullseye, and the process of shooting holes in it is not only skill, which is comforting, but revenge, which is sweet.

Because I grew up on a frontier even cruder than Weber Canyon, and was halved and quartered away from wholeness at least as early as Benny DeVoto, I think I can imagine him as a boy. Probably he was a little brattish, he showed off before girls, teachers, and God; he was contentious, captious, critical, quick to scorn; he affected superiorities and was constantly in controversies and in his bad spells was desolated that some people didn't like him. He was devoted to certain people, ideas, books, with a fanatical devotion, an ardent, unreasonable extremity. He got crushes on girls and for a week or a month was in a frenzy to immolate himself, and within another week or month had discovered that the blonde goddess was dimwitted. Nevertheless his real friendships were affectionate, lasting, and utterly loyal—there have been few people to whom friendship meant more. He read furiously, always beyond his years, and if he used his reading to impress people, that would not be strange. The fact is, he couldn't *not* read. His brain was as busy as a wood-pecker, it pecked at him all day and at night perched ominously just above the lintel of sleep, as disturbing as Poe's raven. Probably even at ten or twelve he had migraines—certainly he had them later. He was a problem to his parents and a terror to the conventional and a despair to his teachers, and he learned early, being an outsider, and different, to fling the acid of his scorn into the face of provincial Ogden, already too small a world for him.

He tried the University of Utah for a year, and that too, in 1914–1915, was such a small world that he stirred it like a porpoise in a Paddock Pool. After one year he was off to Harvard, and now he found himself for the first time in a world profoundly, self-consciously, intellectual. If he did not quite grapple with Greek and Hebrew verbs all day and then take a walk in Mount Auburn Cemetery for recreation, he did the equivalent. He devoured books. He was inspired by great teachers, including Copey, and he met people of his own age whom he could not cow: boys as bright as he, better read, better disciplined, boys who tamed some of his exuberances and shamed him out of some of his provincial prejudices, but who at the same time—and this would be sweet—found him something new and special, amusing or arresting, a wild man from the West, a sensitive intellectual out of the howling wilderness of Utah. He never quite got over the role—and the role, observe, was a double one.

At Harvard he crossed a sort of intellectual South Pass the way it was first crossed in fact—eastward—and saw something of what opened up beyond. On the dubious side, he was corroborated in his literary and ide-

[260]

alistic posturing: ("Thank God for Harvard. It has given me a thorough-going contempt for these externals. Harvard took me and turned me inward, showed me the heart of things, set burning a lamp in the sanctuary of the ideal. Harvard has shown me that the flesh is nothing beside the spirit . . ."). But he learned too that his native West was interesting, even romantic, to Cambridge eyes and to the eyes of nostalgia, and that it was a splendid place for illustrating pure aspiration dragged down by philistinism. He began to play aficionado about his country, as a hundred thousand western boys have played it in eastern colleges. Being Benny DeVoto, he would have taken the trouble to back up his brags or his diatribes with reading; somewhere very early he began to read western history, geography, exploration, travel, and he read them avidly all his life. (Once he told me cynically that as a journalist he had learned to make a fact go a long way, which was true. It was also true that few people ever collect as many facts about their specialty as he collected about the West. He was loaded, a learned man, and he had the ease with his information that great familiarity brings. In Robert Frost's phrase, he could swing what he knew.)

At Harvard too (I am guessing, but I would back my guess with a bet) he was confirmed in a habit that regional folklore and personal insecurity had already formed in him: the belief or pretense that true vigor, including intellectual vigor, is always a little bit crude and aggressive. During the course of his career he offended some people with the consequences of that assumption, which remained part of his critical method. He scared a lot of others with his cartwheeling and shooting, and some of them never did comprehend that often he was only riding up in his warpaint to shake hands.

Finally Harvard must have encouraged him, in his role of western wild man, to hunt the picturesque and sulphurous phrasing of a man who split a plank every time he spit. Impolite western literature furnished him excellent models, including Mark Twain; there have been few if any moderns who could handle spreadeagle invective as Benny could.

Whatever poses he adopted or roles he assumed, the self-doubting youth was still there, and would remain there. Among the DeVoto Papers is a series of letters written to his parents when he was in OCS camp at Camp Lee, Virginia, in 1918. Even to one who knew and loved Benny well, they are a revelation. As a son, however much unrest he might have given his parents (and he was fond of remarking later that the only torture worse than being a parent was being a child), he was an agonizedly affectionate son. In those letters he throbs and yearns and aspires in a way that begins by being almost embarrassing and ends by being touching. If there was ever a boy who needed love, faith, praise, reassurance, and who hoped to deserve them, hoped humbly to earn them, it was he. The need for the safety and reassurance of friends, too, persisted throughout his life. His letters were often intensely personal, a pouring out of aspiration, confession, self-analysis, self-blame, a release of gas from the submerged affection-craving boy, freed in the privacy of love or friendship from the necessity of deceptive belches and hoots and catcalls.

One of the tenderest things I know about Benny—one of the tenderest things I ever heard about anybody—is unfortunately sequestered in the Stanford Library vaults for a good many years because of the personal nature of some of its references. This is the correspondence between Benny and Kate Sterne, a shut-in tubercular patient who had written him a fan letter to which Benny, as he always did, courteously replied. She wrote again, he replied again, and before long he was periodically relaxing after a hard day's work by writing her long eruptive midnight letters. He took down his hair and said what he thought about those who had offended or slighted or pleased him, he wept for lost battles and exulted for victories, he analyzed people and events and policies and regions, assessed reputations, let air out of balloons. The correspondence continued from 1933 until 1944, when Kate Sterne died. Some day it will make a touching and wonderful book, because the invalid became for Benny the most intimate confidante, and his letters constitute a secret, indiscreet, uninhibited diary of eleven of his most active years. What is more to the point here, they kept Kate Sterne alive and mentally engaged long after she might have been expected to be dead. He dedicated *The Year of Decision, 1846* to her, he told her things that he would never have put in print and that he perhaps never told another living soul. And he never met her, not so much as to say good day.

To young Bernard DeVoto, wild intellectual from the Rocky Mountains, rebel, iconoclast, and idealist, the war came like a tornado that uproots trees and houses. He enlisted in a tumult of patriotism. It is hard to remember and believe the faith that young men once had that they might save the world for democracy. Benny had that faith, had it like *paralysis agitans*. Quite seriously, he was ready to die with an inspiring phrase on his lips. Accentuating the spirit, he immediately began a novel, writing it in his head because boot camp gave him no time for pen and paper, "a novel of my own country, the wide and ample theatre of the hills, the peaks and valleys, the mountain streams, the railroads, above all the people . . . If ever there was a labor of love it is the construction of this book, into which I am putting all the knowledge that has come to me . . . Already I have written much of a unique book, of a book which touches depths of feeling I had not know[n], which is the expression of my most outstretched aspiration . . ."

It does not sound like the DeVoto we know. And yet this was the tender thing that never quit living in Benny's shell. From Camp Lee he wrote asking his family to preserve his letters for their possible historical value, and he corresponded thereafter with posterity's perhaps-critical eye on him: "What kind of a man do these missives show me to be? Is there any hope, do you think, for my ultimate salvation?" He took pride in bearing up under heat and fatigue, and we see suddenly that in Ogden this wild man was probably thought a sissy: "I am no weakling after all, despite the sneers I have known in the past." As the camp progressed and he found he could measure himself against the others without apology, he grew cocky, and out of one letter scrawled in a tent in the breathless Virginia heat bursts a salvo of pure DeVoto, in color and tone, exuberance and hyperbole, a foretaste of the bumptiousness of his maturity:

> What need shall I have of a wife? I have learned to cook my meals and wash my dishes, to make my bed and sweep the floor, to clean, wash, and mend my clothes, to arrange

all my belongings and possessions with a neatness and accuracy unknown to women. Why should I ever call a doctor? I know how to keep myself trim and healthy, know the infallibility of iodine and C.C. pills—the Army's own medicines—and know all the approved methods of treating every injury from dysentery to disembowellment, from sunstroke to a cracked knuckle. Practical rubbing up against all kinds of men, the lectures of many officers, and the clean thoughts of a healthy body have taught me more ethics and morality than any minister possibly could. I am or am becoming astronomer and surveyor, Indian scout and clerk, statistician and prospector, woodsman, artist, farmer—every trade and employment within the seven seas. I dare go alone into the wilderness confident that, within a week, I could build me a forty room villa with lawns, garden and garage: fit it out with furniture; grow, kill, and cook my own food; set up a religion and code of laws; establish industry and train an army; organize departments of public health and finance—and, in short, build me a State with no other tools than an intrenching spade and a cartridge belt.

Posterity might wink, but the cockiness, like some other DeVoto exaggerations, was built on facts. He graduated 7th—apologizing to his parents for not doing better—in a class of 150. But he did not get overseas; he was too good a rifle shot, he had improved the loneliness of Ogden to too good purpose, and he wound up in Camp Perry, Ohio, as a musketry instructor.

He did not know it, but that was as close as he would ever get to going abroad. He would make certain Prohibition-years excursions into Canada in search of the rye and bourbon that he called the two greatest American inventions ("How is it that every time I go to Canada the word gets around the neighborhood by osmosis and I have a hundred solicitous friends?") and in the later years of World War II he would suffer himself to be inoculated against typhoid, tetanus, yellow fever, and other plagues, preparatory to going to Africa to write the history of the African campaigns for the War Department. But something happened to that. He did not go, and he never got off the continent of North America. It was just as well. On that continent he could be an expert and a specialist.

After the Armistice Lieutenant DeVoto went back to Harvard to finish, and was told by a member of the faculty not to take himself too seriously, and resolved to follow that advice. After that he returned to Ogden to write his first novel ("a disgustingly immature production for one who asserts so much maturity as I"), to fall in love and be jilted ("The fiction of romantic love is not likely again to impose on me"), to address the University Club on American liberty and get himself expelled, to conduct with vigor his war against all that Ogden stood for ("Do not forget that at best I am a spore in Utah, not adapted to the environment, a maverick who may not run with the herd, unbranded, given an ill name. These people are not my people, their God is not mine . . ."), to suffer a nervous collapse ("I have a peculiar capacity for suffering in those areas of personality which neither anatomy nor psychology has yet been able to describe— areas inextricably tangled with religion and sex and faith and poetry"), and in general to take himself very seriously indeed. He was emancipated by an offer to teach English at Northwestern, and so fled the Babylonian captivity of his native city. He found places where his mind could work effectively, if not in peace—Evanston, New York, especially Cambridge—and settled into furious pursuit of the distinction that he yearned for. From there on, it is the career we know.

The weight and effect of a maverick's career is not immediately assessable, and in DeVoto's case the assessment, when it comes, will have to be a composite one, for no single biographer or critic is likely to be able to follow him into all the corners of American life where he had authority or exerted influence. Nevertheless the outlines of his lasting reputation seem already reasonably clear. At least it may be worth while to indicate one's personal preferences, to state what seems most important as one looks back over the work of a man who remains so stubbornly alive. When he died, one's first thought after the shock of loss was "Who will do his work? Who can carry on what he did?" For it was never so apparent as when death stopped it that for many years he had done at least three men's work, and that it would take three very good men indeed to replace him—that in fact there was not an adequate replacement for any fraction of him.

As a novelist he does not seem truly important, though it was novelist he set out to be. He used to tell students that until a man had written five novels he had no right to call himself a novelist, by which he meant a pro. By that definition Benny qualified, for under his own name he published six and wrote a seventh and part of an eighth, and under the pseudonym of John August he wrote four others. He made a clear distinction between his serious novels and those he wrote as serial entertainments for the magazines—not that he wanted to play demi-virgin, but that his magazine serials were frankly written for money and he did not value them. His serious novels he did value; the inscriptions to his father in copies of his first three books indicate awareness that performance has not quite lived up to desire, but they insist that these are honest books, as true to fact as he can make them, as good as he can do. They also reflect his preoccupation with the West, for *The Crooked Mile* and *The House of Sun-Goes-Down* chronicle the development of a western town not unlike Ogden, *The Chariot of Fire* is the story of a frontier prophet and martyr not unlike Joseph Smith, and even the last one, *Mountain Time*, which begins in a New York hospital, brings its hero Cy Kinsman back to his western birthplace for a sort of reconciliation of the exile that Benny himself had gone through.

These are all honest books and competent ones, and except for *The Crooked Mile*, which sprawls rather badly toward the end, they are well-carpentered, witty, packed with observation and ideas. But for me at least the thrill of life is not in them. The eloquence sounds a little wrong when put in the mouths of fictional characters, the dialogue often glitters but seldom falls exactly right on the ear. There is some dreams-of-glory posturing, especially in the early ones: Benny's heroes have a facility for attracting gorgeous women and for knocking down stupids, sots, and other denizens of the modern West. *Mountain Time*, which seems to me the best of the five novels, contains a detailed and persuasive look at the medical profession, besides characters who move and talk with a great deal more naturalness. But Cy Kinsman in that novel tends to repeat Gordon Abbey of *The Crooked Mile*, and the paralysis of the will that marks them both seems more a contrivance to delay a denouement than something the characters couldn't help.

In short, the fault in these novels seems to me to be that they lean too hard on contrivance, they never quite become life, they are tainted—*et ego peccavi*, Benny!—with the literary, a thing that Benny himself despised. The romantic idealist of the youthful letters, the literary young man from Copey's class, shows through more clearly in the novels than in any of the other writings, and it is an inescapable fact that DeVoto is less sure in his handling of emotional situations in the novels than he is, say, in the reporting of Mark Twain's *Wanderjahre*, of the hardships of the Mormon migration, or the ecology of fur hunters. *Mark Twain's America*, which came between his third and fourth novels, showed him for the first time at something like his full powers. He must himself have recognized that he wrote much better, more authoritatively, more pungently, more importantly, when he could not only write out of the western experience that he knew best, but when he could speak in his own tone of voice, without the ventriloquisms of fiction. Then information, lyricism, irony, indignation, the habit of hyperbole and picturesque phasemaking, could all come together, and Benny's emotional attitudes, though they are evident, are evident at some distance; they inform the facts but are not dwelt on; they produce something very like the tone and inflection of a voice, the stop and flow and rise and fall and thunder and hush of a knowing, intelligent, committed, and unremittingly interested observer.

DeVoto's first significant notice came not because of his novels but because of his essays in *American Mercury*, *Harper's*, and other magazines. They are the beginning of his lifelong career in social criticism and pamphleteering; the essay on Utah that I read in 1926 was one of them, and it, like dozens of others, was never collected and is not likely to be. Typical is what happened to a whole series of angry essays on education written during the five years at Northwestern. Reviewing them in 1936 for possible inclusion in *Forays and Rebuttals*, Benny found most of them "outrageously over-simplified" and others, such as the much anthologized "The Co-Eds: God Bless Them," to be "in some part untrue, in greater part obvious and irrelevant, and in no part profound." Less than a third of his essay production up to that time seemed to him worth reprinting, and his judgment was probably right. But even with a casualty rate of 66 percent, DeVoto's essays in social criticism, including the magnificent series on western land problems and conservation reprinted in *The Easy Chair* just before his death, retain an astonishing vitality. I doubt that any body of like essays from the twenties, thirties, and forties would prove, on examination, to have dated so little, and some of them in their time were of robust usefulness in causes that I cannot but think good.

Who spoke any more forthrightly or effectively against irresponsible Congressional red-hunting than Benny did in "Guilt by Distinction," a mordant undressing of the Reece Committee? Who among us did not cheer when in "Due Notice to the FBI" Benny spoke our minds? ("Representatives of the FBI and of other official investigating bodies have questioned me, in the past, about a number of people and I have answered their questions. That's over. . . . If it is my duty as a citizen to tell what I know about someone, I will perform that duty under subpoena, in open

court, before that person and his attorney . . .") Whether
he was fighting the battle of freedom or protesting the
pasteurization of cheese, exposing the land-grab plans of
western stock interests or bringing to bear lessons of history upon the problems of the present, DeVoto as essayist
performed public services greater than those of most public servants, and during his twenty years in the "Easy
Chair" he built up not only an effective information organization but an enormous and respectful countrywide
audience. When students of the future come to sift the
scores of essays that he threw off at white heat all his
life, a good many are going to be found to be not only
reprintable but as near as such things come to being permanent, a part of the tradition, a part of the literature. "I
stand on the facts," Benny said about his rejected education articles. "I should not care to stand on all the conclusions." Of a couple of fat bookfuls of his total production he could stand on the conclusions as well, and on some
of them he would not even have to grant the customary
discount.

The essayist who began as an amusing wild man grew
into one of the most respected voices of the public conscience. His parallel and interwoven career as a literary
critic does not show the same upward and rising curve.
He fell away from literary criticism, in fact, as he fell
away from fiction, because at bottom he was suspicious of
it. His first successful book, *Mark Twain's America,* he
called neither history nor biography nor literary criticism,
though it was in some part all three, but an "essay in the
correction of ideas." In that book his mind was speaking
not only against a critical and psychological theory and
not only against Van Wyck Brooks, but against a whole

[271]

habit of mind and—never forget it—against the irresponsible literary romantic in his own house. An anti-literary
bias, a sometimes belligerent philistinism, marked much of
his criticism and marred some of it. Whether he was at-
tacking Malcolm Cowley, in a review of *Exile's Return*,
for assuming that the expatriates constituted a whole
American writing generation, or whether he was tempes-
tuously rejecting Thomas Wolfe's undiscipline in "Genius
is Not Enough," he hammered at the need for knowledge,
information, facts, and on top of those, professional discipline. Never having been abroad, he looked with skepti-
cism upon the exiles; too often feeling truly lost, he did
not want to be part of any lost generation. And anyway,
his exile did not reach so far. He had found in New England an intellectual climate that he liked and in which he
could work; and in the American scene, past and present,
he had found adequate subject matter. Not to find these
things seemed to him a literary affectation; and he knew
something about literary poses, for he had been there.

So the best of Benny's criticism is related to the most
American of all our writers, Mark Twain, of whose papers
he was curator from 1938 to 1946. Already addicted to
the disciplines of history, he based *Mark Twain's America*,
as he said, solidly on the works themselves, as he based
Mark Twain in Eruption and *Mark Twain at Work* solidly
on the manuscript papers. Even in his examination of the
despairing backgrounds of *The Mysterious Stranger*, one
of the most speculative of his literary studies, he built his
speculation on a foundation of manuscripts, false starts,
scraps, letters; and when he started what other scholars
have turned into a continuing search for the key to the

composition of *Huckleberry Finn* he proceeded from evidence, not from a theory.

All his life, that is, he had a quarrel with the habit of making literary judgments about life, what he finally came to call the "literary fallacy." The little book by that title, first given as a series of lectures at the University of Indiana, was the summation of ideas implicit or explicit in all his criticism from *Mark Twain's America* on, and it more or less marked DeVoto's retirement from literary criticism. It is a book which must be taken at the customary discount, and it precipitated a painful literary quarrel. Also, in some eyes it marked Benny as a philistine. If being a philistine means valuing facts and suspecting attitudinizers, he was; a belligerent one of a kind it is healthy to have around. Presented with dream boats, he was likely to make pragmatic tests such as stepping on the starter to see if the motor ran.

Philistine or not, he was a healthy and skeptical influence in a profession likely to be full of hot air; Mark Twain criticism could use him right now. Though he was perhaps somewhat less important as a literary critic than as a gadfly of the public conscience, he was still a critic of range, depth, vigor, and a consistent point of view, and in the area which he made his specialty he was major. But in neither social criticism nor literary criticism was he so important as in history. There he brought off something monumental, massive, grandly conceived and beautifully controlled, a three-volume history of the West as imagination and reality and realization. *The Course of Empire*, *Across the Wide Missouri*, and *The Year of Decision: 1846* seem to me to warrant all the superlatives that they have consistently won; they belong on the shelf that contains only Prescott, Bancroft, Motley, Adams, and Parkman, and they are not unworthy of the company they find there. In every way they were the climax of Benny DeVoto's career, and with them he won the absolute distinction that he aspired to. The novels seem, in view of this achievement, like experiments in the tricks of dramatizing action and revealing character; the literary criticism like a course in the estimating of documents; the historical essays like finger exercises; the edition of Lewis and Clark's *Journals* like an encore. The real program of this career was the trilogy of histories.

They are, for one thing, incredibly learned. Their pages are a web of cross-reference and allusion, packed with facts, crowded with brilliant historical portraits. A lifetime of reading and study is distilled in them, and the mistrust with which Benny regarded his romantic and literary lesser half led him to work by preference from original documents, to the sharp intensification of dramatic effect. There is, moreover, more than mere information; these are not merely history as record, they are history as literature. And here the frontier boyhood and the personal acquaintance with country and weather, landscape and coloring and quality of light, drouth and distance, paid off. These histories are related to Parkman's in their quality of personal participation, in the way history can be felt on the skin and in the muscles because the author himself has been able to imagine it that way, having taken the trouble to live as much of it as possible himself.

This way, at least, the exile who never fully admitted he was an exile came home. This is a better and fuller reconciliation than he arranged for his character Cy Kinsman, who rather unrealistically wound up teaching physiology in a cow college. Reconciliation might have proceeded even farther if Benny had lived a little longer, for when he died he was working on the manuscript of a book to be called *The Western Paradox*. Except for one "Easy Chair" on literary cowboys, it had got no farther than a rough draft, and Mrs. DeVoto decided, wisely. I think, not to let it be published. Reconciliation or not, the full fusion of western past and western present, of the local realities and the exiled intelligence, it would have been anticlimactic unless he had been able to take it through the second and third drafts that put the sting into his prose and the bite into his ideas. And even without it, he had done enough. More than enough.

6

The Book and
the Great Community

Years ago, in Saskatchewan, we used to look for a trouble-some winter when the horses grew a heavy pelt of hair, when the muskrats built high in the sloughs, and when the antelope started drifting from the north in October. Omens of a cultural kind have lately made us anticipate a bad winter of the spirit. Formed as we have been by the book, believing with Milton that "a good book is the precious life-blood of a master-spirit, embalmed and treasured up on purpose to a life beyond life," we find ourselves living through a period which seems to value very little either traditional knowledge, wisdom, and eloquence, or the printed book which has been their carrier. And so it strikes me that to erect a great library in the year 1968 is an act of stubborn and sassy faith, an affirmation in the spirit of the philosopher who said, "If I knew the world was going to end tomorrow, I would plant a tree."

This is not the great age of books. They have been for a good while now drifting from the north before the breath of the media, and writers as well as librarians have been growing coats of protective hair. A rather small percentage of Americans read books, and many of those who do read, read non-books, or treat real books as if they were non-books. The paperback revolution that has made everything available has also tended to make everything expendable, like a used magazine. The American device of built-in obsolescence is operative even in literature. And there is always Marshall McLuhan, confidently predicting the Gutenberg Götterdämmerung, the end of print, with all that it has historically meant in terms of sequence, rationality, and tradition. If you are bent upon losing your head rather than keeping it, you do not need the alphabet.

Yet a librarian could be forgiven for thinking that the trouble is not too few books and too few readers, but too many of both. The presses of America alone turn out 25,-ooo titles a year, and what respectable library can confine itself to the books of its own nation? These days, if we read, we must read the world, and that will multiply the titles by a factor of six or eight or ten. Assuming that not all of these are frivolous, or irrelevant to the concerns of educated Americans, and assuming that we have money to buy them and shelves to put them on, there is still the massive problem of selection. You can't preserve them all. Anyone who has had a stack card in the Library of Congress, and has pursued one single book through those labyrinthine miles of stacks, under streets and into annexes and through annexes of annexes, knows the nightmare of total inclusiveness. Then there is the problem of what to throw away, and when. One explosive science, biology, proliferates into print at so frenzied a pace that the mere abstracts of a mere month's articles fill a volume the size of a telephone book. Much of that, indispensable this year, is worthless next. Here the problem is not to store knowledge permanently, but to store it briefly and then throw most of it away.

If we solve the difficulties of selection and space and money and disposal, there is still the problem of retrieval, and that multiplies as readers do. Only 15% of Americans read books, but that 15% equals thirty million people. Watch the bedlam activity in a great metropolitan library such as the New York Public, and you conclude that your notion of the librarian as ruminative, tranquil, rubbersoled, quietly dusty, gently helpful, needs revision. These people are required every day to build a great haystack in which, ever afterward, they will be able to find every single needle.

But if those were the only difficulties attending the preservation and distribution of books, no one would be dismayed. They may be eased by decentralization, miniaturization, standardized cataloguing procedures, computerized retrieval, and other means; and if they cannot be completely solved, that should not bother us. Neither can any other real problem. What is harder for a book-centered generation or a book-centered intellectual class to cope with is the contemporary cultural climate that increasingly disregards the book and depreciates the traditions it reflects.

This climate, described and in fact celebrated by McLuhan, may be, as he thinks, a function of the mass media. In its neglect of print in favor of the image, and in its growing neglect of the eye in favor of the ear, it very probably is. The image is immediate, it needs no complicated symbolic system such as words to communicate its message; and the ear is at least as immediate as the image, and increasingly appealed to. You will find plenty of American homes without bookshelves, but few without a television set, a radio, and probably a stereo. But in its general rejection of the conventional, its emphasis on the present and distrust of the past, its faith in the spontaneous, innovative, and impromptu, as well as in its lively inventiveness, the generation raised on the media is only extending to the limit, and perhaps to absurdity, tendencies that have always been distinctly American, and that in fact have traditionally distinguished western nations from the nations of the East.

The Commission for the Year 2000, looking into present and future for the American Academy of Arts and Sciences, remarks that "a sense of historical time is absent from American thought." We have not only looked with suspicion on the dead hand of the past, we have been unwilling to admit that we cannot make the most profound social changes by a simple act of will or law. Instant Reform is as American a product as instant coffee. We have been as willing to legislate morality, or try to, as we have been to tear down obsolete buildings or retool plants. Thus contemporary dissenters show a family resemblance to the dissenters who left England for Holland in the seventeenth century, and left Holland for America, and left the Atlantic colonies (or Nauvoo, to bring the parallel closer home) for the wilderness. In repudiating their heritage they assert it, for it is a heritage of questioning and rebellion. The Haight-Ashbury district, the capital of the Flower People, has its relationship not only to all bohemias, but to the Massachusetts Bay Colony, mad as that comparison seems.

No young person respects history as much as do people who have lived a little of it. "Why do you care where you came from or what your ancestors did?" a girl asked me when I was trying to explain to a group of students my reasons for writing a somewhat personal history book, *Wolf Willow.* "Isn't it what you *are* that matters? *Now?*"

Now. It is a big word with the young, almost as big a word as wow. Between them, those two words seem sometimes to comprehend the responses of a whole generation. Television's greatest hour, the show that above all others satisfied the demand for instantness as well as violent sensation, was Jack Ruby's shooting of Lee Harvey Oswald. The characteristic modern art form is the happening, which can't be programmed or repeated, but only participated in. Musicians celebrate silence over sound, or noise over music. Painters assert accident over design, a fiercely pure non-art over any sort of technique or manipulation. Pop artists transfer real objects into the art frame with so little organization or change that as Wright Morris suggests, the result differs hardly at all from window dressing. And the Berlin artist who exhibited himself as "a perfect living total work of art" was not thinking of himself as the complex end-product of biological, historical, and cultural forces, and still less as a creator or maker. He was thinking of himself as a happening. He would be right at home in San Francisco.

There is an obvious reason why the young have been able to seize power from the old in this generation as they have not been able to in the past, and the reason is not the media. The young now simply outnumber us, they find they can outvote us as the immigrant Irish found, about 1870, that they could outvote the Boston Yankees. They can not only outvote us, they can outbuy us, outmarch us, outshout us, and in general handle us. They are wooed by advertisers and politicians, they put the fear of God into university administrations, they challenge parents and police.

Forty-seven percent of Americans are under twenty-five. In 1970 more than half will be. Possessed of the power of numbers, they have naturally learned to exercise it. And it is easy for a generation coming of age in a time of bitter social crisis, and having a somewhat inadequate knowledge of history, to think that it invented idealism and commitment. It is easy to discard elderly counsels along with elderly error and timidity and failure. To trust no one over thirty becomes not only a declaration of personal independence but a moral imperative. Iconoclasm can become as compulsive as any other form of conventional behavior, and the voice of the young hormone is sometimes mistaken for the voice of God. The elders, outvoted, disregarded, held in contempt, watch this youth revolution from the sidelines, dismayed and aghast. Or else they try to join it, adopting cosmetically young ideas and some version of Carnaby Street costume or Haight-Ashbury hairdo, in order to get rich from it or win its votes.

I have said that the majority of Americans read no books at all. The youth who trusts no one over thirty may, since he is often an intellectual of sorts, but he does not read the books his elders admire. He reads in some counter-tradition, Zen or otherwise, and quotes from the Tibetan Book of the Dead, or he reads his own kind, books written in the spirit of intransigent modernity—purified of moral taboos, conventional "taste," traditional techniques, and sometimes coherence. Time, a traditional means of order, is melted down into the simultaneity of solipsism or the drugged consciousness. Form means nothing—what is admired is anything that turns the reader on, and this may be better done by irrational than by formal means. Greek rationalism sets as Afro-Asian mysticism rises, and words that were coined to convey meanings are made to serve as substitutes for strobe lights and over-amplified guitars. The virtue of anything—art, costume, life-style, sexual habits, entertainment, conversation—inheres in its novelty, its capacity to shock or titillate, and its promotion of states of ecstasy.

All of which only reminds an elder with some historical sense of Robert Frost's remark that there are no new ways to be new.

Nevertheless, the elder must reserve judgment. This generation is probably as good as other generations, and will make its own contributions. But it cannot long continue the pretense that it is breaking entirely with the Establishment and the past. It will have to re-discover history, it will have to re-establish contact with the tradition it aspires to alter drastically or to destroy. Above all, it will have to acknowledge the absurdity of its cult of total individual freedom. The irresponsible individual "doing his thing" without reference to other individuals or to society is neither new nor viable. Neither is the activist bent upon instant and total reform by means which amount to threat and coercion. Anarchy, pursued very long, is a form of suicide both individual and social.

For no risk, as Josiah Royce once said, is ever private or individual, and no accomplishment is merely personal.

What saves us at any level of human life is union, mutual responsibility, what St. Paul called charity. The detached individual, Royce wrote,

> is an essentially lost being. That ethical truth lies at the basis of the Pauline doctrine of original sin. It lies also at the basis of the pessimism with which the ancient southern Buddhism of the original founder of that faith . . . viewed the life of man. The essence of the life of the detached individual is, as Gotama Buddha said, an unquenchable desire for bliss, a desire which 'hastens to enjoyment, and in enjoyment pines to feel desire.' Train such a detached individual by some form of high civilized cultivation, and you merely show him what Paul called 'the law.' The law thus shown he hereupon finds to be in opposition to his self-will. Sin, as the Pauline phrase has it, 'revives.'

The Buddha, unlike some of his contemporary western followers, found the salvation of the detached individual to lie in the resignation of all desires. Our own tradition pushes us toward the more dynamic solution of an organized and indoctrinated social interdependence, St. Paul's "charity." More of that human bond than he knows remains in the dropout who has "had" this civilization and wants no more of it. More of it than he would admit survives in the activist bent upon tearing down the imperfect political and social structure and erecting a perfect society where it stood. More of it than he imagines motivates the hippie who believes he has emancipated himself into total freedom and the life of pure sensation. Except for a few minor matters such as Christian faith and chastity, he is a dim copy of St. Francis of Assisi.

So there is virtue in the creation of a great library, even

in a time which questions or repudiates so much of the tradition, which has made a specialty of the non-book, which has cultivated instant communication and has taken speed-reading courses that will let it read *Hamlet* in twelve minutes—if it hasn't already read *Hamlet* in comic book form. Bright as the media are, they have little memory and little thought: their most thoughtful programs are likely to take the form of the open-end discussion, a form as inconclusive and random as the happening. Thought is neither instant nor noisy, and it is not very often tribal or communal in the fashion admired by McLuhan. It thrives best in solitude, in quiet, and in the company of the past, the great community of recorded human experience. That recorded experience is essential whether one hopes to re-assert some aspect of it, or attack it. "Like giants," Robert Frost said, "we are always hurling experience ahead of us to pave the future with against the day when we may want to strike a line of purpose across it for somewhere."

It is profoundly right that this splendid library should arise in this city, to serve this community's spiritual and intellectual needs, for nowhere in the United States is the community spirit stronger or the respect for tradition greater. The people of Utah came here as communities on the march, aspiring to build a greater community, and they have retained the virtues of solidarity and mutual responsibility that many American cities never had, or have lost. As one who spent his youth in this city, I can testify to the things it offered even to an outsider, a waif. Security may be as great a social need as independence, stability as essential a commodity as change.

For the fact is, if it is the necessity of the young to challenge and risk, it is the obligation of the old to conserve, not only for their own sake but for the sake of the young who at the moment want anything rather than conservation. No society is healthy without both the will to create anew and the will to save the best of the old: it is not the triumph of either tendency, but the constant, elastic tension between the two that should be called our great tradition. In this society we may confidently count on the will to change. It is one of the strengths of our civilization, and as I have already said, history lines up in support of the rebel. What we have in somewhat smaller measure, perhaps in these years dangerously small measure, is the will to hold fast to what our parents or grandparents found good and workable. It is every bit as necessary as reform.

Konrad Lorenz, the great student of animal behavior, has shown that personal affection, love, friendship, even the very fact of individuation, arise on this earth only in those species which by nature carry a heavy charge of aggression. In certain species of fish, lizards, and birds, as well as in mammals, love arises, literally, as a corrective of hate, which otherwise would lead mate to destroy mate, and the species to commit suicide. In species which do not achieve this bond of affection—which means species in which the territorial and protective aggression does not appear—there are no individuals, only units, like the anonymous members of a school of fish.

Except as we belong to a tradition and a community—and perhaps except as we bear some sort of constructive hostility to those bonds—we are nothing. We have no language, no history, no lore, no legend, no myth, no custom, no religion, no art, no species memory. But the moment our built-in emotions of fear and aggression are modulated to the need of companionship and mating and protection of the young, we have begun to form, in the most rudimentary way, the community of men, for which another name is the Kingdom of God. We are both bound and emancipated by that membership. It is probably bad anthropology, but I like to think that some of the hand-prints painted in ochre on Utah cliffs were made by primitive men and women making an assertion of their simultaneous and joined identity. And if their sons, escaping in anger from the harsh domination of the family and the tribe, should dip their own palms in ochre and press their own marks on the cliff to demonstrate that their hand and their strength is greater than their father's, so be it. Maybe it is bigger. But it is well to have daddy's handprint there for a beginning and a gauge.

That is what a library is about. It seems to me one of the noblest activities of any culture: measure of what has been, indication of what may be, testimonial to our purposes that are shared even in antagonism, reassurance that *homo sapiens* has been and will remain sapient.